family
of outcasts

family of outcasts

A NEW THEORY OF DELINQUENCY

Seymour Rubenfeld

The Free Press
New York
Collier-Macmillan Limited
London

A DIVISION OF THE MACMILLAN COMPANY

Printed in the United States of America

Collier-Macmillan Canada, Ltd., Toronto, Ontario

Library of Congress Catalog Card Number: 65-20000

to Florence

my wife and,
in this instance,
my midwife

preface

national values, neurosis, and delinquency

FORMER Secretary of Health, Education, and Welfare Ribicoff testified before the House Committee on Labor and Education on behalf of the Juvenile Delinquency Act of 1961 that according to preliminary information for 1960 almost 750,000 individual children, excluding repeaters and including traffic violators, were referred to the nation's courts for delinquent acts. In 1956 Bloch and Flynn, after carefully examining available data for 1948–52, had predicted that by 1960 as many as 575,000 young people might be brought before the courts. The youngsters had clearly outstripped the statisticians' expectations. Secretary Ribicoff estimated that at the delinquency rates current in 1960, three to four million children would come before the courts in this decade. His prediction may err on the conservative side, for each year a larger proportion of an increasing child population is getting into trouble. The number of children aged ten to seventeen increased less than 50 percent between 1948 and 1960, but the number of cases of delinquency in that age group more than doubled.

The Secretary's testimony, as well as other sources, also indicates certain broad characteristics of our young offenders. To a disproportionate degree, children of the poor (although those who live in the suburbs may know how court dockets are crowded with cases of children from comfortable middle-class homes), Negro; and from our decaying inner-city ghettos. They are bored with, fighting, or have dropped out of school; and they are usually ages fourteen to seventeen, just prior to assuming whatever adult roles are available to them.

During the 1950s the Cornell University Department of Psychiatry conducted lengthy home interviews with a sample of 1,660 adults representing 111,000 residents of a two hundred-block area in New York City, with a wide range of income. The Midtown Manhattan Study showed that a very large majority of the respondents, whether their economic class level was low, middle, or high, had some kind of definable psychiatric symptom and that only a small minority could be classified as "well" (Langner and Michael).

The press and popular magazines have familiarized most people with the scholars' and professionals' basic explanations for delinquency. Young law violators are the victims of improper upbringing, or they have been raised in neighborhoods where crime has become a way of life, or they have become so discouraged about their chances for legitimate success that they turn to other ways of acquiring prestige and profit. But we understand less about the surprising amount of mental and emotional disturbance among adults that the Midtown Manhattan Study revealed. Does society make many adults neurotic? If so, are the social pressures at all similar to those that make many of their children delinquent?

It may be so. All of people's actions are a pursuit of values; people realize themselves (and are happy) when their actions are consonant with their ideals and values; and they suffer when what they have to do seems unnecessary or unsatisfying or when they are not really sure their values are worthwhile. Whether an older person communicates his discontent in mental illness or a younger one by means of crime, the form that personal dissatisfaction takes may be less important than the fact that each is conveying his pursuit, or his loss, of values to orient his life. The businessman's ulcers are as much a record of a desperate importance attached to acquiring goods and services as are the arrest convictions of a younger housebreaker.

Both the businessman's gastrointestinal record and the delinquent's police record bear witness to what people do to each other as well as to themselves, and what their parents have done with them, in living up to goals they deem admirable or necessary. If we assume that some people everywhere in our society are uncertain as to life's meaning or purpose (And what social commentary worth its salt does not take up these questions?) then executive suites and slum streets may have something else in common. Their occupants sometimes damage the well-being, the health, and the human and property rights of others in their search for ways of redeeming themselves. Sociology and the press have amply documented both delinquency and white-collar crime. Perhaps how to live and let live is something people learn only when they are more comfortable inside their own skins than many are now.

Delinquency and personality disorder may be with us until people up and down the status levels in our society contrive less oppressive versions of ideals about which they are more sure and then introduce their children to them. Take, for example, the community action programs in some of our major cities, underwritten in part by funds allocated under the Delinquency Act of 1961, which are intended to reduce delinquency among underprivileged youths. These programs center on opening up educational and work opportunities for economically lower-class persons, or attempting to render childhood and family experience more satisfying, or trying to make these people readier to learn payable skills. It is questionable whether these efforts alone will do the trick. Defining the problem of delinquency (or, for that matter, neurosis) as a malfunction which can be "fixed" will get us only so far.

We are faced with a matter of cultural growth and development as well as with issues of social inequity. People can only go as far, in rearranging their own and others' lives, as they understand what has happened in their own lives and what they want to happen. In some ways the anthropologist Walter Miller, of all contemporary scientific writers on delinquency, comes closest to seeing the problem of lower-class delinquency as a pursuit of personal values. He has insisted that lower-class people are not our society's excrescence, that they have a culture and an ideology all their own, and more recently has tried to explain some of the behavior of delinquents in this group as an enactment of knightly virtues. Can anything be "done"? Will opening up education and job opportunities for lower-class persons cause them to relinquish their values? Or will their values cause many of them to renounce the new opportunities and cause an eventual rewriting of the opportunities programs as well?

Consider for a moment how long, and with what bloody effort, Western peoples struggled to overcome their loyalties to the gens and to tribal and religious totems, and to idealize the nation-state instead. Also compare your thoughts about an eventual world order, or even a federation of Western nations, with your emotional conviction about the differences among peoples and with present happenings inside the Western Alliance. Arthur Miller's play *The Crucible* is a story of the price one man had to pay to adhere to the ideals of love and rationality in the face of the demonic purity and piety of seventeenth-century Salem. People's values and ideals, and their prejudices, are the terms they come up with, in a given time and place, in trying to live together.

People as individuals, or as members of economic classes or citizens of nations, negotiate constantly with each other, in friendship, competition, pillage, and murder, to establish and renew their values. They bring to the negotiation their prior ideals and the meanings they have attached to themselves through these values; they try to foist their values on each other, or they redefine their working relations by new overarching beliefs and purposes. Something like this happened in Europe when its nations decided to substitute a Common Market for generations of bloodletting, and it happens when white Americans take silent pride in seeing a Negro enter their favorite restaurant, heretofore not open to him.

But negotiating new values and defining our personal reasons for being take time. They have to wait on what develops in the economic system between the classes and upon the personalities of representatives and leaders. The Negro civil rights movement, for instance, has to grapple not only with political disfranchisement but also with economic dispossession. Negro economic discontent may have to wait for economic change, possibly for automation to throw more white workers off assembly lines. Only then perhaps will working-class whites throw off the caste ideology they have maintained toward the Negro since the Reconstruction and align themselves with Negroes in a common working-class movement. (Economic competition and the origins of Jim Crow are discussed in Simpson and Yinger, pp. 140–45.)

Many economically marginal persons at whom the opportunities programs are aimed may want some kind of job, but they may not want to become working-class people. Profoundly, they may wish that their lives were different, but their ideology militates against the wish. They will not collaborate with the rest of society for their own betterment because they have made a virtue of harsh necessity. Some have learned, for example, to value their impoverished leisure because higher economic groups have, for too many years or even generations, left too little room for them in the economic life of the country.

Many of the "privileged" are also straitjacketed in their contemporary value systems. Many entrepreneurs and professionals and their wives engage in a compulsive and prodigal preoccupation with self, in all its outer and inner aspects, that betrays an underlying ambiguity of purpose and that makes living inordinately hard on themselves, on their children and on everyone else, including the underprivileged. We do not just have a commitment to, or even an exaggeration of, the value of "success." Rather, we have an enthrallment, an enslavement, to celebrating the ego, personal power, individual competence, whether in work games, play games, or sex games.

This Celebration of the Self is a less complimentary way of talking about, but perhaps just a more extreme form of, the ideal of self-fulfillment which we have enshrined in our culture. It has its obvious usefulness in letting people do things differently from the way their forebears did them, just as their ancestors' glorification of ascetic hard work in the Protestant ethic allowed them to develop capitalism, as the German sociologist Max Weber has shown us. Both ideals were a long time in coming, have been with us in varying ways for four centuries and more, and are likely to go on for some time determining human events—childrearing, relations between and within our economic classes, inner experience. Our American activism—"If you don't like it, fix it"—may encourage us to adjust income level for some people here, fix up the neuroses of some parents and teach their disaffected children to share in the American Dream there, bring white management to the bargaining table with colored outcasts elsewhere; but we cannot hurry the great mass of people along any faster than they can live, learn, and invent.

We cannot get much further ahead of ourselves than where we are. And perhaps the incubuses of our history burden us more than we realize. The puppet play of striving for middle-class success may be a personal version of the doctrine of manifest destiny, in the name of which earlier white Americans broke everything—continent, aborigine—to their will and turned the Caribbean into *mare nostrum.* Middle-class respectability may be Calvinist predestination secularized—effort and propriety save the pilgrim daily from being like the disreputable poor. Working- and lower-class men, descendants of European and southern Negro serfs, would like to sustain feudalism in their households: Children are, and women should be though they are not, vassals who bend to the manor lord's authority. The social and religious ideology of Black America, according to the symbols and styles of its best writers and store-front church liturgies and sermons, has been saturated with the Hebrew mythos and with primitive Christianity, provided by plantation masters. A people chosen by a just and vengeful overlord suffer for love of him until he delivers them; man born of woman is immolated by male authority because of his mother-love of the oppressed. The legend of the Hebrews had already justified the pacifism and submission of another people, the Jews of the Diaspora. The story of Christ comforted the Negro, subjugated by white men, and bound him inescapably to others of his color. But both stories interfered with self-deliverance. After all, a wanderer does not want to overthrow a pharaoh, but merely wants to escape him; and how can a humble sufferer become a Pharisee? Someone has remarked that psychotherapy is a process that displaces one personal myth with another that is less self-injurious. If a class's social and economic function (or functionlessness) could be changed, would its members find new myths, or must myth-making and substitution be a step in social and economic change? Both, I suppose, but probably neither alone.

If there have been times in the Christian West when very large numbers of people knew their common ends and how to pursue them daily, intervening decades and centuries have invalidated that style and purpose for us, or have mingled memory, record, and romance: crashing lance and blazing pennon, rioting peasants in a Brueghel painting, our Frontier. People today seem to aim wide of an inner mark that might assure and renew them. Their class ideologies reflect these deflected purposes. If they do not openly envy another class's possibilities, they act as if they mistrust their own, as if they have misplaced their loyalties but must cling to a brave pretense nevertheless. Young people may have their grievances against these pretensions.

Many lower-class men and women have as little faith in each other's reliability as they do in an employer's or the slumlord's. Their often unstable marriages lack dignity and caring; they may take as little pride and comfort in possessing each other as they do in holding a decent job (when they can get one) or owning a well-kept household. They sometimes show their children an unreasoning or cruel inconsistency. The delinquent acts of their growing children are no more cynical and disloyal than some of the experiences they have had and seen at home.

Working-class marriages are often more stable, and here there is pride of ownership and earning power. But the adults may so mistrust any friend or neighbor trying to get ahead that they may not accept local leadership for the common good, as, for example, when it means allowing a slum clearance program to destroy their neighborhood. (Gans describes such an event in a community of Italian-American working people.) When a working-class father insists on being his own boss and expects blind obedience from his sons, it is no wonder that when some of these boys become adolescent they launch a rebellion on the streets.

Many high school-educated and economically lower middle-class people are encouraged when they see the other fellow get ahead, and they work hard together in fund-raising activities for church or school. However, they are under a yoke of adhering to what is "acceptable" in their work and marriage relationships—in obeisance to the Protestant ethic and in emulation of their "betters" who have achieved greater financial and educational success than they. Some of them carry self-discipline so far that their married lives are emotional wastelands. Their teenage children, who may demand more enriching purposes, may be strangers to them—resentful strangers who express a vague feeling of having been wronged by their parents in the adolescent cliché, trite and true, that they are given too little "freedom." Feeling vaguely wrong themselves in school and around teachers, these children hunt for diversion and escape from the "square" world they never made.

Then there is the upper middle-class business manager and professional, enslaved to proving his originality and importance to himself, his wife, and his equals—but often not to his children. One-man (and one-woman) shows must limit the number of performances, as a matter of sheer endurance. Besides, children's patience as an audience is soon exhausted; they must get in the act or out of the theater. And they are out, night after night, drag-racing through suburbia, trying to find in their car engines, in sexuality, and even in the police some honest purpose and strength underneath surface show and glitter.

The moral of this capsule class commentary (and caricature) is that we are all caught up in a time of ceaseless change, and that many of us are bobbing restlessly on the strings of our dissatisfactions. It is probably not civilization that makes us discontent, as Freud suggested, but social change, because it never lets us rest. Freud was really inveighing against the oppressive morality of his time and place. The "Victorian" conscience proved to be temporary, just as our self-fulfillment will probably become something else in two more generations.

Ideological obligation is tentative only for a culture; it almost always endures for at least one generation. A man may become so possessed by his compromise that he burns witches speaking in tongues or voices the language of illness to a psychiatrist to exorcise his alien individuality. A teen-age son's delinquencies may represent the same strivings his father disowns in himself. Each in his way is uttering a cry against the sacrifices he must make to available values. Every set of values, as I tried to suggest about the shibboleths of our social classes, carries its own freedoms and restraints.

We ought to consider why constraints sometimes make freedoms bitter ashes—for some (among the poor), the freedom simply to survive; for workingmen and their families, the freedom from bondage; for white-collar people, the freedom to advance beyond their fathers' stations, to learn, to cultivate pleasure, to realize talents. The reason may be that, because every social change we make is a parting of the ways, we also have to break faith with others and ourselves.

It seems that as children grow and marry their parents are left further and further behind. Often the children do not nicely fit the pace and values of the great cities to which they remove themselves. Corporate enterprise and purposes mutate; suburban living follows fashion. Newcomers have to force a fit, and to do this they often have to cultivate a doubt about those personal beliefs that dictate the forms their private feelings and reactions will take, lest inner experience become outer differentness. Each person is directed to the other, hoping to find out what meaning he has and therefore what he ought to believe, because he cannot give meaning to himself. It cannot work, because he knows his friend is in the same predicament. How can he trust a friend's judgment any better than his own? He can pretend that he is impressed with his and his friend's private pomp and display; but our young satirists, playwrights, and novelists, like Feiffer, Albee, and Updike, keep showing us the emptiness inherent in this.

There is no end of misgivings. The Joneses keep going up; Mrs. Jones leaves one *Kaffeeklatsch* for one of higher status. What, she wonders, will her new neighbors think of her parvenu opinions and tastes? What do the old neighbors think of each other as they gather around a kitchen table with her empty place? What, they wonder, does she have that they haven't, by way of husband and self? The conversation turns to the safe subject of children and childrearing. But this morning it is a little less safe. Self-doubt turns a question of right and wrong mothering into the possibility of being a right or wrong kind of person. The peacemakers in the group find an escape hatch: They reduce the issue to a matter of taste. After all, normal means normative, and that may simply reflect preference. The clique happily accepts this redefinition of the question, but it is settled to no one's satisfaction. In fifteen minutes each woman is alone in her kitchen with her child, and in six hours will be in her living room and bedroom with her husband.

As to the men, even if they are sure of their niche in Topsy bureaucracies, they are borne on a current the direction of which none can be sure. A man markets himself, his skills, or both; he cannot be sure that what he has and is today will not be obsolescent tomorrow. He is a quasi-anonymous specialist or technician who has to concentrate and narrow his energies on mattering to someone else as well as to himself over the clamor of a thousand other personalities and their interests. And quickly. Isn't there a prevalent conviction that manhood has a fixed depreciation schedule built in? If so, is it possible for a man to believe he has value, but only of a provisional kind? Room here for a captive, workaday imagination, but not for a free one. Compared to all the inventing men do for a livelihood, what have they come up with recently to enhance their one and only life together? In rolling seas, batten down the hatches and for heaven's sake don't rock the boat.

Accumulate these ports of call and these voyages and the adjustments they require over a lifetime or two, and the casualties in personal disorder, whether legal or psychiatric, mount up. One reason for this is that the best short-term way of dealing with alarming doubts and desires to live some other way, disturbing because they press us to renounce current values, is to deny their existence. I am referring to the process of repression, to "filing it and forgetting it." I think it is the way we force our discontent out of awareness that lends the compulsive quality to extravagant self-absorption. A person can never repress enough, or protest too much, when reality reminds him daily on what weak reeds his values rest. And so hard-won virtues become vicious necessities; the roles enact the person, because he has disowned his reservations and his power of dissent. People shape their social selves to fit the fashion until they have so far invaded their own privacy that their ways of being take refuge in the even more private symbols of psychiatric symptoms.

What people do to each other in their ax-grinding extends beyond their private lives and into society. Some of the differences between our haves and have-nots result from the attitudes a group adopts, what they believe the people in the other group are like, and how the two groups interact. Three parables may make my meaning clearer.

First, as to what interaction is: An experimental psychologist is training a rat to depress a bar in a laboratory cage; he is, in the jargon, "shaping" its random behavior. When the rat brushes the lever, the experimenter delivers a food pellet; when the animal climbs up against the bar, he delivers more pellets, the while noting time intervals, other behavior of the animal, and so on. Finally, the rat approximates a pushing motion on the lever. The experimenter delivers an increased number of pellets, makes copious notes, and reloads his food magazine in preparation for the next stage of the experiment. It is a diverting exercise to demonstrate logically that it is in fact the man who is shaping the rat.

Second, regarding the meaning we give to another: A couple are bewildered and alarmed by their adolescent boy's misbehavior. He is on probation for having been caught speeding in the family car, which he took without permission. He is failing in school and surly to teachers; he flies into rages with his mother and verbally abuses her. They seek professional help. The therapist hears the mother complain that her son seems to goad her until she is driven to retaliate angrily. He puts two and two together, explains neatly that some teen-agers cannot tolerate their parents' protective supervision yet mistrust themselves, suggests to them that their son seems to be crying out for external controls, and recommends a program of consistent rule-setting, punishment, and reward. It works. A couple of months later the boy and the therapist are discussing his past misdeeds and their meaning. The boy brings up the subject of his parents' recent firmness. The therapist gives him a significant look: "You asked for it, you know." The boy considers this, from his present, after-the-fact safety, his friendship for the therapist, and his parents' current approval, and says, "Sure. That's right. I needed somebody to tell me what to do and what not to do." The therapist leans back and puffs his pipe. I suggest that no one will know, least of all the boy, what his previous misbehavior was all about.

Third, as to the attitudes or poses we sometimes strike: Four teen-age boys in a canoe were throwing large firecrackers at people who were having an evening swimming party in a fashionable lake-and-residential area. The party's host, a strong swimmer, announced, "Let's get them Indian style," and dived into the water. He was found dead in the water thirty minutes later, his skull fractured by a blunt object like a canoe paddle. Lest you leap to assumptions, as the therapist did in parable number two, let me say that as of this writing the boys have been absolved, and the murderer remains unknown. The questions I have are, what was his purpose in taking after four adolescents who were throwing cherry bombs at people? Why didn't he call the cops? What was this successful businessman and father enacting or seeking to prove in identifying himself as an Indian on a raiding expedition?

People posture before their friends and genuflect to their romanticized images of themselves. They think they are shaping worlds, not realizing that they are potter's clay too. They impute qualities to another person that may not be there, to suit their convenience, and sometimes the other person acts as if the imputations are true because it suits his convenience.

While this is being written (August, 1963), Senator Byrd of West Virginia, a proprietor of welfare piety, is calling for a Congressional investigation into what he considers a wholesale exploitation of Federal-State welfare funds. Last year he propounded an attitude toward District of Columbia welfare operations: His driving concern was only to improve on the efficient management and distribution of funds. (Proper merchandising of public generosity, reorganizing bureaucratic assembly lines, quality control of the dole—all working ideals of the American industrial genius, inventively extended to a new category of consumers, the poor.) The Senator was not interested in depriving the deserving poor, but able-bodied people should be out earning their way, in keeping with the industrious, white Anglo-American ideal.

His staff investigators, disciples of efficiency in giving and getting, uncovered shocking abuses of the public conscience. A very large number of these supposedly indigent mothers had strapping, healthy men living with them. In many cases these men, or other women in the household, had other sources of income—they obtained occasional day work, for example, on road gangs or as domestics—and still barefacedly took the handouts. They had the cheek to covet middle-class goods; they paid for new cars and brand-new television sets with welfare checks. (That they do without brooms, buckets, mops, and toilet paper to taste the manna testifies to their impious impurity.) The Senator's hounds of heaven had run the sordid truth to earth: The depraved deprived were collecting unemployment compensation—and unemployability compensation.

After revelations of this sort the professionals in charity, in the District, in Newburgh, and in Chicago, shaped things up. In the District they purified the welfare department to its foundations. They generated a tumult of new regulations in the offices of the District managers, forced out slipshod bureaucrats who had not swept the pigeon roosts out of their church spires, hired a whole new brigade of full-time investigators of the unfair poor. With this triumph behind him the Senator trumpets a greater crusade.

(Four months after the above was written, *The Washington Post* editorialized on one sequel to the local pogrom against disreputables of the year before. The number of delinquent and dependent children placed in foster homes and District of Columbia institutions had increased about twenty percent during the past year. This increase was about five times as rapid as the increase in the number of children living in Washington. "Senator Byrd of West Virginia," the *Post* editorial writer commented, "has forced upon our city a series of welfare budgets greatly expanding the institutions and foster homes, while ruthlessly reducing the program to maintain indigent children in their own homes with their own parents. . . . These children are the flotsam of a silent disaster: the Welfare Department's wild purge of its relief rolls" (editorial, "The Silent Disaster," Tuesday, December 10, 1963, a dual commentary, on the abuse of an urban population by a satrap and on the treatment of an American outcast).

The controlled ones shape the pellet-dispensing behavior of the controllers. To begin with, masses of them are Negro; too many for too long have practiced living with white ideology regarding them and, after a fashion, living off that ideology. If, after they have emigrated from certain serfdom to the uncertain cities, they discover they can survive, they have no reason to return—sharecropping promises no better reputation and worse drudgery. Better to be shifty than shiftless—at least the former commands the respectful attention of the law. But even more, they have now become the urban poor. They are the inheritors of an ideological contempt for the masters of the cities that comes down to us unchanged through Shakespeare, Dickens, Zola, Shaw, and Brecht: Sleek, idle, cruelly oppressive, and selfish, the owners use their morality to put a club into their hired, uniformed bully boys' hands. Self-respect requires man, woman, and child to outwit, outrun, and plunder at every turn. The enterprising ones snatch purses, roll marks, or rob liquor stores, steal cars or unemployability compensation. If they are caught they get a clean, dry pallet, steady work, and regular meals. The timorous and the humbled among them look to the welfare ministries and the public clinics. There are more ways than one to push the lever or skin a fat cat.

The middle class believes that the lower-class Negro sees or makes no other choice but a life of unfitness. The middle class has had a remedy for this unworthiness, or at least a purgative. It has established the pale of discrimination within cities, certain occupations, and schools. The program has worked, just as it did with the Jew in Eastern Europe. Every day that the discriminated submit to restrictions they leave the society and its riches to those who want it and in the way they want it, and what is more, they justify the restrictions. They look, talk, dress, and act in alien ways; they accept inferiority; they obviously do not belong. Surely it is an act of Christian charity to suffer them in the same land with us.

They are like squatters on the rocky foothills of our domain. It seems to be a part of our middle-class ideology, just as it has been with every economically important group in history, to believe that the whole society belongs to us. Since we own so much of the hard and soft goods and run the people and things that make and distribute goods, we believe that we are backbone, heart, and brains of the Great Experiment, the workers, paid attendants on our guts and genius, and the poor an excrescence, a Darwinian failure and tribute. By what other scheme of values could men without work for their hands be considered a side-effect of automation? How else explain an urban developer who chooses a parking lot, an office building, or luxury apartments for a slum area? Or the extreme respect that the American Bar Association has paid the racial status quo? (Until this year, its House of Delegates condemned both the integrationists and the segregationists with fine impartiality.) Or the organization of our American doctors staking out private property signs around the illnesses of the indigent aged?

What is good for the middle class is good for the country. If they take care of their own, the things that really matter will look after themselves, and the devil take the hindmost. It is in excesses of civilized generosity, in luxuries of surplus energy left over from necessary efforts, that the owners of the cities underwrite aid for the poor. However, the realization may be dawning that social injustice grown too great can tear apart even the most stable social orders; perhaps, also, there is a glimmering awareness that when only some benefit, present values are atrophying, signaling an eventual withering of the whole society.

This beginning responsiveness to the ways we endanger our way of life creates only a search for new ideological accommodations to each other; it does not make them. Meanwhile the entrepreneurs and experts keep worshipping their household gods in the same ways, go on writing new songs in praise of self, treating most people as consumers of their economic experiments, and ignoring the ones left over because they do not produce or consume enough to count. And the leftovers go on finding their ways of extorting sustenance; their stillborn talents and strength await the better life hereafter. It is the same between parent and child when some disaster in training and caring has destroyed their mutuality; they try forcing their wills on each other, or they try to abandon each other, but each suffers in his futile effort to complete himself without the other's help.

Why are men too unemployable to produce and consume enough? Ideology becomes a deeply personal matter. When society has no faith in or use for a man's will to work, that man falters. What else is he good for? And bad for? He casts about, runs experiments of his own, comes up with his own working hypotheses about what he is, many of them based on his experiences in uselessness, in being an industrial byproduct. His woman loses faith in him, and with their mutuality gone the couple settle on alternately extorting from and neglecting each other. The children are raised in the image of their parents' meaning to themselves and one another, and in their parents' conception of the usefulness and value of a male and female human life. We call the consequences psychological disorder. What the children do about their lot and how they act on and against their parents' values and their own prospective valuelessness to society are sometimes called delinquency.

acknowledgments

There are several people to whom I owe thanks for their help with this book. Donald Cook encouraged me to attempt a statement of my theoretical views, and gave my first, groping efforts the moral support they needed. Raymond Gould, of the National Institute of Mental Health, aided me in many ways and supported my efforts through to the completion of an earlier version of the manuscript. Herbert Gans encouraged me to seek publication and made some very valuable suggestions regarding the work.

I want to express my gratitude to a number of others who took the time to read the earlier version, and who made invaluable comments. In addition to Joseph Abrahams, who taught me many things that have become a part of the book, and to Herbert Gans, there were Roger Burton, Martin Gold, Jacob Hurwitz, Arthur Kassoff, Irving Kaufman, Hilan Lewis, Professor Walter Reckless, David Twain and Isaiah Zimmerman. I also owe Kenneth Artiss and Isaiah Zimmerman the memory of an enormously exciting discussion on a summer evening in 1963, much of which has found its way into the Preface.

Mrs. Cynthia Smith typed the bulk of the manuscript, faithfully and well. I also thank Mrs. Marian Buckner and Mrs. Natalie Van West for their typing assistance.

Finally, I wish to express my gratitude to International Universities Press for permission to quote from E. H. Erikson, "Identity and the Life Cycle: Selected Papers," which appeared in *Psychological Issues*, Vol. 1 (1959); to W. W. Norton & Company, Inc., and to The Hogarth Press Ltd for permission to quote from E. H. Erikson, *Childhood and Society*, 1950; to Basic Books, Inc., for permission to quote from A. Inkeles, "Personality and Social Structure," from *Sociology Today*, edited by Robert K. Merton, Leonard Broom, and Leonard S. Cottrell, Jr., Basic Books, New York, 1959; to The Free Press for permission to quote from R. A. Cloward and L. E. Ohlin, *Delinquency and Opportunity: A Theory of Delinquent Gangs*, 1960, and from H. J. Gans, *The Urban Villagers: Group and Class in the Life of Italian-Americans*, 1962; to *Psychiatry* for permission to quote from T. Parsons, "Social Structure and the Development of Personality: Freud's Contribution to the Integration of Psychology and Sociology," in Vol. 15 (1952); to the National Society for the Study of Education for permission to quote from A. Davis, "Socialization and Adolescent Personality," *Adolescence, 43rd Yearbook*, Part I, 1944; to Holt, Rinehart and Winston, Inc., and to Routledge & Kegan Paul Ltd for permission to quote from E. Fromm, *The Sane Society*, 1955; to Houghton Mifflin Company for permission to quote from "Patterns" by Amy Lowell; and to Herbert J. Gans for permission to quote from an early draft of *The Urban Villagers*.

S.R.

contents

part one

a psychocultural theory

OVERVIEW

This is a technical book and, as nearly as I can make it, a scientific one. It is written in the hope and belief that if various technicians of behavior can settle questions of fact and decide differences of doctrine, they will speak with a clearer voice about what needs to be done. Therefore, the book is not about what to do; it is an organized speculation on certain realities, and an assault on certain scientific dogmas and conventions, addressed to those who are trained and paid to think and plan. Personal opinions are probably everywhere throughout, but from here on I make an effort to support them with facts—or at least to keep opinions unobtrusive.

The theory is a polygamous marriage of theories. I lack the resources, and most of the pretensions, to create new theories of personality and society. I also have the belief that a theoretical work has to be very, very good to blaze trails that are all new; otherwise, it soon becomes a neglected and an overgrown byway. Humbly, then, it is hoped that this work may break a logjam or two in the mainstream (even if it has to miscegenate scientific as well as literary metaphors to do it).

A word about a principal partner to the marriage, psychoanalytic theory.

Psychoanalytic theory is the richest source of scientific understanding regarding personality functioning, and the most widely accepted, that we have at present, in spite of criticisms regarding its construction. It seems to me that if delinquents are to be helped we need as full an understanding as we can get of how society and the individual shape each other.

Sometimes one hears that what is needed is a social-psychological theory of delinquency. What we also need is to draw together and apply what is *already* known and thought to be true about man's psychological workings. We may already know what is at stake for society in social problems such as delinquency. Perhaps only after we grasp the multiple factors at play in such a problem will we begin to take a full inventory of resources and changes needed—or see whether indeed some things should and can be altered in our society as it is now constituted.

There may also be a proselytizing and an evangelical reason for appealing to psychoanalytic theory. Those who spend their professional lives dealing with personality functioning need to be shown, in the language they use daily, how much their advice and counsel may be needed in thinking through and planning delinquency intervention programs. It is my impression that the scientific planning staffs for these efforts contain every kind of behavioral-science and -practice talent except that of therapists and students of personality.

Educators, social workers, political scientists, anthropologists, sociologists—these, it seems to me, are usually in charge; the clinicians make their consultation visits, train line workers, perhaps assist in planning the clinical side of follow-up studies, and then retire to the insularity of campus and practice. If this is true, intervention must suffer because the basic dimensions of problems are left ill-defined. This theory, then, is offered in the further hope of making easier thinking, talking, and planning in the most refined psychological terms needed *while at the same time* grappling with the social aspects of large-scale intervention.

What follows is a summary of the next three chapters, and of the theory in this book, so that the reader may orient himself (and brace himself) for a presentation that will have to be discursive at times.

Summary

The simplest way of categorizing this theory is to view it as a containment theory of delinquency, after Reckless—one that takes into account both the internal and the external controls on behavior. Certain limitations in a strictly sociological view of delinquency detract from an understanding of inner controls and from an understanding of the relation between inner and outer realities—the relation of the individual to his environment. A principal sociological definition of personality is that the self is socially defined. Although valuable so far as it goes, the definition overlooks the importance of intrapsychic and interpersonal continuities as contributors to cultural continuity and change. Sociological theorists of delinquency tend to be social determinists; they believe that culture and society shape behavior and that personality factors, when they enter in at all, do so as intervening variables. This represents only one view of human reality, and a questionable one at that. Partly as a result of this view, sociological theorists tend also to be quite relativistic about personality, chalking it off as a side effect of a particular environment and not measurable against any general yardstick of psychological functioning.

The theory of this book adopts somewhat different premises about human realities. It assumes instead that both individual and societal behavior result from interdependent forces, none of which is ontologically prior: technological and cultural, institutional, interpersonal and intrapsychic. Whether or not a particular item in one of these categories can be specified as emergent from items in the other categories, it must be dealt with in its own terms, because once arisen, it will persist in an interdependent relation to other factors and affect all the others.

For example, the prejudices of whites have determined their

socioeconomic relations with Negroes as much as socioeconomic relations have determined prejudices. Prejudices, or other psychosocial factors, may be anachronistic to current material and social realities—certainly racial prejudice is a factor in unemployment of Negroes at a time of relatively full employment, but such factors must be understood, and dealt with, as separate forces.

Chapter 2 is an effort to translate discontent with prevailing norms—pressures, in other words, to deviant behavior—into psychological terms. Cohen and Cloward and Ohlin seem to propose that repudiation of conformity negates the personal consequences of having previously subscribed to a social system in which the individual has been a failure. It is equally possible, however, that people may blame the legitimate social system and become disaffected from it, but at the same time may not entirely rid themselves of their rejection of self resulting from personal failure within the system.

Blaming the system might then also operate as a way of projecting negative evaluations of the self, a defensive relief of unpleasant inner experience without renunciation of these evaluations. Social discontent (status or position discontent, in the terms of the two major, current sociological theories of delinquency) may therefore be *objective*, or it may be an *externalized self-discontent*.

Disadvantaged people may join their externalizations in new ideologies, so that illegitimate beliefs and values may subserve the function of projections. Self-discontent may arise when a person compromises his ego capacities for trusting, autonomous, assertive, and/or competent dealings with others in adapting to restraints that institutional norms put on his freedom of action. In this theory, then, self-discontent means experiencing those feelings of ego deficiency that Erikson describes—distrust, doubt and shame, guilt, and inferiority. Externalizing is seen as a living-out of rebellion against these inner limitations, alternative to *symbolic* rebellion in psychiatric symptoms.

This is not meant to be a theory only of lower-class delinquency. The economically deprived are not the only ones in our society who suffer from normative restraints on their ego resources; each social class may have institutionalized disadvantages affecting it. Accordingly, constraints which may affect each social class respectively are specified; possible internalizations of these restraints and consequent ego adaptations to conscience demands are described; and forms of externalization, within each class, for each kind of psychocultural adaptation are mentioned.

There may also be subcultural traditions, once functional in organizing ego strengths but now anachronistic, which may operate as cultural (vs. structural) restraints on freedom of action. Four, which may affect different class subcultures, are named.

Erikson has also proposed four other ego crises that people undergo in adolescence and adulthood. These are conceived to be *psychological* ends, states of psychosocial integration, toward which adults strive by *means* of the four types of ego strength acquired earlier. The economically disadvantaged are often barred from conventional adult activities; in their disbarment from "success" they may be deprived of both psychological ends and means. As a result they may suffer greater compromises of ego functioning than privileged people.

At the same time, however, any proposal that simple, logical connections exist between constraint, social class, and specific ego functions has to be qualified: An individual at any class level may experience multiple ego limitations, including those of adult, "integrative" functions, as a result of any one constraint. Research on the psychosocial effects of constraints would probably have to entail factor- or cluster-analytic methods, as in much current psychological research on delinquent typologies.

In other words, the theory at this stage is frankly heuristic and illustrative. The theory generates three basic kinds of rebellion and deviance: rebellion expressed in symptoms, deviance as externalization, and deviance based on objective social discontent. In this view, opportunity theory encompasses only the last.

Chapter 3 discusses the emergence of delinquency in a context of discontented socialization agents. Parents may transmit their self-limiting psychocultural adaptations to their children through the modifications they make in socialization practices. Symbolizing parents enforce similarly indirect expressions of ego limitations on their children. "Disturbed" delinquents may be those who display a mixture of symbolizing and externalizing behavior, the latter as an acting-out of covert parental rebellion *and* of developmental fixations, induced in the child.

The meaning of "developmental fixations" is broadened at this point in the theoretical presentation to include not only ego limitations but also correlated arrests of psychosexual needs. It is argued that this does not require assumptions about fixed instinctual development, but rather that compromises and restrictions imposed by parents on the child's ego and superego functioning focalize and detain what are, basically, very pliable primary drives.

Externalizing parents may allow their children great latitude to act out, to externalize, ego deficiencies and fixated needs, which these parents at the same time induce through their childbearing practices. Some of these children are probably included in the category of so-called "normal," "subcultural" delinquents in studies of typology. There may be proportionally more symbolizing than externalizing parents in the middle than in the lower classes.

It is also possible that some parents, during their own adolescence, may have renounced conventional cultural goals so thoroughly that they were also able to throw off forms of self-rejection. They may then have experienced an objective social discontent, and they may raise children who have relatively mature personalities but deviant ideals, children who are themselves objectively discontented.

In the young of deprived backgrounds, regressive trends resulting from fixated needs and limited egos, along with social and cultural processes, codetermine delinquency as a specific deviant outcome. Pessimistic and alienated ideologies state a deprived subculture's structural relations to the larger culture, *and also* subserve blaming others for inner restrictions of conscience and ego. These ideologies promote further surrenders of ego function, this time of learning capacities, which handicap deprived children in acquiring an education and tie them more strongly to their subculture.

These alienated values and beliefs also endorse antisocial conduct among older members of the potential delinquents' subculture. The ideologies and normative behaviors reintegrate externalized expressions of ego insecurity in some of the young; the young are also prompted to regress to certain kinds of satisfactions by sentiments suggesting the same needs in older members of the subculture; and these young people's externalizing and living-out of fixated needs may also be their effort to resist the integrative failure that a prospective adult lower-class identity represents to them.

Thus, lower-class delinquency is a living-through of subcultural sentiments and a limited (and self-limiting) resistance to unrewarding prospects. Misconceptions shared by social scientists about nativism in psychoanalytic theory are discussed, as well as developments in psychoanalytic theory, to justify this ego-psychological interpretation of subcultural delinquency.

chapter 1

introduction

DURING the past ten years Reckless and his students have formulated a basic point of view about the causes of delinquency, which he has named a "containment" theory. The simplest way to categorize the theory of this book is to label it a containment theory. What Reckless means by the term, essentially, is that delinquency is behavior that violates norms and/or laws, and that violative behavior is ordinarily contained by two sets of forces, one inside the individual, the other environmental. The non-delinquent individual is constructed in such a way that he resists temptations to break the law and is inclined to seek his satisfactions within it; his environment controls him, through police power and other punishing agents, and he is supported and shaped in a conforming direction by the values, goals, and practices of others to whom he is loyal. What makes most delinquents, on the other hand, is not a failure in one or the other control system, but a combination of circumstances, both outer and inner: The individual is pushed by his lack of restraint and his interest in illegal activity, and pulled by his social world into inventing deviant ways of obtaining various important satisfactions.

Reckless at once generalizes and dismisses the arguments between sociologist and psychologist by restating limitations of each position in his own terms. One, he says, is talking about the "pull" and the other about the "push," and each is clutching at half the elephant. The sociologist points out to the psychologist that the individual delinquents in whom he identifies personal malfunctions also have very realistic and appropriate reasons for acting as they do; and the psychologist rejoins that, realistic or not, their behavior is an outcome of personalities that are put together in different ways from many conforming young peoples' personalities. Reckless suggests that, when either expert talks about his favorite kind of delinquent, the kind that most closely fits his version of the facts, he is explaining some small number of cases at an extreme of a spectrum. The suggestion is a persuasive one, because although our special interests may draw us to study the "push"or the "pull" of delinquency, our knowledge and experience, both personal and professional, inform us that reality is usually more complex than theory.

An Autobiographical Aside

I suppose that our theoretical tastes are all tempered by the personal experiences we have had, and at the risk of boring the reader with irrelevant autobiography I should like to indicate some of mine. Like other psychologists I was trained to concentrate on individual differences and on continuities within an individual. I paid attention to similarities in characteristics that a person displays at different ages and in varying social situations, and to connections between seemingly dissimilar characteristics. I suppose, too, that like other technicians I have a tendency to reify or otherwise enshrine basic concepts; I must remind myself, for example, that "ego" in a technical sense is not a thing but a shorthand symbol for a bewildering variety of personal processes. It is easier, of course, to identify the same frailty in someone else, as when a sociologist talks about disembodied and mysteriously pervasive normative structures, a subject to which I shall happily return later.

I had an apprenticeship in the treatment of delinquents under a psychoanalyst, Dr. Joseph Abrahams, who not only had a way of reconciling most of what they said and did with the terms of psychoanalytic theory but also had intriguing ideas about the ways in which drives and character adapt to history. I became interested in some modal characteristics of delinquent boys from different sociocultural backgrounds—the ruthlessness and mother-worship of some very tough Negro slum delinquents; the passion and errant knighthood of some boys of Italian, Polish, Mexican, and Puerto Rican descent; the distance from (more than dislike of) their fathers and the stiff self-consciousness of some delinquent and near-delinquent boys of lower-middle class "Anglo" background; the articulate desperation of some privileged adolescents who seemed, in their defiance, to be probing for solidity behind what they felt to be snares and delusions.

While I was making these observations I became acquainted with the sociology of delinquency. I experienced a disconcerting figure-ground reversal; what had been "background" now seemed of central importance. The concentration of delinquency in the urban slum, economic deprivation and discontent, the gang as a folkway, and lower-class life styles as coherent culture patterns —these seemed to be the grand organizing forms, and individual differences appeared to be no more than minor. They were of interest like the delinquent act, but, like the act, not very important or meaningful out of their sociocultural context. Otto Pollak has observed that when one kind of specialist becomes absorbed in another's conceptual framework he goes through a period of positive transference in which he attributes greater explanatory power to the new set of concepts than to his own. My romance with ideas about society and culture (some will think, after reading further, that I was perhaps a fickle or shallow lover) was the stimulus for the thoughts that have gone into this work. The fact, for example, that there are very high rates of psychological disorder among other groups in society than lower-class delinquents, and some evidence that lower-class non-delinquents may have comparable rates of disturbance, suggested first that psychopathology might then explain everything and, therefore, nothing. Subsequently, the question of kinds of pathology became more important; after that the concept of psychopathology seemed to confuse more than to clarify some of the true relations of men to their culture and personal histories, and to obscure the significance of culture and history as human processes.

The thought that the personality patterns of delinquents were not very useful explanatory variables gave way to the consideration that their usefulness depended on what one was trying to explain, why one wanted to explain it, and at what level of cultural-historical development the inquirer found the concepts and information he needed when he began his inquiry. I wanted to understand delinquency as objectively as I could (which meant, to borrow a piece of a definition of objectivity that Erikson applied in another context, to understand it from the most advanced viewpoints of behavioral science that I could comprehend), and I hoped that the understanding would afford me a clearer opinion about what types of intervention might be most useful and possible. (There is little of the latter, by the way, in this book.) My doubts about the value of psychological factors were less a permanent disenchantment with them than a serious reconsideration of a sociological conception of personality that was different from and even at odds with the one I had learned and been using. Instead of the continuities within a person among his characteristics and across his lifetime, I looked at the connection between person and group. I realized once more how strikingly people come to differ in their various conformities, given their fundamentally similar potentials (which, I must admit, is another article of faith; there may be constitutional differences—see, for example, Sheldon's work on delinquent somatotypes—which are beyond the scope and interest of this effort).

Sociological Man—A Chameleon

If one reads the social students of delinquency with a careful eye on relations between self and society (and they must take a position about personality, even if it is not their primary interest), one gets the impression that they are not talking about a conception of personality that is simply more convenient for organizing the data in which they are interested, but one that they think is generally more useful and truer than a personality theory based on ideas about enduring inner needs and internal objects. I am referring, for instance, to Cloward and Ohlin's discussion of delinquency and to Cohen and Short's statement (1961) of a sociological consensus regarding the components of the self. They assume that an individual's expressive style, his motives, and his conduct standards are molded by his groups. So far so good; these premises are not open to question, at least not by a psychologist who has tried to absorb the viewpoints of H. S. Sullivan and Erikson. But it seems to me that they also assume that if a person moves, or is moved, from one social context to another the slate will be written anew by the changed social forces in the new situation. It is as if they have taken the sound observation that people in different groups differ as individuals and have made the unsound inference that a given individual is as changeable as his environment.

This may seem an absurd imputation about the views of scientists who have sought social explanations for lower-class adolescents' extraordinarily durable resistance to efforts to reduce their delinquency. The only explanation I offer is that there is a basic incompatibility in the social scientists' conceptions of the individual in his group which is not yet reconciled. For example, Cloward and Ohlin's book is a theoretical statement and only touches on issues of intervention, yet it seems fair to say that their argument rests on the idea that if the environment were improved and opportunities given to deprived youth, the incentives for illegal behavior, the really necessary and sufficient causes of delinquency, would be removed or reduced. Of further interest is the fact that the detailed proposal for the Mobilization For Youth action program in New York City, an application of opportunity structure theory, contained serious consideration of measures for changing self-defeating adaptations to a deprived environment. These adaptations, as they are spelled out in the proposal, amount to nothing less than self-perpetuating personality patterns which are independent of changes in external conditions; the psychologist Gordon Allport's concept of functional autonomy of motives and attitudes is explicitly used in the proposal to explain this kind of adjustment. Yet, the notion of self-defeating personality patterns is mentioned once, on page 39 of the original presentation of opportunity theory, and is given very little weight, even implicitly, anywhere in the work.

There are only two explicit references in Cloward and Ohlin's work to the idea that childhood experience may leave any lasting effects. One is a passing rejection of the argument that delinquency is a result of primitive or unsocialized impulses. (I reject it, too. It is pretty much a straw-man reservation, as will be made clear in Chapter 3.) They do recognize, and attempt to rebut, the thesis that socialization in female-based households may lead to problems of masculine identification in lower-class male youths, but beyond this they are silent on the subject of intrapsychic processes that might reach from childhood to a delinquent act in adolescence. Their treatment of delinquent aggressive behavior, for example, is entirely confined to situational factors present in adolescence (with one glaringly veiled exception, which I shall take up later). It is particularly notable that no reference is made to the unconscious. This concept has been indispensable in almost every system of thought about the continuity of personality since Freud. Clearly, Cloward and Ohlin felt that the concept was unnecessary in their explanation of delinquent behavior.

Cohen also seems to reject out of hand unconscious processes when he dismisses "vague and dubious displacement theories" of motivation to delinquent behavior. One of Cohen and Short's criticisms of psychoanalytic theory, in their paper on the social determinants of the self mentioned above, is that its assumptions about the operations of the unconscious are unprovable. Presumably, the type of proof these writers have in mind is an empirical one. The existence of the unconscious can no more be proved than can Cohen's proposal that the lower-class delinquents develop a reaction-formation against middle-class norms; both are intervening-variable constructs, cannot be directly observed, must be inferred from evidence, but are useful in organizing what can be directly observed. As to empirical documentation of the existence of the unconscious, there are almost seventy years of psychoanalytic case observations. As to its usefulness, it is a cornerstone, as I have said, of explanations regarding connections among an individual's personality characteristics and behavior in differing group situations and over periods of time. When we say that a person has displaced aggression from one object to another, we mean that the person has transferred aggressive feelings and purposes to a subjectively similar and more convenient substitute target, *and* that the inner shuttling of affect and aim is not readily verbalizable by the actor to himself or someone else. The transfer has the advantage of sparing the person a knowledge of what he intended toward the original object of his aggression. Our own experience may tell us that this is a neat way of explaining some of our own behavior and that of others whom we are able to observe over extended periods of time. This is one psychological process premised on the existence of the unconscious that Cohen has rejected, even though he has employed another, reaction-formation, that also assumes its existence—an example of his incompatible conceptions about personality.

As I reconsidered the plausibility of unconsciously mediated processes like displacement, it seemed that what really was being questioned—and ignored—was the basic notion that an inner reality and constancy also shape the flux of outer events. It seemed to me that the social and cultural students of delinquency had invented a psychology of their own that did not take dynamic psychiatry seriously. It was a psychology that gave credence, in assuming that the most significant elements of the self were those that were socially sharable, only to those purposes and feelings that were consciously admissible by an adult.

Even H. Bloch, a sociologist who, in his handbook on delinquency (with Flynn) and in his theory of delinquency (with Niederhoffer), has given careful thought to psychological factors as an aspect of an adolescent status crisis in our culture, seems to have misunderstood and discarded the main body of psychoanalytic observation and reconstruction of child development. In his work on social disorganization he constructs a detailed model of socialization and then pronounces at the end of it:

> *The emergence of the sex drive impinges upon the psychogenetic organization after it has already become firmly entrenched.* 1. The sex drive thus becomes canalized according to the already existent network of roles, attitudes, and wishes. 2. The Freudian contribution, thus [sic], must be utilized in relation to the system we have set up. . . . The manifold Freudian conceptions . . . in fact . . . are already becoming "respectable citizens" under the sociological reformative influence (pp. 118–9).

This version of the Freudian contribution, and particularly of the psychoanalytic definition of sexuality, would make little sense to a psychoanalyst.

Axelrad criticized an older generation of sociologists of delinquency in a succinct way: Shaw, Thrasher, and Whyte "avoided the problem of the relation of culture to personality. . . . [They] have been conspicuous for a reliance upon an extreme form of environmentalism, a bland lack of concern about unconscious factors, and a deterministic scheme based on a rather primitive form of learning theory" (p. 31). I think the writings of contemporary social students of delinquency warrant the same criticism on all counts.

Personality Perseveres

It seems to me that a psychology that has been simplified into the terms of an individual's situationally defined roles, rules, and goals does indeed avoid the relation of personality to cultural events. It simplifies that relation as well. This kind of psychology does not envisage a person as an actor, but rather as a reactor. Social scientists who employ this kind of psychology have rejected Freud's misconception of man against civilization but have replaced it with another, that of civilization (or culture, or society) over man. Perhaps because they have been primarily interested in the ways in which social forces determine each other, they have apparently assumed that social determinism is fundamental in human affairs. At least, they do not seem to have given any systematic consideration to the possibility that psychological and social processes may be interwoven in the causation of any human event. I think it is fair to say that the principal proposition of earlier transmission theorists of delinquency, Shaw and McKay and Sutherland, was that groups make individuals behave as they do. I think that W. B. Miller also takes this as a central tenet in his description of the culture patterns and patterning of lower-class people, including delinquents.

Certainly, the power relation between a group and any particular individual is clear and dictates the direction in which most of the efforts to influence will flow. It is one way of looking at matters that clarifies certain effects—for example, observing that delinquency is often a socially conforming act. But the relation can just as well be reversed; that is, men shape the behavior of groups. When sociologists exaggerate the importance of social forces and neglect others, they are creating a "social man," just as earlier economic philosophers invented an "economic man" and the Freudians an "instinctual man." Contemporary social theorists of delinquency like Cohen and Cloward and Ohlin have introduced important new concepts of individual participation in the evolution of delinquent groups; they have gone beyond assimilation of delinquent social forms to assay the ways the forms are constructed. However, they imagine that only situational factors are integrated in collective delinquent behavior. As long as they maintain that delinquents are most responsive to factors like rejection by middle-class people and barriers to opportunities for legitimate economic activity, these theorists will be postulating a social man.

Much of this sociology is very relativistic. It assumes that people at different social class levels, for example, are different only in that which can be sociologically defined but are the same in other respects, or that their other characteristics are not comparable. Cohen and Short, for instance, offer in contention with psychodynamic explanations the presumption that all or most people have personality problems; they neglect the fact that though personality processes may be as common as grass they may nonetheless be essential as intervening variables. This sociological relativism assigns to the group a life of its own separate from the personalities of members. A possibility overlooked is that earlier external conditions may have been different, generating new forces affecting the nature of the group.

These emergent forces are the strivings and relationship potentials of individuals and the kinds of satisfaction they need *as they enter the group*. These personal inclinations are not entirely definable in socioeconomic terms. One major weakness in Sutherland's transmission theory of delinquency was his suggestion that intensity of association between individual and gang is a condition of assimilation of group codes. Intensity of contact may not be related to environmental factors as totally as, say, Sutherland's frequency of contact; intensity is at least a partial function of personality factors, that is, of the attractiveness of the individual to the group and their attraction to him. Similarly, Cloward and Ohlin talk about needs for clothes, cars, and girls, which are not, psychologically speaking, needs at all but instrumentalities for satisfying needs that are left undefined. These "needs" may be sufficient for the authors' purposes, but there may be other needs equally important to the psychocultural process that makes delinquents.

The Subcultural Experience

Cohen's and Cloward and Ohlin's definitions of gang resolutions of adolescent problems of adjustment are highly profitable heuristic devices, because, as I have said, they have moved the sociology of delinquency away from paradigms of assimilation and imitation. Their theories are also sociological myths that pay insufficient attention to the continuity of individuals through their group experiences. Lower-class adolescent gangs do not get together because they have been rejected by the middle class or because middle-class means and/or ends of economic success have been barred to them. Some of these youths have been ganging together since they were two years old (W. B. Miller *a;* Gans). There probably could be no collective repudiation of conformity and no delinquent group resolutions without years of earlier attachment to peers and without a welding of personal styles and group ways.

The individual selects the group that will shape him. He progresses through a series of such group selections (except for the first, his family, and perhaps the second, his early childhood peer group, which may be considered given and which partly determine his subsequent choices); or he passes with his peers through a progression of group functions, depending on the goals of particular importance in each era of his life. Regarding "goals," I am thinking not only of socially defined roles and interests appropriate to each age grade in a particular subculture but also of stages of growth that must be surmounted in personality development (E. H. Erikson, 1950; 1959).

I think this progression of functions is implicit in the sociological concepts of role patterning or role sequences. Each subculture probably has two, three, or more "tracks" of such role sequences, programed for different relationship styles and different goal orientations, each track with a schedule for psychosocial and group functions and with scheduled revisions in orienting values and views of the world. The corner boy-college boy distinction in the lower class (Whyte) is probably a cross-sectional view of two such tracks at adolescence. Two lower-class progressions may be: school misbehavior and truancy in childhood, undifferentiated group delinquency (vandalism, theft, and gang fighting) in adolescence, economic marginality and petty criminality in adulthood; or, school misbehavior and petty theft in childhood, criminalistic group delinquency in adolescence, participation in organized crime in adulthood. The individual, progressively differentiated by his past experience, schedules himself for one or another of these tracks, depending on which one promises, through its styles and goals, to fulfill his purposes and capacities as they have been shaped so far.

A gang boy has years of negotiating issues of authority and subordination (sociologically, years of accepting and repudiating norms) behind him by the time he reaches adolescence. The ways in which he and his peers both have and have not dealt with parents, adults, and older children are early entries in their adolescent catalogue of beliefs and values. Together, they have been negotiating with sources of power and satisfaction since childhood, and by now they ought to have clear, if implicit, ideas and attitudes about how they must and should assert their own interests. The ordering of sociological propositions about the formation of delinquent norms can be reversed in this light: Delinquent groups do not repudiate conventional norms because of deprivation; they are in a deprived relation to educational and job opportunities because they previously repudiated norms that are part of a conforming child's preparation for school and job success. They do not evolve delinquent solutions because they have become alienated from conventional views and standards; they are alienated because they have evolved or have been patterned in ways that may or may not have been delinquent but that did deviate from a subcultural track that would lead to successful conformity.

Delinquency is a part of a fabric of commitment woven from earliest experience; it extends into personal relationships as well as into social views. Specific issues, both psychosocial and socioeconomic, confront an adolescent and stimulate him to redefine the arena and the objects of the game, but its rules have been undergoing definition since his infancy.

Reality vs. Realisms

Available sociological models, in short, show a direct participation of the delinquent in antisocial norms, without implications for his personality. I am trying to suggest that some delinquents participate in more intimate ways in the anomie of their subcultures and in the resulting creation of antisocial norms. I have already indicated two ways in which personality processes may have determining importance: personality as an intervening variable between social conditions and delinquent response; and interdetermining or feedback systems, in which personal responses to socioeconomic deprivation may independently introduce modifications in group beliefs and attitudes that were initially more direct, social responses to the same deprived conditions. Much more needs to be said, even in an introductory way, about the relation between personality and culture as it pertains to delinquency, and what I have to say about it here might be called the multiple levels of human reality.

Every elementary statistics text teaches that correlation is not causation. According to the pragmatic criterion, what is important is what helps us to solve our problems. But I want to consider further what might be important (logically determining) on the basis of facts and concepts at our disposal.

From a pragmatic standpoint all professional observers of delinquency, regardless of discipline, have to arrive at their respective conclusions empirically. Except for action programs, there is little opportunity to manipulate variables experimentally and to distinguish cause from concomitant. The sociological theories are one way of describing human interaction and its outcome, and action research will tell whether that description is sufficiently complete for all practical purposes.

I do not believe that there is anything basic about socioeconomic structure or culture patterns, unless the inquirer wants to know how either of these large systems affects subsystems within them, or unless he wants to understand the integration of either at the conceptual level of society or culture. If we want to understand how a social system developed, an analysis of that system with only sociological constructs, like the interacting effects of value, belief, and normative subsystems within the whole, will explain the system in terms of itself and be in some sense circular. A set of norms may be invoked to explain the emergence of other norms, but the "antecedent" norms may be partly definable by the norms they are supposed to have generated. If lower-class delinquency as a normative system is a response to conventional norms, it may also be argued that conventional respectability is a response to lower-class standards. It seems to me that we must turn to other factors to understand how the normative distinctions originated and why they continually change.

(The same criticism may be made of classical psychoanalytic theory. When psychological disorder is defined in terms of the solipsistic circle of id, ego, and superego without regard for the impact of sociocultural change on these factors, a logical problem of endless regress is generated. I interpret Merton's criticism of Freudian theory in the opening paragraphs of his paper on anomie as a posing of the question, How did the socializers become disturbed to begin with?)

Such a self-enclosed analysis seems clear only to the specialist, because usually the concepts he is employing are those most familiar to him; his analysis may be well integrated, but he has restricted himself to one level of reality and has consequently simplified his problem.

Economic systems, to choose another example, are not entirely explainable in terms of economic forces. The development of Communism in Russia has had something to do with sadomasochistic and other authoritarian elements in the Russian "soul," judging from Erikson's (1950) study of Gorky and from the historic relations between Russian peasants and their feudal masters. Lenin's uncompromising split with the more moderate Mensheviks may have been partly determined by as highly personal an event as the execution of Lenin's older brother during Lenin's formative years. And Freud's psychology of women may be meaningfully discussed in terms of his having been an exalted Victorian male and of the suppression of women in his time. Ibsen's works, viewed as a social commentary on the inhibitions and frustrations of bourgeois Victorian women, render Freud's observations on the innate envy and moral inferiority of women more understandable. Closer to home, as Cloward and Ohlin say, the toughness and the exaggerated protestations of virility expressed by some lower-class gang boys may be related to the absence of more conventional ways of acquiring prestige. It is likely that these characteristics are also related to the fact that these boys spent their childhoods under the domination of matriarchs (W. B. Miller *b*; Rohrer and Edmonson). Toynbee has commented that "The meaning of a thing can be sought for only in some field outside the thing that we are trying to interpret and understand." We might enrich our understanding of delinquency if we consider the interaction effects of social values, beliefs, and norms; subcultural traditions and customs; interpersonal strivings; and intrapsychic structures. My theory is a probe in that direction.

Interpersonal Aspects of Class Distinctions

For example, Cohen and Hodges and W. B. Miller attribute the weaker marital relationship in the lower class to the economic insecurity of the men, who have had to travel away from their homes to find work and at periods have been unable to support their families. As a result, these authors suggest, the men and women involved have learned, essentially, to do without each other. In other words these writers are specifying the economic relation of these men to the larger system as determining the separate companions, interests, and decisions that they and their wives have to develop.

This is an important area for delinquency theory because in the view of some, notably Miller himself, some male delinquent behavior may represent an effort to allay sex role anxiety resulting from family backgrounds in which the mother was the central figure. Is it possible that the economic relations of lower-class men with their employers might have personal effects that could be expected to influence these men's interpersonal affairs, including their marital relationships?

The economic relation of employer and employee is also related to a value system and a world view, such as the Protestant ethic, which prescribes (and in a sense determines) the employer's single obligation to pay an unskilled laborer for his work. What other values and views determine the economic relation? Discrimination against minorities frequently serves economic interests. Historically, the white slaveholder and currently many white employers and merchants justify some of their business practices by their biases. Prejudice as a system of beliefs could not exist without the capacity of the ego to create and maintain elaborate distortions of reality. Most of the familiar defense mechanisms, repression, displacement, projection, etc., have been used to explain how people can sustain their stereotypes of minorities when they interact with members of these groups. (These mechanisms may function as intervening variables in the generation of any belief system, and are implied by all the delinquent techniques for neutralizing guilt, described by Sykes and Matza, which are functional beliefs.)

Furthermore, employer and employee negotiate their economic agreements at other levels besides the economic, that is, besides deciding on the value of labor. The employer may selectively perceive and act in ways, and expect and require certain types of behavior by the employee, that will support his economically functional stereotypes. This is Merton's self-fulfilling prophesy operating at an interpersonal level.

Many Negro employees, caste members a few generations removed from being chattel, have had very little choice but to accept the legitimacy of whites' economic power. Since white economic activity and rights have been grounded on claims to superiority and on attributions of Negro inferiority, the Negro, in the act of accepting the legitimacy of white economic power, has had to make some accommodation to stereotypes regarding himself. The psychosocial aspects of this accommodation have been well described (Davis and Dollard; Kardiner, *et al.*, 1945, 1951; Karon). Negroes have identified with standard American (white Anglo-Saxon) beliefs and norms, and since some traditional American attitudes toward them have been persecutory, this has meant an identification with the aggressor, resulting in self-rejection. Self-rejection is a psychological adaptation to, and a deep internalization of, the role expectancies of prejudiced and economically powerful whites. Because the adaptation prepares one party to negotiate more securely, it can be said that Negro self-rejection may codetermine the economic relations of whites and Negroes.

Cultural Anachronisms and Class Distinctions

The historic power balance between slaveholder and slave almost required that the Negro, in order to survive, assimilate white attitudes toward himself. But power and privilege have been accumulating in Negro hands for a hundred years, however begrudged and inadequate. There is some indirect evidence that Negroes' self-attitudes are being maintained in projections about monolithic discriminatory practices. Aside from the psychological speculation, at least it may be true that some Negroes are maintaining convictions about their disbarment that are anachronistic; that is, they believe there are fewer opportunities than actually exist. There have been reports in the popular press that business and industry are willing to hire more Negroes, but cannot find enough who are sufficiently trained to fill the job openings. I assume here, with Cloward and Ohlin (pp. 121–24), that beliefs about opportunities influence educational aspiration.

Obviously a factor of culture lag may be involved here; job opportunities may have opened up too recently to have affected Negroes' beliefs, and there may be a discrepancy between job opportunities and restricted access to higher education and skilled job training. I should like to assume for a moment that the lags are not so great as to account for all of Negroes' skepticism, assuming the existence of that skepticism. The persistence of such non-functional beliefs, which do not reflect changes in socioeconomic realities, has been repeatedly documented in the anthropological literature and in the history of minority groups in this country.

A striking example of the latter is the way the Dakota Sioux have continued to socialize their children to the values of a warrior society, which has been dead almost as long as slavery, despite the anomie and the personal unhappiness created by the conflict between old and new values and despite the at times ruthless efforts of the government to root out the old culture (MacGregor, *et al.*). Regarding the Dakota Sioux, Erikson has said that it is one of the most paradoxical problems of human evolution that virtues which were originally designed to safeguard an individual's or a group's self-preservation become rigid under the pressure of anachronistic fears of extinction and thus can render a people unable to adapt to changed necessities (1950, p. 113).

Cloward and Ohlin recognize the importance of such anachronisms when they discuss a continuing disparagement of educational aspiration among some American minorities. "Although these cultural orientations," they say, "persist as major obstacles to the utilization of opportunity, it should be remembered that they emerged initially as adaptive responses to socially structured deprivations" (p. 103).

Whether or not these authors have entirely accounted for the origins of these cultural traditions, their comment does not meet the problem of emergence squarely. For if such subcultural patterns persist in the face of changes in actual opportunities, they are affecting lower-class deprivation as variables independent of socioeconomic conditions. Nor is it likely that the most efficient way of altering such beliefs is a further improvement, from the minority's standpoint, of socioeconomic conditions. It seems to me, therefore, that for both practical as well as theoretical reasons we need to know more about the psychological and cultural forces that maintain such subcultural systems of belief.

Self-Rejection as an Identity

The most frequently described effect of the Negro's identification with his white persecutor is his adoption of the white's evaluation of the Negro, *i.e.*, that he is bad or inferior. Stereotyping, however, involves not only negative evaluations but also negative images. In the vicious circle of stereotyping, the white person has attributed to the Negro those qualities most abhorred in his own culture: uncleanliness and stupidity, justifying white aggression; leading in turn to guilt, fear of retaliation, and further hostility on the part of whites. Further, in the case of the male, cruel and gross sensuality; and, regarding the Negro female (sometimes to justify the white man's violation of his own standards in taking her), wantonness and general impulsivity. (Sociologically this attribution of traits might be rendered as the maintenance and elaboration of beliefs supporting the economic norms.)

If data show that Negroes internalized these evaluations, uncounted numbers of them must also have absorbed the stereotypes. This was socioeconomic reality, too, and if Negroes had very little opportunity to formulate, let alone validate, some other conception of themselves, it would have been either psychologically appropriate (realistic) or inevitable for them to try to *live inside the stereotype*. That is, the most reliable means of obtaining satisfaction and security may have been to conform to the pejorative definition (as in the lower-class subservience of an Uncle Tom or the middle-class subservience of a white man's Negro). Moreover, the avoidance of one set of definitions might lead to the imposition of others equally negatively defined (childish bum, dirty rapist). In *To Kill a Mockingbird* (Lee), once the prosecuting attorney maneuvered the Negro defendant into pitting his truth against his white accuser's lies, the white jury's condemnation of him as a rapist became tragically inevitable. In a clinical context the confirmation of what Erikson calls a negative identity may be seen fairly commonly in those capable middle-class youths who are school failures; one or both of their parents may have been underachievers and may be endlessly dissatisfied with and derogatory about their children's school efforts.

Respecting the Multiple Levels of Human Reality

Earlier I indicated my personal belief that social structure is not fundamental in causing human behavior. Social structure is no more "there" than personality structure; it is not reality; it is a set of useful constructs for ordering certain aspects of reality. I also said we might avoid circularity and enrich our understanding of origins and changes of social structure by examining other aspects of human realities than social structure. As examples we have considered how prejudice and stereotyping are constituents of the assertion and acceptance of socioeconomic norms between white and Negro.

A social scientist might say that these psychosocial aspects were dependent variables, determined by socioeconomic conditions, in the way, for example, that Cloward and Ohlin account for the emergence of negative attitudes toward education among some minorities. Conversely, however, I have suggested that prejudice as an ideology makes the socioeconomic norms possible, because ideology, like rationalizations, sanctions actions from which people might otherwise abstain (de Sausseure). Like rationalizations, of course, the emergence of an ideology presupposes the possibility of and the desire to take the action it legitimizes. Consequently, an interactional description might be constructed: An economic opportunity, for the white person, exists (implying pre-existing values and beliefs about the significance of such opportunities); he can exploit it more fully with cheap labor; he creates, and the Negro accepts, a set of beliefs regarding the laborer's inferiority to legitimize the employer's low wages (or, historically, bare subsistence for slaves).

The social scientist is in a position to describe the consensualized and collective aspects of action. He can describe the social, economic, and cultural forces impinging on decision-making and the impact of decisions on these collective structures and processes. The specialist in personality, on the other hand, is equipped with special methods, concepts, and interests to describe the inner and interpersonal processes by which a decision is reached and its interpersonal effects. (This is not to say that sociologists cannot be expert psychological observers, as will be seen in Chapter 3.) What is known about self-rejection as a component of Negro accommodation to the norms, for example, has been uncovered by psychological investigation (Brenman; Clark and Clark; Goff; Kardiner and Ovesey; Karon; Myers and Yochelson; Radke and Trager). *Sociological concepts cannot adequately define the human energies that generate a belief system and the energies that a belief system mobilizes in the formation and maintenance of values and norms.*

The next chapter will summarize a set of propositions regarding psychological processes which may be interrelated with the social emergence of deviance. It will summarize, in other words, the general theory in this book. Negro self-rejection is only one instance, although perhaps the one most often examined, of self-injurious personal adaptations to social systems. (I mean by the latter term a related set of beliefs, values, and norms to which people may subscribe.) There have been many other minority groups who have been economically exploited for the creation of capital in the history of this country; all of them have been objects of prejudice and stereotyping, as social distance studies have consistently shown. Furthermore, there are several other types of structural disadvantage, besides lack of economic opportunity, for groups not now subject to minority stereotyping. These disadvantages may also promote self-derogatory adaptations. These personal adaptations are the bases, in the theory to be presented, for types of personal dissidence within a social system and for pressures toward deviance from it.

chapter 2

psychosocial pressures to deviance

Sociological Models of Deviance: Partial or General Theories?

ONE of Merton's purposes in his paper on anomie is to demonstrate how deviant behavior might result from disadvantages in the social system for the deviant individual rather than from psychological disturbance. He is unequivocally opposed to any psychological explanation that would claim that most deviants have poorly repressed instincts, that man's nature is antisocial; that much seems clear. However, it is also clear that he speaks as a social scientist, delineating what interests him and leaving other determinants to other specialists.

He states at the outset: "Should [the search for social pressures toward non-conformity] be at all successful, *some* forms of deviant behavior will be found to be as psychologically normal as conformist behavior, and the *equation* of deviation and abnormality will be put in question" (p. 126; my italics). Later he comments, "But we should note again . . . that we are here examining *modes of adaptation* to contradictions in the cultural and social structure: we are not focusing on character or personality types. . . . though the psychodynamic mechanisms of (a ritualistic) adaptation have been fairly well identified and linked with patterns of discipline and socialization in the family, much sociological research is still required to explain why these patterns are presumably more frequent in certain social strata and groups than in others" (pp. 141, 142). He does not exclude personality factors from deviant behavior.

On the other hand Cohen, to some extent, and Cloward and Ohlin, more clearly, seem to polarize psychological disorder and delinquency. These authors seem to suggest that motivation to deviance comes to one fundamental "either-or" issue: Is a person impelled to act out of internal frustration and strains (which may then be expressed in psychiatrically definable symptoms), or does he act against external, *i.e.*, social-structural, impediments to his satisfaction (as when he participates in gang delinquency)? Cohen puts the polarity this way: "the connection we suggest between status-frustration and the aggressiveness of the delinquent subculture seems to us more plausible than many frustration-aggression hypotheses because it involves no obscure and dubious 'displacement' of aggression against 'substitute' targets" (p. 132).

Cloward and Ohlin dichotomize the respective consequences of blaming self or the system for personal failure:

> Whether the "failure" blames the social order *or* himself is of central importance to the understanding of deviant conduct. When a person ascribes his failure to injustice in the social system, he may . . . become alienated from the established set of social norms . . . The individual who locates the source of failure in his own inadequacy, on the other hand, feels pressure to change himself rather than the system. Suffering from loss of self-esteem, he must either *develop mechanisms that will protect him from these feelings of personal inadequacy* or work toward eliminating them by developing greater personal competence . . . attributing failure to one's own faults reveals an attitude supporting the legitimacy of the existing norms (pp. 111, 112; my italics).

W. B. Miller also dichotomizes "psychopathological" and "normal." Since psychiatry considers such symptomatic expressions of aggression as withdrawal, depression, alcoholism, addiction, prejudice, and projection to be abnormal, then typical forms of aggression in the gang must be normal. "From this perspective, this type of adolescent group appears not as a defective or pathological organism, but as a highly effective device for accommodating [the] universal human problem [of aggression]" (Miller, *et al.*, p. 298).

Psychological Antecedents of Social Discontent

To pursue an alternative line of thinking, every defection from a social system implies a prior commitment to that system, either by an individual or by his subcultural predecessors. By the same logic as that expressed in the passage from Cloward and Ohlin just quoted, an individual who accepts the legitimacy of a social system in which he is prevented from reaching goals that the system enjoins, may (although not necessarily must) blame himself for his failure *before* he withdraws his loyalty to the system. The process of social disaffection may be preceded and mediated by a dissatisfaction with self as a participant in the system.

That is, a person may rid himself of the self-disparagement resulting from his relatively poor performance by attributing its cause to circumstances over which he has relatively little control, such as social barriers to opportunity. In such a case we should then say that the person's sense of unjust deprivation (Cloward and Ohlin, pp. 113ff.) regarding restrictions on his chances for success by conforming is indeed a reaction to such barriers but is not a fully accurate expression of his private reactions to limitations on opportunity. He has projected the causes of personal failure and has *externalized his reaction to failure;* that is, he blames others or the system not instead of, but as a displacement from, himself.

The person's alienation from a frustrating system and its resulting social consequences may be as Cloward and Ohlin describe them—the alienation determines the individual on a path of deviant behavior—but the purpose of the person's disaffection and the psychological processes involved may be other than they indicate. Projection is a defensive process that wards off but does not resolve a conflict state. To the extent that a person has internalized cultural goals, to the extent that he has identified with them in his conscience, he may not succeed in renouncing a negative evaluation of self. Perceiving his failure to approach the system's ideals, he may be able to repress the evaluation only by this process of projection and externalization.

Camus, in his philosophical analysis of rebellion, tries to distinguish between the values implicit in revolt and those involved in revenge. Rebellion, he says, affirms the positive in man while revenge expresses resentment, which is marked by feelings of impotence, passivity, and envy. "Resentment is always resentment against oneself," Camus says (p. 23). He admits, however, that some acts of rebellion are motivated by resentment. Whereas Cloward and Ohlin suggest in the passage quoted above that all deviance is an affirmation of self against the social system, the theory of this book agrees with Camus: Some deviance also involves resentment which is directed as much against the self as against others. This whole theory is simply an elaboration of the latter, alternative assumption.

Self-Discontent as a Latent Social Function

Merton has anticipated attempted rapprochements such as this, between personality and social process, in his methodological analysis of functionalism (pp. 21–81). He points out, "Too often, a single term has been used to symbolize different concepts, just as the same concept has been symbolized by different terms" (p. 22). Further, "just as the same item [of social or cultural forms] may have multiple functions, so may the same function be diversely fulfilled by alternative items" (p. 35). Failure to recognize the manifest and latent functions that a given piece of a social or cultural order can serve, or the possibility that one function is served by several different pieces, confuses the distinction, Merton says, "between conscious *motivations* for social behavior and its *objective consequences*. . . . How easily, and how unfortunately, the sociologist may identify *motives* and [social] *functions*. . . . The motive and the function vary independently . . . [and when this is forgotten] sociologists [may] confuse the subjective categories of motivation with the objective categories of function" (p. 61, Merton's italics). "Inclusion of motives in [a] descriptive account helps explain the *psychological motives subserved* by [a social] pattern" (p. 59, my italics).

Cohen uses the concept "status discontent" to indicate lower-class youths' antipathy to middle-class evaluations of them, and Cloward and Ohlin speak of "position discontent" to conceptualize lower-class youths' resentment of barriers to attainment of success goals. I am suggesting that both these terms are used in such a way that they may symbolize socially relevant discontent *and* dissatisfaction with self. The terminology obscures self-discontent as a *sociologically latent* function of success barriers that provides the *personal motivation* to the establishment of illegitimate social systems. The whole process of delinquent development, then—social disaffection, repudiation, establishment of new ideological and normative systems—is seen here as subserving the psychologically motivating qualities inherent in the self-discontent of individuals who had been living within the legitimate sociocultural system. Furthermore, I shall try to indicate that some personality characteristics of some delinquents may be functionally related to structural restraints rising out of the social order; that the *items*, to use Merton's terms, of socialization and resulting personality configurations in the young may be fulfilling the same *function* of alienation from the social system as do status and position discontent sociologically defined.

Psychopathology and Externalized Discontent

I am following another lead, suggested by Erikson: "I have indicated in detail how . . . adolescent conflicts find a temporary 'solution' in borderline conditions [disturbed reactions verging on extremely severe neurotic and psychotic states]. I would like to point out to psychopathologists that we can probably learn a lot from juxtaposing 'borderline conditions' and 'delinquency'—in a way comparable to Freud's original juxtaposition of hysteria and perversion. In both pairs, the first expresses by inaction and displacement what the second 'lives out' " (Witmer and Kotinsky, p. 11, fn.). Instead of *presuming* that the internal strains toward delinquency are opposed to those leading to psychological disturbance, I have tried to compare data about delinquents with psychopathological symptoms, to see whether there is any commonality of underlying personal states. I then reasoned backwards, to socialization conditions which might have precipitated those personal states; and, also juxtaposing psychological stress reactions and the reactions of adults undergoing unrelenting socioeconomic disadvantages, I tried to work "forward" to personal adaptations that might affect the socialization of their children.

This is a theory of delinquency in a sociocultural context; it does not assume, as Cohen's theory seems to, that prospective delinquents generally become alienated because of direct contact with social frustrations. The process of projection and *externalized discontent* may apply not only to adolescents who are about to enter a system that seems to omen sacrifice without due compensation, but also to their parents and other adults who provide the social reality in which the potential delinquents grow up.

Personal Functions of Ideology

Merton describes the social conditions that generate ideologies which legitimize deviant behavior as conditions that justify illegitimate means to general cultural goals, or create new, illegitimate goals, or do both. But a new ideology may, at least initially, function as a means of expressing states of tension and personal unhappiness resulting from adherence to the ideology it replaces. Thus, according to De Saussure, the Protestant Reformation may have increased the individual's opportunity to free himself from poverty by legitimizing his desire to throw off his father's authority. The Reformation permitted the individual to come closer to God the Father by suppressing ecclesiastic authority; even his submission to Calvinistic predestination may have functioned as a denial of personal responsibility for outdoing his father by amassing greater wealth.

It is important to note that a new ideology does not immediately release an adherent from the personal mold in which he was cast;

it is possible that he and his descendants may have to compensate, through the new ideology, for archaic claims of conscience until the old ideals and guilts are gradually renounced in successive identity crises over several generations. This, it seems to me, is the implication of anachronistic traditions in some subcultures; of witch-hunts during the first two centuries of Protestantism in Europe and America (an historic instance of externalized guilt); of heavy reliance on dogmatism during the Reformation, which De Saussure specifically mentions as a possible defense mechanism. It is important to note this, I think, because old insults to self-esteem may persist in displaced forms even in long-established illegitimate social systems, such as organized crime; the professional criminal may, as it were, have stopped living inside an older stereotype that had been applied to him or his parents when he or they were disfavored participants in the legitimate system, but the stereotype may go on living inside him, or indeed, living him.

Normative Constraints and Adaptive Personal Limitations

The self-rejection of the Negro is a prototype of self-discontent produced by the legitimate sociocultural system; neither racial caste nor socioeconomic deprivation is the only institutionalized handicap imposed by the prevailing ideology. Institutionalized restraints on people's capacities to negotiate with others for satisfaction of needs and strivings—restraints, in other words, on their ego resources—can be cited at every socioeconomic level, from the deprived to the privileged. It is hoped that a consideration of these restrictions on ego function from an integrated theoretical standpoint will help to clarify not only lower-class delinquency but middle-class delinquency as well.

I propose that any adult who has participated in a social system which enjoins certain goals but sets many limitations on access to them runs the risk of compromising his ego capacities in trying to conform to the institutionalized restraints that exist for people of his status level, whatever his relative social advantages. Which limitations of ego functioning he accepts and internalizes are likely to bear a relation to the particular institutional barriers to achievement that fall most heavily on people at his class level.

I am adopting the premise of Merton's paper on bureaucratic personality that "man is to a very important degree controlled by his social relations to the instruments of production" (p. 152). The emphasis on sentiments supporting the goals of an organization, he says,

> leads to a transference of the sentiments from the aims of the organization onto the particular details of behavior required by the rules. Adherence to the rules, originally conceived of as a means, becomes transferred into an end-in-itself; there occurs the familiar process of displacement of goals whereby "an instrumental value becomes a terminal value" (pp. 155).

This is a powerful enough postulate to generalize, for heuristic purposes, to relations between personality and other structured restraints besides bureaucratic organization.

An adult whose action is restrained in our society, with its universalistic goals, may blame himself, that is, disparage himself for his personal limitations and be discontented with them rather than accepting them fatalistically as, for example, members of a rigid caste society might. (The stability of Eastern caste systems, according to H. A. Gould, has depended partly on the preponderance of ascriptive criteria for stratification over achievement criteria.) Psychologically, there are no limits that a person in our system must place on his ego-ideal except those that his maturity and experience may have imposed on his narcissism.

While, however, a person may adopt and maintain certain aspirations (to advance his status, if he is in the middle class; to increase his economic success, if he is in a lower one), he may modify his conscience in other ways by idealizing (attributing moral validity to) those norms that restrict his relations with more powerful members of the social structure. These ideologically based superego demands and prohibitions (in the sense that they flow from normative restraints predicated on collectively held beliefs and values) are the internal forces that restrict his capacities for personal action and interpersonal negotiation. The kind of self-disparagement will depend on which ego functions have been weakened.

The Functional Equivalence of Differing Personal Adaptations

A person may rely on either negative or positive ego attributes in performing a function. Whether an individual occupies a more or less favored position in the social structure, he may subordinate himself trustfully or fearfully, may assume authority benignly or harshly. We could say that he has either subjugated himself to a conscience which is primitive in certain respects or been guided by a relatively flexible and permissive one. A privileged, prejudiced person may or may not have an authoritarian personality (the concept and some of the research pertaining to it are reviewed in Simpson and Yinger), and deprived people may also differ in this dimension (see Cohen and Hodges on authoritarianism among blue-collar people). The functions of a given social status are usually broadly enough defined to permit its occupants a variety of interpersonal styles; in fact, when we consider some of the institutional restrictions, we shall see that certain limitations on ego function may be very useful in performing some occupational roles. At the very least—and this is the point of this paragraph—because a person may rely on either his ego weaknesses or his ego strengths in occupying a status, these personal attributes may be indiscriminable sociologically and may therefore, for sociological purposes, be considered functional equivalents.

Terms

When I refer to ego strengths vs. ego limitations, weakness, or vulnerability, I am following the routes mapped by Erikson in his topography of ego functioning. I use the concept of superego prohibitions to mean the internal representation of not only the environmental conditions that regulate a person's behavior, but also those conditions under which he experiences accrued defeats during his ego development or under which he accepts compromises in his ego functioning. A person's feelings of distrust, shame, doubt, guilt, and inferiority regarding himself and others are unpleasant internal states which may prompt defensive behavior or self-defeating ways of dealing with others; they may also be viewed as indicators of the person's subjugation to his conscience.

Ego-ideal and ideals are either internalized beliefs and values, mediated by prior socialization and identification with others in adolescence and adulthood to maximize ego strengths and accomplishments, or a positive moral valuation placed on ways of dealing with others—adaptations to institutional restraints—which constrict ego operations and ultimately contribute to a sense of personal defeat.

Ego Accommodation to Mutuality vs. Conflict. An adult as well as a child may undergo an injurious personal adaptation to a situation, if it continues long enough. The ego, whether young or old, has the widest latitude for development and use of capacities in situations that permit negotiations for mutual satisfaction—in situations where individuals reciprocally regulate themselves in and through their regulation of the other. (The level of regulation and the issues to be negotiated among the parties concerned depend, of course, on the level of ego development of each. A child who successfully acquires control of his sphincters and some feelings of competent individuality in the coordination of his gross musculature is one whose parents have confirmed, in their dealings with him, that he has achieved a certain limited independence from them.) An adult, like a child, is handicapped in his ego functioning in situations where interdependence and collaboration have been limited, where the other parties disjoin their interests from his and are able, through their relative power, to coerce his adherence to their decisions. In the social structure, people may derive their power from ideologically based norms that bind lower-status individuals to certain prescribed interactions; the more powerful, as mediators of institutional restraints, may then interact in disjunctive and coercive ways with those of lower status.

Symptoms or Externalizations: Further Analogies. The externalization of discontent is viewed as a "lived-out" analog of psychologically disturbed behavior. The disturbed individual displaces the expression of his conflict state to symbolic objects or acts (the hostile and extortive interpersonal intent, which remains repressed, is sometimes referred to as "secondary gains" [Szasz]).

The externalizer projects his own interference with his ego functioning into others about him, and is able to obtain temporary surcease from his inner state by blaming others for his troubles and by discharging his discontent in forms of aggression (of disjunction and coercion) against them. Both symptom and externalization, however, remain enslaved by the claims of conscience and yield only limited satisfactions. The externalizing person remains subservient to his conscience in the kinds of accusations he levels first against himself and then, by projection, against social subordinates, peers, and authority figures; he lives out the particular kinds of restrictions he has placed on his own action by alienating himself from others' interests and by attempting to coerce them in the same ways in which his conscience, alienated from some of his ego resources, has coerced his own ego.

The advantages of externalizing as a means of coping with internal conflict alternative to symbolic expression ("psychopathology") are several. The symbolizer may succeed in mobilizing the intervention of special enabling agents (such as psychiatrists) and may succeed in having himself withdrawn from conflict-provoking situations and placed in a more secure environment (such as a mental hospital), but if he does so, he must undergo a social labeling process (Kai Erikson) that will deprive him of many adult privileges and satisfactions.

The externalizer, on the other hand, retains his socioeconomic status and with it his functionality and adult freedoms. He is able to avoid the more categoric attribution of unfitness that many psychiatric patients must suffer and is able thereby to maintain greater self-esteem. His denial and living-out of conflict may ward off certain unpleasant subjective states much more successfully than do the coping mechanisms of a psychologically disturbed individual; they may even bring the externalizer the satisfaction of realistic accomplishments when he joins cause with other externalizers (such as the rewards of conformity to, and status advance in, an illegitimate social system). The support of the externalizing person's distortions by other externalizers helps him also to maintain his ego intact and to avoid the frightening feelings of identity disruption that a neurotic or psychotic person may experience.

There remains the question of the differences between persons who externalize and those who symbolize. That is, why are some persons' projections realistic—aimed at real people and situations and organized with considerable amounts of fact and reasoning—while others' are patently paranoid—containing bizarre ideas about fantasied referents? Let me emphasize that though the intrapsychic processes involved in externalization may be clarified by analogy to those underlying psychologically disturbed behavior, I am by no means asserting that the people involved suffer from the same severity of conscience or of ego deficiency. (As a matter of fact, the worst possible misconstruction one might put on this theoretical treatment of pressures toward deviance would be to interpret it as an argument that self-discontented people are "sick.")

We might expect that the conscience of a symbolizing person will be more demanding and repressive than that of an externalizing person, and that his ego will be similarly more intimidated in seeking realistic satisfactions. This might result from a consistently more repressive socialization, one which permits the growing individual fewer ego achievements and which, on the whole, does not tolerate even the less indirect forms of counteraggression against parents and siblings. We might also infer, from the psychocultural viewpoint of this book, that this repressive experience in the family may mediate a relatively greater oppression of certain categories of people inherent in different social systems—as for instance the higher incidence of certain forms of hysteria among women than among men in Victorian Europe (see Szasz for a discussion of possible psychocultural relationships), and the higher degree of psychiatric impairment among low socioeconomic groups in our society (Langner and Michael).

Preconditions for the Emergence of Self-Discontent. A final problem in positing this kind of externalizing adaptation (and it may be the foremost in importance) is to elucidate the conditions under which only certain people may become self-blaming. For it is most likely false to assume that all people subjected to structural disadvantage succumb in the manner being considered, no matter how severe a strain social realities impose on them. As Bettleheim suggested in a *Harper's* article, even though most European Jews may have submitted in a masochistic and sheep-like way to mass extermination, there still were individual instances of realistic resistance and the collective resistance of the Warsaw Ghetto uprising. More relevant to our considerations, no study of delinquency incidence has shown that *all* youth in any high-delinquency area become delinquent; Reckless was able to locate in such areas conforming youth whose families and personalities seemed relatively insulated from the deviant and (presumably) personally disordered lives around them. Besides, it may be hard for some readers to believe that any adult personalities may be damaged by situational stress, even though Bettelheim's (1958) classic observations of regressive behavior among concentration camp inmates offers empirical support, and findings regarding adverse intrapsychic reactions of some subjects in sensory deprivation research provide some experimental support (Kubzansky, pp. 67–78, in Biderman and Zimmer).

I should like to appeal to the concept of individual predisposition as one condition which may differentiate those who make self-compromising responses to structural strains from those who do not. Those adults whose ego functions have already been limited in conforming to archaic but still extant ideologies, as mentioned a little back, would be less well equipped to negotiate current oppressive social conditions resourcefully; they would be more likely to surrender behaviors that might have given them feelings of trust and competence again. The predisposition, then, would be an ego incapacity in the adult related to anachronistic subcultural traditions. (Four such psychological adaptations to subcultural anachronisms are discussed on pp. 56–58.) Such a *culturally* compromised adult might assimilate *structural* compromises of individual action into his ego and conscience.

There is obviously some risk of circularity in this reasoning; but it is not suggested that the question of personal maladaptation to society reverts back endlessly and atavistically to psychological ancestry. Just as institutionalized restrictions do not come about overnight, neither do belief and values systems, and it is probable that self-defeating adaptations to ideologies and attendant norms develop cumulatively, perhaps over several generations. What may begin as a situational stress reaction or as a relatively small concession to current sociocultural conditions in one adult may be transmitted in his socialization of his children and elaborated by them in their identity decisions, in what may be a progressive *characterological erosion* in a chain of connected lifetimes.

Strict sociological analyses may view action primarily as response to contemporaneous forces—group norms and values impinging on the actor at the moment—and tend to err in the other direction, that is, by diminishing or even ignoring the relevance of personal, familial, and subcultural history. This is the conceptual error of sociological realism to which I have alluded and which will be discussed more fully later. Without discussing why he thinks so, Cohen, for instance, apparently assumes that displacement explanations of delinquency are vague and dubious in contrast to middle-class rejection; I wonder why he finds the superiority of situational analysis of pressures to deviance self-evident.

Cloward and Ohlin are subject to the same conceptualizing bias in singling out the desire for material goods and money as the most important frustration underlying lower-class delinquency. Since it is hard to believe that these desires become intense to a person much before the age of ten, one is left to wonder whether nothing happened to a delinquent before that age which might also have some bearing on his deviance. Again, Cloward's (1960) theory of inmate social organization in prisons assumes that the illegitimate character of the system results from relatively contemporaneous deprivations and status degradations imposed on the inmates as law offenders, and that earlier socialization is in a sense irrelevant. Not only do his and Ohlin's theory of delinquency and W. B. Miller's find illegitimate norms and social goals in lower-class enculturation, but there is also good empirical basis to infer that psychocultural experience is important in the social organization of illegitimate behavior, at least so far as inmate social systems are concerned (Rubenfeld and Stafford).

Overview of Table 1. In approaching a step-by-step exposition of Table 1 (and in contemplating an explanation of a later table) I am reminded, uncomfortably, of Erikson's remark to the effect that diagrams acquire a life of their own. I confess (or externalize my discontent by retorting beforehand) that I am not highly confident that I have isolated as clearly as possible the essential entry under each heading; I suppose that is why there are sometimes several terms in one category, rather than the crystallized polarities one finds in Erikson's tables. But it is hoped that several terms will indicate the nature of the variables involved better than one, and it should be understood that all entries are subject to revision, by myself or others.

Table 1—The Externalization of Self-Discontent

EGO CAPACITIES				IDEALIZATIONS					
Strengths (Virtues)	*Weaknesses*	*Ideologically Based Restrictions*	*Socio-economic Class Affected**	*Discouraged*	*Encouraged*	*Self-Experiences; Attributions to Status Equals & Subordinates*	*Projected Attributions to Superiors*	*Counter-idealizations*	*Externalizations*
trust (hope)	distrust	exclusion distance	LL LL	communality petition	self-interest grandiosity	untrustworthiness isolation unworthiness	selfishness insensitiveness	"trouble, toughness smartness, fate, excitement, autonomy" (W. B. Miller)	exploitation
autonomy (will)	shame, doubt	economic & political dispossession	LL, UL	expression of self-interest spontaneous contribution	scrupulosity	helplessness insignificance presumptuousness	intransigence extortiveness	willfulness wariness	constringency negativism
		subordination, work routinization	UL, LM						
initiative (purpose)	guilt	culture conflict	UL, LM	assumption of responsibility	authoritarianism	impugnation rivalrousness transgression envy	jealousy vengefulness	arrogation	rebellion
		centralization of authority	UL, LM, UM						
		work bureaucratization	LM, UM						
industry (skill)	inferiority	technological change culture change	UL, UM UM	usage familiarity	technicism status "abstractification" (Fromm)	ineptitude uselessness maneuvering	coldness pragmatism	"technical ruthlessness" (Erikson)	"innovation" (Merton) contriving

The several headings across the table, after the first two indicating ego attributes according to Erikson, indicate the sequence in the emergence of externalized discontent. Ideologically derived structural restrictions affect class levels differentially; the restrictions may exert pressures to limit the scope of personal action; these limitations on interaction may be internalized in the form of constrictive superego ideals and prohibitions; the ways in which a person may derogate himself or, by projection, those of lower status, peers, and of higher status, will reflect the compromises of his ego.

The actual externalization (and by this I mean action, following on and to be distinguished from projective attribution) consists of two steps. The actors formulate counterideals that justify the externalization of their forms of aggression. Collectively these counterideals are *incipient illegitimate ideologies.* They are incipient justifications, that is, with respect to illegitimate means (norms) and/or ends (goals), permitting some action against the legitimate system while enjoining adherence to conformity in other respects; but they may also be fairly well-developed ideologies supporting deviant but not primarily illegitimate social subsystems, such as the lower-class culture. (These ideological developments may represent a step in the transition to delinquent social systems, that is, a withdrawal of moral sentiments supporting conventional norms while adherence to these norms is maintained for other reasons, such as expediency. See Cloward and Ohlin's valuable distinctions between the moral validity and the legitimacy of social norms, pp. 18–19 and *passim.*)

This may sound like a lot of terminological hairsplitting, but I wish to avoid the question, at least for the moment, of whether lower-class culture is a "reaction-formation" to socioeconomic deprivation, or whether it has a cultural integrity of its own, as W. B. Miller insists. I have already indicated that collective beliefs and values, in the sense in which I am concerned with them, serve other human interests beside personal reactions to stress. Miller's lower-class "focal concerns" may certainly subserve other functions besides externalization of discontent, but they may also serve that purpose for some lower-class people.

I also want to reiterate, by viewing the counterideals as incipient illegitimate ideologies, the general position taken here that delinquency occurs in a predisposing context; that the beliefs and values held by a prospective delinquent's socializers are the seedbed for specifically delinquent social systems. I mean also to suggest that externalized discontent may be a link in the evolution of adult illegitimate social systems, such as organized crime.

The second step in externalization is the living-out of what was originally an internal conflict. The person aggresses against others in ways that reflect his sacrificed ego skills. He now seeks to extort from others responses which he is no longer able to negotiate successfully.

THE EXTERNALIZATION OF SELF-DISTRUST. In the first horizontal of Table 1, it is suggested that higher socioeconomic classes exclude many lower-lower (LL) class individuals, especially colored, from participation in many aspects of the legitimate sociocultural system. This ostracism also involves distantiation from lower-lower class people in all ways—interpersonal, social, physical. These restrictions may represent an attack on LL people's basic ego capacity to trust. Their inclinations to engage in communal religious, social, and economic activities with higher-status whites are discouraged (really, tabooed); any petition or protest for improvement of conditions or righting of inequities, whether individual or collective, to higher-status authorities, whether in business (landlords, employers) or government (police), is more likely to be treated with disrespect, to be denied or even punished, than are pleas or complaints by higher-status people; the futility of asking for help when all are in need may also discourage communality among LLs, especially as prohibitions against a sense of relatedness to a larger whole begin to be internalized.

An LL may, correlatively, find it adaptive to idealize an interest in self and to divest himself of strong attachments to others, since their capacity to increase his security is limited and therefore undependable; and, to idealize unrealistic and grandiose wishes for status and comfort, since structural barriers to opportunity are so great that they have little power to limit and direct ambition, and because such private grandiosity offers at least fantasied gratification. (Kardiner and Ovesey and Karon provide data on compartmentalized fantasy activity among Negroes in deprived circumstances. See also Finestone on the self-isolated grandiosity of LL Negro males.)

Neighborhood pimps and gamblers, who often enjoy reputations of being "high livers and big spenders," are usually local heroes to LL corner-group adult and adolescent males. Their repute and prestige in these groups may represent not only acceptance of illegitimate means to success; these figures may also personify the grandiose, "leisure class" ideals of some of these LL males.

(See Matza and Sykes, 1961, on delinquency as a pursuit of leisure-class values. These authors argue that the "youth culture" represents the open pursuit by youth of generally but covertly valued leisure goals, and that in this sense delinquents are acting on very widely held values. They suggest that one reason why some adolescents pursue leisure goals in illegitimate, or delinquent, ways may lie in the personality characteristics of these youths: "It is possible that leisure values are typically converted into delinquent behavior when such values are coupled with frustrations and resentment. This is more than a matter of being deprived in socio-economic terms" [Matza and Sykes, p. 719]. Their point of view is compatible with mine, but lacks psychological specificity. I am suggesting that the frustrations and resentments resulting from outcaste status and dispossession may lead to a self-interested and grandiose idealization of leisure. See also B. M. Spinley's findings regarding narcissistic trends in, among others, London slum dwellers.)

The feelings of untrustworthiness, isolation, and unworthiness, resulting from a sacrifice of personal means of relating to larger collectivities and by contrast of realities with ideals, may be measurable in such indices of despair and pessimism as the Srole anomie items. Just as these items have a projective quality ("these days a person doesn't really know whom he can count on"), so the same self-feelings may be attributed to peers as traits and motivating qualities. (This might have a feedback effect on slum disorganization.) Again, perhaps aided by a selective perception overdetermined by his inner experiences, an externalizing LL may attribute qualities of selfishness and insensitiveness similar to his own to higher-status authorities with whom he must have contact. As already suggested, reality may lend massive support to these projections. In this way, *externalized self-discontent may be precursor and companion to status discontent* (Cohen) *or position discontent* (Cloward and Ohlin).

I am ready to nominate W. B. Miller's list of lower-class "focal concerns" to the category of counteridealizations in the externalizing of distrust. As I have suggested, these subcultural concerns may well serve the multiple functions of a semi-independent social system, but they also imply that some adherents may be objectifying personal problems in the environment and living out distrust of peers and authorities. These focal concerns (Miller, 1958) suggest that: Preoccupation with insecurity and defiance (fate, trouble) hardens an LL against aggression (toughness); an alienated looking-out-for-oneself (smartness) predisposes an individual to exploitativeness; a high valuation on impulsive and episodic living (excitement), perhaps may be his diversion from inner isolation. Also, his autonomy seems mainly to be covert dependency wishes.

Thus armed with justifications, a lower-class corner-group male may exploit a lower-class woman, taking what she has to offer without making a binding commitment to her in return; by petty and sporadic theft and by absenteeism and unproductiveness, he may exploit local merchants and employers as best he can. The lower-class matriarch, for her part, may adopt a cynical and exploitative attitude toward the male in the household (see Rohrer and Edmonson on the matriarchal subculture), and may exploit her children's dependency to increase her sense of importance.

Structural Strains Toward Shame and Self-Doubt. Structural restraints on autonomy of action may produce abiding feelings related to shame and doubt in some upper-lower (UL) working-class and some lower middle-class (LM) people (see second horizontal in Table 1). Such people have relatively little control over the economic enterprises that use their labor, or over political processes that involve their interests, or over redevelopment and public service programs that might affect them adversely (economic and political dispossession is clearly a fact of LL life as well, and may add to a sense of hopelessness in LLs). They must take orders, even if these are poor ones, in most aspects of their work (subordination). White-collar work, whether clerical or involving sales or service, and blue-collar work below a skilled technical level can be so repetitive and may constitute such a fractional part of a complex economic process, as in an assembly line, that the worker may acquire a mechanical, routinized attitude toward his effort. (Rank-and-file union members have a collective impact on economic activity, but they may also feel very much subordinated in their relation to entrenched union leadership.)

Self-interested criticisms or challenges of policies at work, union meetings, or city hall may be met with indifference or retaliation. A worker may also be discouraged from contributing suggestions for improvements or change (spontaneous contribution, in the table) and restrained from developing a sense of proprietorship in economic, governmental, and labor organizations. Dispossession, subordination, and routinization may, on the other hand, encourage him to put a high value on scrupulosity, not in the sense of having moral scruples but rather as a doubting quality of mind that remains vigilant against rash errors of judgment.

The UL or LM who internalizes these pressures as prohibitions and ideals may correspondingly limit his interpersonal behavior. He may sacrifice his sense of volition and independent-mindedness in his dealings with higher-status people. As a result, he may have to cope with feelings of being unable to help himself adequately and of being unimportant in his relations with the higher status. He might suppress inclinations to express a difference of opinion or to speak up for himself on the grounds that this would be considered an affront and be ridiculed (helplessness, insignificance, presumptuousness).

Structural Strains Toward Guilt. People do not follow straight lines either in their behavior or in diagrams. There are other norm-related restrictions in the social structure which may affect other ego capacities of people at these class levels. Before we proceed to projections and externalizations that may accompany shame and self-doubt, it might be well to consider structural strains upon individual initiative and sense of purpose to promote feelings related to guilt (the third horizontal in Table 1). We might then examine the combined effects of guilt, shame, and doubt on the UL and LM respectively.

The southern and eastern European immigrant laborer, coming as he did from rigid, caste-like social orders, would have had relatively little or no difficulty accepting qualities of diffidence and deference which may be part of a worker's adaptation. (I can remember, as a small child, accompanying my father, a merchant, when he had business dealings with first-generation Americans who were Polish farmers and Italian workingmen; I was impressed then with the extreme respect which they accorded him and the honorific titles by which they addressed him.) Their children, however, second-generation Americans, assimilated an egalitarian ethos which spurned such subservient manners. They would have had to go against their parents' own ego-ideals and expectations of them in not accepting a caste-like resignation to low status in the new country, and perhaps also in feeling a position discontent regarding the squalid, deprived circumstances of an immigrant ghetto.

I am suggesting that feelings of guilt may be a psychological correlative of culture conflict. Archaic ideals may be passed on, in the identification of the child with the conscience of his parents, and not easily renounced. Guilt may be an unconscious determinant in the persistence of working-class ethnic subcultures, such as that of the Italian-American "urban villagers" that Gans describes: If second- and third-generation Americans are disloyal to their forefathers' ways, they can at least remain faithful to each other.

Culture conflict may still be with us, although more attenuated than that existing between immigrant parents and their children. The UL today who maintains ties to an ethnic subculture may be pulled toward assimilation into the general culture as much as his father was pulled formerly away from immigrant parents. The pull is there; Gans reports that defections away from the neighborhood and into the middle class continue.

LMs of UL origin may also experience their own mobility as disloyal, especially if they are ashamed of their class background and fervently deny it and if their parents had no particular upward aspirations for them. Thus, culture conflict may remain an active force, inducing guilt in upwardly aspiring people who initiate, or who may just contemplate, moves away from their reference groups.

Other structural restraints may block initiative directly and lead to guilt-related feelings eventually. The compartmentalization of functions in large business and government organizations (bureaucratization) and restrictions on the decision-making powers of those managers directly in charge of workers (centralization of authority) may create a certain rigidity and formality which stultifies assertive action on the part of ULs and LMs. A white- or blue-collar worker may feel that it is wrong to assume responsibility while, on the other hand, he idealizes some aspects of authoritarianism: unquestioning submission to authority; conventionality of beliefs, values, and perceptions that would simplify issues of obedience and conformity; intolerance of ambiguity and anti-intraceptiveness that might counterweigh imaginative approaches to change. (Merton makes comparable inferences regarding the bureaucratic personality, pp. 151–60.)

The UL or LM who divests himself of capacities for seizing the initiative may be vulnerable to feeling (and being) outdone by others in competition. Reluctance to espouse his own cause without feeling guilty about it may subject him to rivalrous feelings: He may not only want to defeat a competitor but may feel a personal animus toward him. He, more than others, may also envy a relatively successful peer his possessions and victories. Both the envy and the rivalry would predispose a person to projective fear of retaliation. His suppressed sense of purpose may promote feelings that he is transgressing on the interests of others when he seeks to advance his own, and he may, in a similar vein, continually impugn his own motives and feelings.

Externalizations of Shame, Self-Doubt, and Guilt. A UL or LM may project inner experiences of shame, self-doubt, and guilt onto peers. He may think that they consider him incompetent, unimportant, or presumptuous, or that they impute improper motives, rivalrousness, or disloyalty to him. When he needs to disparage them because of his own uncertainty or their imputed (or actual) response to him, he may impugn their motives, attribute rivalrousness or envy to them, or denigrate their competence or importance.

Gans describes several characteristics of the UL community which resemble these processes or which may serve the purposes of externalizers in that group. Adults were continually concerned that their motives and actions might be impugned by friends and neighbors. In peer-group social gatherings individuals took turns edifying themselves before the others, taking care at the same time not to overdo their self-aggrandizement for fear of arousing the others' enmity. The men were extremely sensitive to anything that seemed like an invasion of their autonomy, so much so that they could not organize themselves when the preservation of the community was at stake.

I wonder whether these attributes are not also ascribed to status inferiors such as Negroes, for purposes of self-enhancement and also as an expression of authoritarianism, and thus become elements of the prejudice and stereotyping to which the LL must adapt. (Simpson and Yinger review the evidence of working-class prejudice since the Reconstruction, as well as data regarding the relationship of stereotyping to the authoritarian personality. It is interesting to note that the area in Cambridge, Maryland, that voted most solidly against the local referendum for equal public accommodations for Negroes in September, 1963, was, according to newspaper accounts, a blue-collar district. This particular datum suggests that there is something more to working-class prejudice than a fear of competition for jobs.) UL impugning of and scorn for Negroes' motives, as projective cognitions, could account for much of the social reality behind a Negro LL's selective perception of selfishness and insensitiveness in status superiors, since many representatives of the general culture who have direct contact with LLs, such as policemen and strawbosses on laboring crews, are drawn from UL ranks.

Qualities could be attributed to more powerful figures, such as work authorities and politicians, that might be functionally connected with self-feelings related to shame, doubt, and guilt. These status superiors might be viewed as unbudging in their demands for conformity to rules and relentless in their push for productivity (intransigence and extortiveness); they might also be seen as inordinately jealous of their power and privilege and likely to be punitive if their decisions and opinions are questioned too directly (vengefulness). Here might be the beginning or the interpersonal dimension of a sense of unjust deprivation among some UL and LM workers.

These attributions to those of lower and higher status and to peers may justify sentiments supportive of attitudes and behavior that would be not only deviant but also opposed to the established order. A person who believes that others are trying to presume on him because they think he is helpless or unimportant, or that lower-status people with whom he interacts are unimportant or "uppity," or that authority figures "won't give an inch" or "are trying to push me around" may feel free to adopt some of the same sentiments toward them that he, in his scrupulous and constricting conscience, adopts toward some of his own inclinations. He may wish to oppose or interfere with their autonomy willfully, that is, because it is within his power and not because his interests are affected or harmed in any way. He may also decide that it is only sensible and self-protective to suspect the worst about their intentions (wariness). (Rigid-hostile-suspicious types of obsessive-compulsive characters are common more among lower- than middle-class people, while anxious obsessive-compulsive traits are more common in the middle class; see Langner and Michael.) Similarly, a person who believes that others are impugning his intentions, are trying to interfere with his assertiveness or to defeat his strivings, may feel that it is right to usurp their power if he can, to arrogate prerogatives to himself, and to act arrogantly in the face of opposition. The loyalty of rank-and-file members in some unions to leaders who may be extremely aggressive or threatening in their organizing tactics and other negotiations with employers, and possibly personally corrupt, may involve an identification with a man who personifies arrogation and usurpation.

Willfulness, wariness, and arrogation are counteridealizations which may be embryonic justifications for the formation of illegitimate practices. It is suggested that interpersonally these practices may partake of what may be called constringency, negativism, and rebellion. There may be a class difference in the form of these possible externalizations. LMs, with a socialization and a class subculture that may emphasize conformity, might resort to indirect and more covert forms of retaliation, such as withholding cooperation and passively opposing superiors or peers by overdoing their scrupulosity (constringency).

Merton offers as an example of such behavior how bureaucrats may withhold vital information from an official whom they feel does not adequately recognize their status, or how bureaucrats may swamp an official who tries to dominate them with an unmanageable number of documents (p. 156). A UL, on the other hand, who has perhaps been less regimented in both his childhood and work experiences, may show a more openly rebellious form of negativism. He might be more prone to get into quarrels and fights and wear his grudges on his sleeve, so to speak. It is widely believed that workingmen are much more likely than middle-class people to use their fists to settle an altercation; if there is any truth to this, I wonder whether a more resentful UL would not find it natural to externalize in these ways.

The Externalization of Inferiority. The fourth horizontal suggests some of the possible relations between structural restraints and personal adaptations in upper middle-class (UM) people. Those who have the greatest vested interest in the instrumentalities and the rewards of the social system may be the most vulnerable to adverse effects of its changes. (The very wealthy may reap greater rewards, but UM managers operate holdings for the wealthy who are thus relieved of the social and technical instrumentalities of profit-making.) Parsons (1962) has suggested that the profound activism of our society sustains a very high rate of social and cultural differentiation—a proliferation of new skills, roles, and values and of climbing performance expectancies for self and others. The resulting emphasis on technical competence as a measure of human worth carries with it a proportionate risk that a person may devalue himself as an incompetent. A sense of mastery and functional adequacy may give way to a sense of inferiority, because "know-how," "getting things done," and "accomplishing things" are unrelenting aspects of the complex American success image.

It seems to me that the very fact of commitment to unrestrained and undirected technological and cultural change (Keniston) can threaten a sense of skillfulness, because people, like machinery and technology, obsolesce. That is, a person, especially a UM manager or technician who has identified himself with the importance of innovation in methods and products, is under constant pressure to change and update his skills and his contributions to technical and social invention, whether this involves grinding out new productivity levels, merchandising methods, or sales. He may be constrained to view himself as a self-modifying apparatus that must change internally as outer reality is changed. If, as may often happen, he finds it increasingly difficult to discard old knowledge and styles of action and keep up with incessant demands to innovate and to wrest success from encounters with new customers and technical problems, he may experience himself as "slipping," "losing his grip"—as obsolescent.

The personal demands of cultural and technological change may outstrip the adaptive capacities of some UMs. Perhaps it is only young people who can muster the energy and sufficiently identify themselves with the values implicit in change and differentiation to experience a satisfying industriousness. If such a person does not consciously experience inadequacy, it may be because he is searching with increasing desperation for diversions and poses to ward it off—Babbitt and Willie Loman are only two of the personifications of this kind of unquiet desperation that American literature has produced.

Social critics have made observations to the effect that our culture (or at least the part of it that belongs to the Affluent Society rather than to the Other America) adores youthfulness and, conversely, is ashamed of growing old. If these observations are true it may be because the culture defines aging (and cleaving to accustomed ways) as obsolescence. Change may be a very inhospitable climate for other, perhaps latent and age-specific, values that emphasize holding onto what is familiar, tried, and true. The idealization of technical, business, and social inventiveness may render the tastemaker and the goods-and-services vendor victims of their own values—slaves to a "technological drivenness" (Henry), which may generate a great dissatisfaction that must be escaped through compulsive ritualism or, as suggested here, externalization of their inner dilemma.

Riesman and his collaborators have borne witness to the passing of individualism and to the rise of a state of pluralistic ignorance in our culture which is potentially anxious and existentially unstable and uncertain. They have called it other-directedness. Various contemporary psychological critics of society, notably Goodman, Fromm, and Henry, have indicated a variety of personal sacrifices that people may make under the cultural compulsion to produce and consume novelties. One of these, it seems to me, may be that the compulsion to make new things to satisfy what Henry calls the "lopsided preoccupation with amassing wealth"—amassing wealth in order to make and have new things—may lead paradoxically to a disdain for the objects invented and bought. The built-in movableness of individuals and households; the built-in obsolescence of products for "better living"; the ceaseless mutating of job interests, skills, and functions, and of other-directed tastes and styles of life express the desire for change and newness. Each in its way militates against familiarity, in the widest sense interpretable.

Fromm has written of what is perhaps the most profound loss of familiarity as a result of capitalistic enterprise—the loss of man's familiarity with himself. While one may argue about the psychological premises and the generality of Fromm's contentions, his application of the Marxian concept of human alienation, to the extent that it is valid, may be denoted in people's estrangement from specific actions such as engaging themselves with what is familiar and dependable. (Each of the losses in ego function that Erikson proposes may be considered a subtype of self-alienation. However, it is suggested here that the losers suffer not because of frustration of some supra-cultural human needs [which is Fromm's neo-Freudian position and which Merton has criticized] but because people assimilate sentiments by which they disparage themselves, or which block culturally valued action and thus lead eventually to a sense of personal failure.) For despite the current conventions and the routines of conformity which we contrast with deviance, this is an era that has not had time to get used to itself.

People cannot be sure that the social usages they evolve will last. They cannot settle into a dependable network of human relationships any more than they can attach themselves with a sense of permanence to the new house in their suburban stopover. They are discouraged from practicing a well-tried skill or ritual (it is interesting how the latter term has acquired a pejorative connotation) or using a thing so that skill, ritual, or object becomes part of a person's experience of his own functioning competence. We may see the dismantling of skills in the continual retraining of salesmen by their companies; of ritual in the secularization of church activity. This may sound like an appeal to a delusive nostalgia or an implicit invocation of an "intrinsic" human need, but that is not intended; I am suggesting that a person may feel most justly busy when his business involves methods, objects, and people to which he attaches some enduring importance. It seems unlikely to me that a person can take pride in his skills—esteem himself because he does things well, or manages relationships competently, or masters information—unless they are things, relationships, and information that matter to him.

When, on the other hand, a person's expressive and instrumental actions are constantly subordinated to an insatiable hunger for novelty and to economic processes undergoing unceasing rationalization (in the sociological, not psychological, sense), he may be constrained to "abstractify" his relation to his social and technical circumstances. Fromm uses the term to mean the withdrawal of personalized attachment to concrete objects and situations; a person uses himself, others, and his work as instruments for the attainment of some removed goal. (An adaptation to the cultural insistence on novelty and change is an orientation to future satisfactions that discounts the significance of present pleasures and attachments—an updated Protestant ethic.) People may carry their instrumentalism so far that they interfere with occasions of intimacy, because they may view them as sexual exercises in handling themselves and the other (Bettelheim, 1962).

One end-product of abstractifying, according to Fromm, is to reduce the value of one's actions, hence of oneself, to dollars-and-cents terms. Another is a sterile technicism that has little regard for the object, skill, or style itself, but cares only that the technique works, i.e., turns a profit, or profits a person's status, since rank, title, and privilege become more important as relations and activity become less dependably satisfying.

It is possible that, when a person denies himself the satisfactions of usage and familiarity and exaggerates the importance of technicism, status, and abstraction, he is more likely to worry whether he is using his time and energies well, to wonder secretly whether what he does and in a sense is has use, and to view himself and others as objects to be maneuvered and manipulated. He may repress these twinges or reassure himself by insisting that peers and those of lower status are no better than he or are just trying to make him feel inadequate, and that status superiors and authorities are calculating individuals who care only about how much he makes or how profitable he is. Believing this, he must continue to keep up with changes in tastes and in the marketplace, stay on the make and make up to bosses.

"Technical ruthlessness," as the justification for a UM externalizer's retaliatory measures, is a term Erikson uses once (1962) in passing reference to enslavement by the school-age virtue of industriousness: "to consider as good only what works, and to feel accepted only if things work, to manage and be managed" (pp. 5–6). Thus, a gunman may admire his marksmanship; a nation, its overkill capacity. Technical ruthlessness might justify the sharp or dishonest business dealings of some UM "innovators," in Merton's sense of the word (pp. 134–40), and a Machiavellianism on their and their wives' part to achieve financial and social success (contriving).

Anachronistic Traditions as Subcultural Constraints

There is another possible set of constraints on ego function that are not functions of the social structure but rather of the cultural order. I am referring to the cultural anachronisms that may exist in some segments of the population, for archaic ideals and taboos may be transmitted from parent to child over generations, as in the case of the Dakota Sioux (MacGregor, *et al.*). "Freud," Erikson says, "assigned the *internalized perpetuation* of cultural influences to the functions of the 'superego or ego ideal' which was to represent the commands and the prohibitions emanating from the environment and to traditions. [He quotes Freud:] 'The super-ego of the child is not really built upon the model of the parents, but on that of the parents' super-ego; it takes over the same content, it becomes the vehicle of tradition and of all the age-long values which have been handed down in this way from generation to generation. . . . Mankind never lives completely in the present. The *ideologies of the super-ego* perpetuate the past, the traditions of the race and of the people, which yield but slowly to the present and to new developments and, so long as they work through the super-ego, play an important part in man's life'" (E. H. Erikson, 1959, pp. 103–4).

The historical link of LL Negroes to *slavery*, uninterrupted as exclusion from the dominant culture and transmuted into economic degradation, may sustain an unending crisis of distrust. Some Negro LLs may wish to return to a passive and helpless relationship with others, and may therefore persist in the feeling that reality is inhospitable and depriving; in exercising power, they may seek omnipotence, through transmitted identifications with remote plantation masters and overseers, and may provoke hostility and distrust in those they try to tyrannize. (See the portrait of Julia's father in Davis and Dollard.) The women, perhaps with cultural memories of the chivalrous attentions that southern aristocrats paid their women (among whom may have been some Negro LLs' female ancestors) and of an archaic code of honor among men, may feed their present disappointment and distrust of the males they raise and live with on these secret idealizations.

Survival of archetypes from feudalism may restrict the independence and the initiative of those who are the most direct psychocultural descendants of European peasants in our society, the members of ethnic subcultures. (I hope it is clear that I am not appealing to any Jungian mechanisms here.) The paterfamilias, judging from Gans' descriptions, still demands instant submission from his children. It is commonly believed (although Gans does not report it) that some Italian-American mothers are singularly attached to their sons; if so, perhaps this arises partly out of a persisting distance from and resistance to the father in his assumption of an oppressive authority.

Certainly the moral ideology of the Reformation and of Calvinism may still be with us, inhibiting spontaneity, exaggerating the value of scrupulosity, and complicating problems of guilt in middle-class Protestants; Cohen has summarized the modified Protestant ethic which may still prevail among many middle-class Americans. The probable concentration of obsessive-compulsive traits in middle-class people (Langner and Michael) and the sexual inhibitions and anxieties still found in great numbers of psychiatric patients are clinical instances, as middle-class respectability is a sociological instance, of the viability of asceticism and of taboos against sensuality. (The supposedly more austere spirit of the Catholic Church in northern Europe may have provided the ideological force behind the development of similar traits in some American Catholics, those Irish and Germans who are descendants of mid-nineteenth-century immigrants from northern Europe, who may now be most heavily concentrated in the middle class. The sexual primness and the frigidity of women in contemporary English slums, who are immigrant Irish Catholics and Protestants, reported by Kerr and Spinley, is striking and probably relevant.)

Imperialism as an ideological force may not be dead either, even though it is almost a hundred years since U.S. troops slaughtered Indians to secure *lebensraum* for members of the dominant race, and not quite so long since marines went into Central American countries to protect United Fruit. The course of empire may no longer be westward or across oceans, but down the class structure. Reports from impoverished coal mining sections in the eastern part of the United States suggest that great corporations still ruthlessly exploit labor and raw material resources and just as ruthlessly abandon them when they are no longer profitable (feature article, page 1, *The New York Times*, Sunday, October 20, 1963). The commercial redevelopment of inner-city areas, making profit the first concern and cost to lower-class inhabitants secondary, and the continuing opposition of some conservative business interests to advertising controls and to the expenditure of tax revenues on welfare programs suggest that there are those in charge of economic enterprise who insist on defining society as a marketplace. It seems to me that some of the people who embrace these values, and some of those members of the middle class who do not actually possess the economic power but identify with the values of those who engage in these practices, may be truly slaves of industriousness and technical ruthlessness.

Later Stages of Ego Development

These cultural restraints on ego function, and the structural restraints discussed before, have been applied to the four fundamental issues of ego development which, according to Erikson, a person confronts during about the first twelve years of life. Erikson has postulated four later stages of ego growth, which are the achievement of a stable identity vs. identity diffusion, in adolescence; the acquisition of the capacity for intimacy vs. isolation, in young adulthood; generativity (with regard to children, objects, ideas, etc.) vs. self-absorption and integrity vs. despair, in middle and late adulthood.

In his theory of ego development, Erikson adopts the epigenetic principle familiar in physiology as well as in psychoanalysis that full functional harmony within an organism depends on the proper rate and sequence of development in its components. Thus the fate of later ego developments is partly fixed by the outcome of earlier ones (E. H. Erikson, 1950). This corollary assumption is fundamental to Erikson's theory, and it will be so in our considerations later, since, as a containment theory of delinquency, the model presented here is also a socialization theory. The most important reason for the preceding examination of possible psychological factors in the disaffection of adults with the dominant sociocultural order was to set the stage for considering ways in which these self-discontented adults interact with their children so as to predispose them psychologically toward deviant behavior.

The premise that achievements and failures in early ego functions affect crises in later functions is not, however, immediately relevant. Those most affected by the structural strains discussed are working (or adapting to restrictions that deny them work) and raising children and have the first four ego crises behind them and largely decided, for better or worse. (The kinds of cultural restrictions just described, however, might have affected the early functions of these adults since their parents would have taught them these cultural restrictions, in the interpretation put on others' actions and in interaction with the child, and probably at an early age when the anachronistic ideology would acquire the coercive force of myth. This is not to say, on the other hand, that subcultural traditions of this kind might not also receive social reinforcement during adulthood, as in the beliefs and values of informal adult peer groups.)

Despite the fact that we are principally concerned with relatively developed and defined individuals at the moment, it would be logical to assume that the criteria for self-fulfilling adult action (later ego stages) presuppose and include the earlier criteria as subfunctions in adulthood. The adolescent who is in the process of achieving a stable and satisfying identity is able to trust a certain kind of future enough to make a commitment to some values from among those available; he has the singlemindedness and the assertiveness to differentiate himself from elders and peers without fear of leaving too much of value behind or fear of shame or guilt; he is employing his sense of industrious competence to learn the skills inherent in a prospective adult role. Similarly, in the crisis of intimacy, a young adult might fear entering another person or allowing another to know him unless he felt in possession of a secure sexual identity (E. H. Erikson on ego identity, 1959).

Each compromise, then, of an adult's trust, autonomy, initiative, and industry would compromise all his adult ego capacities, since each of the former is a constituent of all the latter. Social and cultural constraints may also affect adult ego functions directly. An adult who devalues the familiar in restless pursuit of new diversion and in productive drivenness may sacrifice ways of defining his identity. When the double sense of self-sameness (Erikson), of inner consistency and outer dependability, is broken up by change, a person may be threatened by a distrust and insignificance he may have put behind him when he made his adolescent commitments. Since social usages by which people familiarize themselves with each other are also provisional and other-directed, opportunities for intimacy are sacrificed. If companionship becomes an instrument—and it may in marriage as well as in business—I wonder whether people do not feel isolated in the patterns they are living, patterns that they are likely to feel are imposed on them by "the times" or some other outer force rather than through their own subscription (". . . for the man who should loose me is dead,/ . . . In a pattern called a war./ Christ! What are patterns for?" cries the woman in Amy Lowell's "Patterns"—the title also of Rod Serling's play about contemporary businessmen). The UM who is absorbed in demonstrating his proficiency in careerism (or in status- and diversion-seeking) may have too little interest in validating his existence with his children, be of little interest to them, and may therefore fail to experience a sense of generativity. During his child-raising years he (and his mate and children, as objects of his externalization) may have to cope with the precursors of despair in middle age.

The private feelings of self-doubt and guilt, with which some LMs and ULs may respond in slavish adaptation to institutional and traditional pressures on them for conformity and submission, may create uncertainty in their identities; cause them to lack the trust and the spontaneity for satisfying intimacy; make them too controlling of themselves and others to negotiate the generation of new relationships, children, original ventures. The thicket of disadvantages growing out of a history and a reality of ostracism and dispossession may hedge in all aspects of an LL's adult ego functioning, as studies of LL multiproblem families indicate. The family is most directly affected by these adult ego dysfunctions, at all class levels, so that the children not only have to grow up with the consequences of ego failure in their parents but also must decide what to do about these unattractive personifications of adulthood when they come to the age of identity formation. In the young, pressures toward deviance, whether symbolized or externalized, may also consist in part of wanting to avoid or forestall the kinds of lives youths may see their parents leading.

An Oversimplification Clarified

I have stated more than once that cultural and structural constraints on adult ego functions may interrupt the course of adult action by upsetting any of the first four "developmental" functions (in contrast with the later four, which I shall call the "integrative" ego operations, because through them the adolescent and adult integrate themselves and are integrated into society). I should like to clarify that statement. Table 1 and the ensuing discussion of it suggest a relatively simple connection between external condition and internal effect: A given structural constraint affects a particular ego capacity and not another; sociocultural exclusion and distance, for example, are described as damaging an LL's ability to trust, but not as injuring his sense of autonomy as well. However, logic tells us that any of the structural barriers named may be mediated in interpersonal ways that could injure any or all four of a person's developmental capacities. I was trying to suggest the more obvious and probable ego malfunctions that might follow from a particular constraint, and then the kinds of externalizing processes that might be built on them; but I did not mean that the malfunctions I related to each structural pressure should be taken as the only, inevitable consequences of that pressure. As constraints, they do not determine but rather predispose toward particular adaptations.

I am submitting the hypotheses that ostracism and perhaps traditions from slavery will promote *at least* distrust in some LLs; work subordination and routinization and perhaps also feudalistic ideals will promote at least self-doubt and shame in some

ULs; and so on. If I forget to remind the reader in the appropriate place later, let me say now that the possibility of multiple personal adaptations within an individual, or among people subjected to the same structural or subcultural pressures, will be an important reservation to bear in mind when I get around to constructing four different delinquency-producing processes and resulting delinquent "types." Each process and type, even though it will be given a specific class-subcultural context, will be built out of the particular developmental malfunction that may *likely* occur among adult socializers experiencing the constraints I have attributed to that class subculture, and should not be viewed as the only process and result that may occur in that context to the exclusion of the other three.

The four processes and their respective personal consequences in the young should, like the findings of much current psychological research in delinquent typologies, be considered trait and behavior clusters which may describe a few adults and their delinquent children in the subcultural context named fully and many delinquents and their parents partially. A given constraint may be hurting other levels of ego operation as well in the real individuals involved. Further, because constraints elsewhere in the social structure and the general culture may induce the same psychological effects that I shall be attributing to a particular subculture, the same traits may be expected to occur among people at other class levels. In short, I shall be constructing paradigms or prototypes for a way of thinking about delinquency, and I expect the prototypes themselves to be modified or discarded should they be subjected to further research and theoretical inquiry.

Severity of Deprivation and Profundity of Ego Injury

One last qualifier regarding this treatment of pressures toward deviance in adults is differentiating the effects of structural barriers. There is still some disagreement among sociologists as to the distribution of delinquency in the social structure. Cohen and

Cloward and Ohlin are inclined to believe that there is more of it in the lower class, but Matza and Sykes (1961), for example, interpret relevant data as indicating that there may be as much hidden delinquency among the privileged as there is overt misbehavior among the deprived. But should it be determined eventually that there is more delinquency in disadvantaged social sectors, the finding might be related to the possibility that the structural constraints we have been considering may be, like economic deprivation, progressively more oppressive and perhaps more debilitating as one looks "down" the social structure. (Professional acquaintance with delinquents of different class backgrounds persuades me that delinquent social forms are more elaborated and entrenched and personal commitment to delinquent ideologies deeper at lower-class levels.)

It seems doubtful to me that the structural constraints mentioned would each carry the same weight. It was H. S. Sullivan, I believe, who somewhere in his writings pointed out that only those who have experienced ostracism may know what an extremely painful and perhaps destructive reaction it may cause; one may contend that LL Negroes have built up elaborate subcultural and personal cushions against this form of rejection, but we may also wonder about the personal cost to them and their forebears before they hit on the most protective counterbeliefs and -values, and about their unconsciously registered perceptions and reactions to the reality of outcast status now.

Erikson has made an observation about doubt and shame similar to Sullivan's; he has suggested that we may overlook how excruciating these emotions may be, because in our culture shame and doubt are early absorbed into a sense of guilt (1959). Various anthropological studies of some preliterate societies have indicated that shaming is a punishment sufficiently powerful that it may be almost the only negative sanction needed for socialization. Those ULs and LMs who are subjected to relatively arbitrary and demanding authority (or who may selectively so perceive the actions of authority because of subcultural predilections), and who may therefore be liable to feeling helpless and insignificant, may be open to much stronger inner attacks on their conforming autonomy than we realize.

It was these considerations that prompted what may have

seemed to some readers an overly neat correlation between social class structure and the developmental order of ego levels in Table 1. It seems to me a worthwhile heuristic hypothesis that the more oppressive and depriving structural and traditional constraints are, the more deeply will they strike at a person's abilities to negotiate with reality.

Psychosocial Means and Ends and Their Obstruction

There is another way to understand the greater effects of constraints on lower class levels and, in turn, the more elaborate development of illegitimate social systems and the possible higher delinquency rates there. I should like to use the distinction between means and ends, but not in Merton's sense. All of a person's ego capacities and skills may be considered means, since it is through their use that he obtains those satisfactions he desires.

The culturally valued goals and satisfactions to which adults aspire may all be parts of the complicated business of "success." These goals are also, psychologically speaking, integrative ends or end-states; because it is through approaching and achieving them that a conforming adult in our culture realizes or negates his integrative ego capacities—his identity, intimacy, generativity, and integrity or wisdom. Our preferred and prestige-conferring forms of communality and companionship, of art, craft, productivity, power, recreation, and knowledgeability are the institutionalized ways by which adults in our society exercise their integrative ego functions.

It is obvious that there are class differentials in the attainability of these integrative end-states, differentials that are directly related to a person's relative economic advantages. A UM's parents will have had the money (assuming that they are UM also) to buy him the education and/or to capitalize a business venture in which he might make enough money to buy a home in a hospitable community and the more expensive kinds of entertainment and leisure activity, to wield influence, to control productivity or practice sought-after professional skills. This might suggest a narrowly middle-class-oriented view of what constitutes satisfying adult activity in our society; but if ULs and LLs have their own subcultural forms of integrative activity, they are also participants in the general culture.

This observation is so often made that we tend to lose sight of the fact that the very *biculturality* denoted is not yet completely understood. In a sense W. B. Miller only denies the problem when he insists on the cultural autonomy of the lower-class milieu. I wonder if it takes us a little closer to the heart of the matter to note that people are probably as capable of embracing two different and even at points incompatible cultural traditions as they are capable of living with psychological conflict. Thus, for instance, Matza and Sykes suggest that many conforming adults are members of a contraculture; in private informal settings, and in their ideals, they may adhere to a "subterranean" leisure ethic as against the Protestant ethic by which they work and accumulate goods and privilege.

To the extent that a disadvantaged LL man or woman admires the manicured, pretty suburban streets he sees on TV, in "family" movies, and other popularized idealizations of the life of a business or professional man or a suburban housewife, he or she probably will believe in the value of the kinds of integrative ends that are represented, and will also know or believe that the ends are blocked for him or her. There are no Negro Ozzie and Harriet. While social and subcultural constraints on personal action may exist at every class level to create ego limitations to match normative and value restrictions, a middle-class person can still hope and plan for respectability, acceptability, some degree of social and economic influence—all the social indicators, the "success symbols" of conventional integrative activity—and enjoy them to the extent that a harried and oppressive self-concept permits, if he is self-discontented.

The middle-class person may have limited psychological means for attaining integrative end-states whereas a lower-class person is often culturally and socially barred from them. The unavailability of *social means* to success—structural barriers to opportunity, in Cloward and Ohlin's sense—may create barriers to *psychosocial means and ends*. The effects of lower-class barriers —of exclusion, distance, dispossession, and work subordination and routinization—may thus compound the pressures to deviance.

A Restatement: Three Forms of Social Repudiation

The individual who is committed to a social system largely out of a sense of personal threat and intimidation is already alienated from that system. He is alienated from some of his personal potentialities by his subscription to the system. Moreover, adherence to a social system with universalistic goals under inner duress, that is, by intimidation of the ego, will inevitably force responses against the system or some part of it, such as work authority, peers, or family. Three forms of rebellion are possible. If a person underwent considerable duress at his parents' hands because of their psychocultural adaptations, he may respond to restraints on his adult ego function with symbolic discontent—neurotic or psychotic behavior that may label him a psychiatric deviant; "normal" anxiety (not in a psychiatric, but in the popular, sense) that may manifest itself in the legion of hysterical symptoms (see Szasz on the hysterias as unconscious malingering) that the general medical practitioner treats with tranquilizers and office counseling; or in those diseases which may have a psychosomatic basis, such as some cardiac, circulatory, and gastrointestinal disorders.

He may consciously repudiate the beliefs, values, and norms governing his behavior in one of two forms. A person may not in fact renounce his definition of self and the demands of his conscience, in which case the rebellion is an externalized, lived-out attempt to deny his inner reality. Another historical example is that of those Germans who during the Weimar Republic and the Thirties found in Nazism a romantic and paranoid solution to several problems at once: the national and personal insult of defeat, economic ruin, and the relation of the German male to his father and mother (see Erikson on Hitler, 1950).

The second kind of conscious repudiation, and the third form of rebellion, is that of a person who has enough ego strength, sufficient accomplishments in mutually satisfying negotiations with others, to reject, rationally and objectively, conventional views and standards about living. He renounces both his negative evaluation of self and destructive claims of conscience in and through a rejection of the social system that has oppressed him. I doubt that this would happen to very many adults, since if they are relatively well satisfied with themselves they are probably obtaining enough satisfactions within the legitimate system to seek some conforming accommodation to it; some of them, with relatively superior ego skills, would surmount the more oppressive social constraints and cultural anachronisms, and repudiation might also be held in check by membership in conforming reference groups. Some socially conforming groups, according to Cloward and Ohlin, do not consider some aspects of the general culture morally valid but accept these aspects for the sake of expediency; their members are then able to live with social and economic constraints, because their self-esteem no longer suffers. Examples may be the hostility of Italian men toward the Church, which has been traditionally allied with property rights and political conservatism, and the cynicism about politicians and businessmen among the conforming Italian workingmen whom Gans observed. It is possible that under extremely depriving conditions, such as those affecting LLs, many adults may become deviant; but it is contended here that few LLs would escape psychological injury and would carry their superego and ego problems over into the social organization of their deviance.

This kind of thoroughgoing renunciation is more likely to occur at adolescence, when a young person whose socialization has granted him a fairly friendly conscience and flexible ego experiences a social discontent which from a psychological standpoint is rational and objective. Conventional prospects look unrewarding and unfair to him, and in his identity crisis he may look inward and be able to throw off any inner oppression that might yoke him to the legitimate system. In terms of the theoretical approach here, opportunity theory gives an adequate account of only these youths' entry into delinquency. In such instances the situational factors described in the sociology of delinquency and crime—socially definable discontent, consensualization, social reinforcement in the peer group, role definitions, and patterning into illegitimate opportunity systems which have their own status criteria—are the necessary and sufficient conditions for the emergence of delinquent behavior, and predisposing psychological factors are secondary or extraneous. Such a person may, like Frenchy Joyeaux in *Out of the Burning*, be forestalling a prospective deprived identity in his delinquency and may eventually, like Frenchy, escape both deprivation and delinquency by a conforming commitment to upward mobility; or he may eventually become a professional criminal, making a commitment to upward mobility in the illegitimate opportunity system described by Cloward and Ohlin.

Throughout the discussion of possible socialization effects following, it must be borne in mind that the adolescent identity crisis, and the accompanying psychosocial moratorium that our culture provides for decisions regarding adult careers (Erikson, 1959), introduces an element of indeterminacy, both for understanding and attempting to predict from childhood experience. This is unfortunate perhaps for science but fortunate for the viability of our culture when the identity decisions have favorable and productive consequences. Slater and Woodside's study of working-class and lower middle-class marriages in London provides numerous striking examples of adults who were apparently able to achieve relative marital stability and upward socioeconomic mobility despite squalid and emotionally sordid childhood experiences. Florence Kluckhohn recorded an amazing anecdote of a woman who seemed to acquire great integrity of character in the face of a lifetime of bad faith and neglect at others' hands. We may take data such as these as evidence of the great ability of people to withstand rejection and brutality and to synthesize an identity out of the strongest elements in their egos and superegos.

chapter 3

the emergence of delinquency

The Transmission of Psychocultural Adaptations

THE psychocultural adaptations of adults are reenacted in interactions with their children. This is a major, substantiated hypothesis of many observations regarding childrearing practices and culture (Kardiner, *et al.;* Linton, Whiting, *et al.*). Mediated by the parents' personalities, the rules and roles governing family organization reflect the sociocultural systems in which the parents participate (See Parsons and Bales' theoretical work, and accompanying data, on the integral relation among society, family, and personality as systems of action.) The historical and current hardships of a group of people may become encoded in the character of their children. These premises underpin the processes of psychological transmission suggested below.

An adult's childrearing practices may reflect his most important ways of relating to himself and to others, in the developmental issues he emphasizes and his ways of resolving them with the child. As we have seen, Freud has suggested that children identify with their parents' consciences; it has also been observed, first by Freud but also by many other students of personality, that parents often take the position of their own consciences, rather than that of their egos seeking satisfaction, in dealings with their children. If a parent enacts his roles with other adults out of self-disparagement and subjugation to a harsh conscience, he may disparage and domineer his child in similar ways; he may build up in the child the same sense of personal defeat and alienation from his potentials that the parent feels.

In the last chapter it was suggested that the potential delinquent may have his first social experiences regarding alienation from conventional beliefs and values, not in his peer group, but with parents who have self-discontentedly repudiated some values supporting conformity. It is also important to recognize the possibility that parents who are not only conforming in their behavior but conventional in their belief and values systems may also induce a self-discontent in their children which might then be mobilized against some aspects of the general culture. These parents have been psychoculturally compromised; they adhere to conventional ideologies by limitations on their ego resources, but have not externalized their own self-discontent.

Their rebellious inclinations are suppressed but are vented symbolically (symptomatically); or, husband and wife may externalize only to each other and their children. Such adults may be pervasively discontented with their own ways of relating to other adults. They do not, however, challenge the beliefs and values underlying their slavish conformity. They may themselves have been raised by oppressive parents and therefore find it very difficult to accept and act on rebellious impulses.

Also, the passing of generations has changed the original oppressive agent. What had been sociocultural constraints for the predecessors became interdictions to the descendants. What might have been social discontent in preceding generations is transmuted into the terms of intrapsychic conflict, interpersonal insecurity, and hostility familiar to psychiatry.

Further, if these parents are middle-class, then structural and class-subcultural realities would support their suppression of further alienation from conventionality. These realities include the compensations of relatively rewarding conformity and the many emphases on conformity in middle-class enculturation. Seward's reviews of data and case materials regarding clinically definable reactions to culture conflict (1956; 1958) provide numerous illustrations of adverse effects on the personalities of people raised by parents whose egos suffered in their psychocultural adaptations.

I am asking, in other words, for a theoretical reappraisal of the assumptions that there are a "normal" and a "disturbed" delinquent (a "sociological" and a "psychological" delinquent, which sounds more like a political division along the lines of spheres of influence than a scientific simplification). Supposedly, the presumed normal delinquent is likely to be lower-class and the disturbed, middle-class. It is suggested that many of the so-called normal or integrated delinquents share the same failures of psychological maturation with their clinically disturbed compeers. They do not give the same signs of intrapsychic conflict because family and subculture support and provide social outlets for the externalization of their self-discontent. They are seemingly less anxious and uncertain, not because their egos are less limited, but because they and their sociocultural contexts have found ways of circumventing oppressive consciences. The "maladapted" delinquent experiences his ego failures more acutely, and is alienated from his sociocultural context; some "conforming" delinquents are alienated from the same ego failures just because they are integrated into group externalizations.

Transmission of Symbolic Discontent

If parents are subject to a private tyranny that overweighs their ego strengths, they may so tyrannize their child that he mistrusts his own and others' freedom. The child may never clearly distinguish between mutual regulation of and unilateral control over relationships. Since his parents forbid him to openly coerce others, as they prohibit themselves, his major methods of trying to dictate the terms of relationships will be symbolic. Profound counter-rejection of the parent is frequently a basis of autistic behavior in children; school phobias are clinically understandable as diffuse efforts to do away with school which separates the child from a dependently controlling mother who has taught him that external reality is filled with threats to his independence and initiative (Coolidge, *et al.*).

At adolescence the child may continue the unconscious rebellion, as seen in the cases of acute identity diffusion, the borderline psychotic states that Erikson discusses, which constitute at least in part an abject refusal to go on in the course parents demand, coupled with an equally abject surrender to the parents' consciences. One such girl said to me, "If I fight my mother's standards, I'm ungrateful; if I join them I see myself the way she does. They're both worse," not daring to define the better alternatives. Or, the adolescent may displace (externalize) the rebellion to beliefs and behavior that may border on delinquency—as in truancy and property violations associated with a pattern of school underachievement—and that are opposed to views and standards which the parents have been trying to enforce.

There may be a class differential in the occurrence of externalization via delinquency at adolescence. Middle-class parents may overemphasize conformity and emotional proprieties in child-rearing much more slavishly than UL and LL parents, although they may at the same time feel free to externalize distrust, self-doubt, and submissiveness in their marital relationship—behavior from which the children may take their cue for dealings with peers or other adults outside the home. Delinquency as an outburst against a rigid conscience may be impulsive and heavily symbolic as well, as in property destruction, assaults, exhibitionism, and voyeurism. Both Hurwitz and Albert Reiss, in their analyses of delinquent types, established a category of individuals who have not repudiated internal conflict regarding conforming attitudes and experience personal insecurity and anxiety. These delinquents are impulsive and destructive; they often come from homes of high socioeconomic level which are in low-delinquency-rate areas.

Parents may also tacitly encourage, or significantly fail to discourage, certain symbol-laden forms of delinquency, such as sexual offenses and assault, because of gaps in their otherwise restrictive consciences or repressed wishes to commit the same acts. I am referring here to the concept of superego lacunae, developed by Adelaide Johnson and Szurek and others. If a parent was reared by parents who enveloped his growing ego capacities and his burgeoning search for new objects of attachment apart from them, overwhelming his freedom in their need to control him, the parent of our delinquent may have infantile or fixated wishes. He may desire sexual and other satisfactions (including aggressive ones) that reflect the patterns of dominance-submission and dependency taught him, and the forms of physical pleasure exaggerated or forbade in the course of parental teaching.

A Clarification of Psychological Premises

I realize that the last two sentences allude to much more than they say. I am trying to suggest that psychocultural adaptations can become quite elaborate and complicated over successive generations, and that they can involve the most intimate and private aspects of personality. Let me make two other, related matters clearer. The use of words like "infantile" and "fixated" and the notion of forbidden physical pleasure may be a red flag to the environmentally-oriented behavioral scientist; such a reader may assume he is asked to subscribe to a Freudian scheme of fixed, asocial or presocial instinctual development. He is not. I adhere to the hypothesis, implicit in much of modern psychoanalytic ego psychology (Erikson; Hartmann; see also Gill's and Rapaport's brief reviews), that the development of primary needs goes hand-in-hand with the development of capacities for object relations—that is, relations with people or with significant parts of them, like breasts, hands, and vocal sounds. Physiological development does not determine cravings for satisfaction any more than it determines capacities for interaction, negotiation, and collaboration with others. As for aggression, developmental psychology has long since demonstrated that the organism has the capacity from birth for what appear to be rage reactions. It is assumed here, not that there is a biologically predetermined schedule of types and objects of destructive aggression, but that aggression always remains a latent capacity; and, that what the person aggresses against and how he aggresses depends on the nature of the frustration, his prior experience, and his level of development of other physiological and psychological functions.

As Erikson has pointed out, classical psychoanalytic thought paid much more attention to the impact of psychosexual development on a person's relations with his environment—his object relations—than to changes in the object relations during psychosexual development. And, it might be added, than to the impact of object relations on libidinal development itself; as Parsons (1952) indicates, the older psychoanalytic premise of fixed instincts has been open to question because of observations which suggest that environmental experience can drastically reorganize fundamental libidinal energies.

However, I accept the principle of epigenesis in human development, unlike the position taken by Parsons in the same paper. Epigenesis assumes, among other things, that the developing organism progresses through a series of pleasurable interests (zones of gratification). The principle also assumes that the particular focalized zone will limit, *but will not determine in some inherent way*, those aspects of the environment that most interest the organism. Still another assumption underlying the epigenetic principle is that the total state of the organism—the useable physiological apparatus and the psychological capacities for introjection, fantasy, and projection—limit the ways in which a person engages his environment (Erikson, 1950).

The psychophysiological stages of development bring different respective *issues of human relations* to the forefront, and each issue is settled by the organism's experience. This is the connection that Erikson's theory of ego development has to libido theory. Psychophysiological developments do not determine the child's relations with his environment. They rather set successive stages and scenery for their enactment and resolution. Thus the infant's helplessness and receptiveness make the issue of trust critical in his experience. But how he eventually feels about getting things from people, and about their trustworthiness, is a matter that is largely decided then and there by what happens between him and his mother, and not by his "orality."

Concepts of infantile sexuality, fixation, and regression may be entertained without involving one in premises concerning fixed human needs (a different matter entirely from not-yet-socialized drives for physical stimulation) and premises about an asocial human nature. An infant has to learn to adjust his (psychosocial) mode of *getting* to his mother's way of giving during the physiological (zonal) stage of interest in mouth-breathing-sensation. When he does so he will be able to integrate the pleasures of receptiveness in subsequent psychosexual developments, and he will also be able to utilize the modes of getting satisfaction and gettings others to do things for him in later psychosocial negotiations. Assuming that the rest of his development is relatively successful, as an adult he will not be marked by either oral *zone* or *mode* fixations.

The successful socialization of the infant's orality, and the crisis of trust, does *not* result from forcing him to give up an unlimited hunger for receptive pleasure, as libido theory has been interpreted. Rather, these matters depend on the mother's and child's mutual regulation of each other. The child's regulation of himself depends on the mother's capacity to accommodate to him—to guide him in how, not how much, to satisfy himself. If mutual regulation is not attained, then oral deprivation may be experienced, as well as a lasting preoccupation with receptive pleasures. If one of the modes of acquiring mouth pleasures—taking in, grabbing hold, holding on, letting go, pushing in (each one of these becomes a primary mode for subsequent erogenous interests, in Erikson's scheme) is disrupted so that it plays less or more than its due part in guiding mother and being guided by her, the person may acquire a lasting mode fixation. He may always, for instance, have strong receptive sexual interests or work relationships; or be grabby, or withholding, or intrusive (Erikson, 1950).

If a person completes one or more stages of development relatively successfully but cannot negotiate a resolution of a new crisis, he may regress to earlier modes and zones of gratification. The regression may be partly compensation, partly a way of smuggling in and out, through regressed behavior, some of his pleasures and ways of relating. For example, the child who is forced into an abject surrender in a toilet-training struggle may become a feeding problem: His mouth becomes a tight sphincter holding out against intrusive foods, because he was forced to let go of his feces against his will (a symbolic protest, by the way, against oppressive parental values and behaviors).

If the child and his socializers cannot reciprocally adjust his ways of ensuring pleasures to their own, then he, his family, and society are stuck with his frightening identifications and projections, his immature objects, and his overdone ways of relating. All are burdened, that is, with his defeats and failures in ego functioning. When, therefore, any of the negative terms in Erikson's glossary are used here it may refer to zone and/or mode fixations or regressions.

Thus a person who is ashamed of or doubts his capacity for autonomous action may hold onto controls over others, hold out against others' independence, be unable to let go of feelings or inclinations, or at least not in an accommodating way, and/or seek "anal" satisfactions in all forms of gratification. He will attend to what can be hoarded up, parceled out, rigidly controlled or submitted to; or what can be disrupted and "messed up" in eating situations, leisure activities, sexual experiences, in clothing, homes and other furnishings of living, in interpersonal relationships in general.

From the point of view in this book then, an "unsocialized impulse" has very little meaning other than as a reference to response latencies; for once any kind of erogenous interest or motor capacity emerges it *must* be socialized—and not "more" or "less" either, because that misconceives the nature of primary motivations, but either favorably or unfavorably for subsequent maturation.

At the beginning of this section I spoke of two matters pertaining to child development that had to be clarified. To proceed to the second one: It was stated earlier that parents' psychocultural adaptations determine which developmental issues will be stressed and how resolved with the child. This assumes that ideologies assimilate and organize the libidinal energies of adults. Beliefs and values draw on libidinal needs for support, and ideologically supported subcultural patterns provide consensualized means and objects for these desires.

Thus the self-distrust of the LL Negro, which has been suggested as his internalized adaptation to outcast status, may promote a wish to be enveloped by an omnipotent, incorporative other, who aggrandizes himself by allowing the LL subject to obtain infantile, passive gratifications. In other words, the LL Negro adapts his orality to his degraded status. This may be an element in his identification with the aggressor; it may be functional for the required compliance of his occupational role; it may also be a component of his highly dramatic religious forms. The last often rely heavily on the Hebrew mythos of being led to the Promised Land by an all-protective God, and on salvation through suffering and surrender of one's fate. ("Were you there when they crucified my Lord" the spiritual goes.)

Thus also, W. B. Miller (*c*) indicates that some of the economic functions and institutions of lower-class culture encourage the establishment of a homosexual element in the personalities of lower-class males. The parent may then prefigure his child's eventual participation in subculture patterns. He may direct the child's ego development toward certain object relations, particular means and objects of satisfaction, that may correspond to the parent's ego adaptations to sociocultural restraints and to the subculture patterns that have grown up around these restraints.

An LL Negro matriarch, for example, may build such attachments into her son. Such sons give many signs of their Oedipal and pre-Oedipal bonds to her. They worship their mothers alone among all adults, and they are continually preoccupied with incest themes, in "playing the dozens" with other gang boys (W. B. Miller, *et al.*). The mother may occasionally violate her son's trust by neglect, harsh treatment, and rejection of him in favor of transitory men. She may interfere with his efforts to distinguish between his own interests and hers when he is with her, and she may also seduce his intrusiveness. In other words, she may fix in her boy the same yearning for union with an omnipotent other that she has established in her own psychocultural adaptation. His dependency on, his identification with, and introjections of her may then play their parts in his preoccupation with receptive homosexuality.

Many child-rearing practices may result from the inventive operation of the primary process, which may shortcut rational thought and find similarities among certain subcultural items, particularly object relations and issues that arise in human growth. For instance, the more prevalent use of corporal punishment in child training (a determinant of marked aggressiveness in some children; see Bandura and Walters) among the lower classes, as contrasted with the withdrawal of affection in the middle classes, may be related to the way such parents subordinate themselves to the sociocultural order. Lower-class parents may unconsciously associate outright suppression of autonomous behaviors that they disapprove of in the child with their own authoritarian adaptation to sociocultural pressures on them for conformity and submission. See, for example, the very strong emphasis that low-income people put on the authoritarian aspects of childrearing, in Langner and Michael, Chap. 16.

Other childrearing practices may be more or less adventitious—accidents, so to speak, of the parent's object relations. The English slum mother's virtual abandonment of her child after weaning, reported by Kerr and Spinley, may result in a permanent impairment of the capacity for trust and intimacy and facilitate a lifelong susceptibility to matriarchal control. This abandonment seems to have more to do with the mother's satisfaction in caring for her next baby, who is totally dependent, and perhaps with the vicarious gratification of her own desire for receiving pleasure passively in caring for an infant, than with a deliberate rejection of the lap baby.

Symbolic Repudiation and Subterranean Family Traditions

It was suggested above that repressed wishes in a parent—consequences possibly of his parents' negotiations with him that fitted their adaptations—may promote delinquent acting-out by the child. The adolescent voyeur or molester may be responding to his mother's seductiveness. This may in turn reflect her hidden rivalry toward her overcontrolling mother, for instance, and her unsettled wishes toward a father who may have wanted too much of her, perhaps because of his dissatisfaction with a marital relationship that was shot through with hostile externalizations.

As an example, an adolescent boy took a little girl to the woods, molested her, and tore up some female underclothes. His mother, who had disliked and feared her domineering mother for as long as she could remember, "knew" that he had torn up the clothes because of anger with a nun with whom he had quarreled at parochial school. The mother also resented her passive and withdrawing husband, the boy's father, because "he would not fight." The social worker described her as a rambunctious, tomboyish person who joked about sliding down a banister after the interview. This boy had always been a special child; "He was a ball of fire as a small child—he never stopped running," and he got into mischief every time she turned around, the mother said. She and her husband were very awkward in sexual matters, apparently in experiencing them as well as talking about them. The boy, obsessed with the subject, was terribly frightened by sex; yet he acted out an intrusive, angry restlessness that matched his mother's. The clinician is familiar enough with these subterranean family traditions. I am suggesting that these traditions may absorb developmental ego functions and object relations into personal adaptations to culture and social structure; that the traditions can work endless variations on identity problems in a family chain, and that they may have something to do with delinquency in adolescent members.

We have, then, according to this analysis, adults whose behavior and conscious attitudes may represent a slavish conformity to social and cultural restraints, and whose rebellion is symbolic. They dictate the terms of growing up to their children, forcing the child into immature attachments or "fixations" and generally forbid all but symbolic resistance, although their self-discontent in their adult statuses and functions may be displaced to externalizing in marital conflict. One or both parents, on the other hand, may rely much more openly in their interpersonal relations, outside the home as well as within it, on externalized denials of their inner intimidation and subservience. In their dealings with the child they may then define him as a *similarly deficient person who is free to externalize his ego limitations and immature wishes.*

Transmission of Externalized Discontent

These parents will not stamp out all overt efforts to aggress against, extort from, or circumvent parental tyranny on the part of their children. Since the parents' inner reality is circumvented in similar ways, they may value, accept, or even approve of the child's adoption of these interpersonal operations. For example, the slum mothers observed by Kerr and Spinley tolerated and overlooked sadistic outbursts of older siblings against younger ones; the mothers themselves attacked a child when he obstructed their wishes. Kerr suggests that the delinquent boy, fussy and effeminate in his identification with "Mum," tries to get away with his offenses just as his Mum gets away with her aggrandizement and impositions within the family.

The mothers are also quick to defend their children's externalizations of apprehensions about controls. The contagious sprees of property destruction in which these children sometimes engage are excused by parents as an adolescent "lark" (Spinley, p. 72). Lest we begin to imagine people who are happily uninhibited (the slum pastoral of some romantic middle-class observers), both these English students list textbook signs of maladjustment—enuresis, night terrors, depression, nailbiting, and other indices of personal anxiety—as well as personality test data that testify to the ego weaknesses and immature attachments of these adolescents.

Externalizations of ego deficiencies in marital discord may be so well-established between externalizing parents, and there may be so many externalizers in deprived groups, that overt alienation, such as blaming and attacking in the marital partnership, may be a subcultural tradition and institution. Rohrer and Edmonson, for instance, report that the LL Negro matriarch is typically distrustful and manipulative toward the man or men who share her bed and board. Almost all the "Mums" in the two English studies cited manipulated or ignored their compliant husbands, except for sexual and other physical requirements; the men in turn withdrew to pubs and prostitutes and let the "Mums" work their will on the children.

Viewed sociologically, this marital alienation may be a direct adaptation to the occupational instability of lower-class males, as W. B. Miller and Cohen and Hodges suggest. Viewed interpersonally, it suggests the operation of sociologically latent functions, to use Merton's term, that subserve the motivations (stemming from the psychocultural adaptations) of the parents. A parent locked into an externalizing marriage may subsequently encourage the child to counterattack as if the other parent had threatened him. I have seen LL Negro boys throw the man of the house out, clearly on their mothers' behalf as well as their own; whereupon the mothers took in new "easy riders" and the sons went out to commit a rash of delinquencies, usually purse-snatchings, housebreakings, and assaults, until they were swallowed up into the correctional process.

The child of externalizing parents may become defined in a general way as well as within the family as an insecure and immature person who is surrounded by, and must cope with, externalizing egos. He develops counter-coercive techniques as a reaction-formation against his felt vulnerability; he develops substitute ideals, based on successfully defeating other alienated egos, as compensation for a complex sense of self-defeat. His "adgression," a child's pre-hostile way of going at things and relationships, becomes aggression when parents and older siblings substitute neglect and coercion for mutuality (Erikson, 1950, pp. 64–65).

Transmission of Objective Social Discontent

A third logical possibility in the psychological transmission of discontent lies in the socialization provided by parents who may have been able to withdraw their moral sentiments of support for a social system that puts them at a disadvantage, and who are therefore able to renounce the system's interpersonal and intrapsychic implications. It would follow from the theoretical position here, as I suggested before, that the least likelihood of adult escape from injurious psychocultural adaptations would exist precisely at those points in the social structure where disadvantages are greatest. It also follows that where structural and subcultural disadvantages are less and freedom to approach integrative end-states are greater, there would be less inner pressure to repudiate the ideology and norms of the legitimate system. Nevertheless, the possibility of adult disaffection with interpersonal disadvantages of the legitimate system remains at all class levels (as does the possibility of a continuation into adulthood and parenthood of this kind of renunciation during the adolescent identity crisis, as discussed at the end of the last chapter).

Table 2—Family Transmission of Discontent

Ego Adaptation	*Negative Conforming Response*	*Negative Deviant Response*	*Positive Response*
Adult Self-Discontent Adult Social Discontent ↓	+ ± if present, suppressed	+ symbolic & externalized + conscious	— ± if present, conscious
Adult Social Behavior ↓	Conformity alienated from social discontent ("Ritualism," Merton)	Deviance alienated from ego failure	Self-realizing conformity or deviance
Socialization of Child's Ego; Superego ↓	Facilitation of failures Overemphasis on conventional ideals	Facilitation of failures Induction of counter-ideals	Facilitation of strengths Induction of non-conforming ideals
Child's Self-Discontent Child's Social Discontent	+ symbolic and/or externalized ± if present, suppressed or conscious	+ symbolic and externalized + conscious	— ± if present, conscious

+ present — absent ± present or absent

Such parents may still conform to the legitimate norms on the grounds of expediency or impracticality of violation, or they may remain loyal to some of them while also embracing illegitimate norms, as in those instances of successful professional criminals who also maintain respectable middle-class family lives. They may raise children with relatively strong and resourceful egos to have values which differ from those of the legitimate system. If these children subsequently experience social discontent, it may be an objective discontent, that is, not overdetermined by kinds of dissatisfaction with self. The child may then turn to delinquency or, depending on the nature of his dissidence and alternate values (as well, certainly, as on other identity elements that may be more easily defined psychologically), to other organized forms of youthful deviance such as political radicalism or Bohemianism (Matza, 1961).

It is likely incorrect to assume, however, that personally freer youths who are more objectively discontented with conventional values and norms avoid delinquency and enter into non-delinquent forms of deviance. Polsky observed that the Beat community in Greenwich Village were experiencing intense identity problems that were related to insecurity and immaturity. Moreover, many blended delinquency and Bohemianism; many were retreatist delinquents, in Cloward and Ohlin's meaning, who supported their use of opiates by thievery.

Discussion of Table 2

Table 2 summarizes the factors which have been discussed in these three forms of *family transmission of discontent*. The adult ego adaptations (top horizontal) refer to the externalization processes discussed in the last chapter. "Negative" indicates the presence in adult personality of the internalized objects (introjections, identifications) which have enforced limitations on those personal action potentials that Erikson's ego attributes subsume. "Conforming" and "deviant" refer to the presence or absence of externalizations. Social discontent indicates the withdrawal of moral sentiments from beliefs and values supporting (some) norms, which may also include some law norms; this discontent may be objective, in a psychological sense, or overdetermined by self-discontent. The negative deviant ego adaptation among adults subsumes all the kinds of externalizations to respective social and cultural constraints which have been proposed; this category in Table 2 does not denote any particular socioeconomic class. There may, however, be relatively more conforming than deviant adults in the middle classes, and more deviant than conforming adults in the lower classes among those who have sacrificed ego capacities in their adaptations to constraints, as has been suggested.

The reference to "Ritualism" under the social behavior of negative conforming parents is meant to indicate a possible relationship (but certainly no perfect symmetry) between a psychological enslavement to conformity and the ritualistic adaptation to culture and social structure that Merton describes in his paper on anomie. The ritualist, according to Merton, allays his acute status anxieties by lowering his level of aspiration. He buries himself in routine and in zealous adherence to institutional norms as a private escape from the "*dangers and frustrations*" (p. 141, my italics) inherent in pursuing cultural goals. By dangers and frustrations Merton has clear reference to normative restraints on action. It is suggested here that some who accomplish this social adaptation lower their aspirations by exaggerating the sentiments, beliefs, and values they attach to normative limits on their action. They do so by internalizing those most oppressive and constricting aspects of the behavior, by authorities and peers, that mediates institutional norms; they thus alienate themselves from conscious acknowledgment of discontent with norms and from some of their ego resources.

I should also like to quote Merton in support of the contentions that there are class differentials in the two ways of handling psychocultural sacrifices, and that the negatively conforming parent may be more rigidly controlling of his children than either the parent who has retained ego flexibilities or the negatively deviant parent:

> If we should expect *lower-class* Americans to exhibit . . . "innovation" [in the face of normative frustrations], we should expect *lower-middle class* Americans to be heavily represented among those making [the] adaptation [of] "ritualism". For it is in the lower middle class that parents typically exert continuous pressure upon children to abide by the moral mandates of the society, and where the social climb upward is less likely to meet with success than among the

middle class. The severe training [for conformity] leads many to carry a heavy burden of anxiety. The socialization patterns of the lower middle class thus promote the very character structure most predisposed toward ritualism (Merton, p. 141).

It need only be added that when parental ritualism is coupled with parental self-discontent, children may be induced to experience a self-dissatisfied rebellion expressed in misbehavior and delinquency before they commit themselves to a continuation of the cycle of negative conformity to which they have been trained.

Requirements of a Delinquency Theory

Thus far a view of the psychological aspects of social discontent has been offered. But what of the emergence of delinquency as the specific deviant vehicle for this discontent? There are many forms of social deviance (Becker; Matza; Polsky), and a theory that assumes it has explained delinquency by describing pressures toward deviance is not properly a theory of delinquency but of deviant behavior, as Cloward and Ohlin point out.

Cloward and Ohlin also devote a good part of their work to a social explanation of three variants on lower-class delinquency, the conflict and retreatist subcultures and gang delinquency-for-a-profit; one might then say that a theory of delinquency is not completed (in the sense that any theory ever is) until it has detailed the processes by which discontented youth make these final differentiations. This theoretical work will be concerned with this last issue least of all, since I assume, with Toby, that the number of youth who constitute such pure strains of delinquent culture is a small minority of all delinquents. The model presented here applies in the lower class to delinquents who may be members of what Cohen has called the parent delinquent subculture, whose participants may engage indiscriminately, as far as group values are concerned, in fighting, retreatism (such as drinking), and stealing. These are, by the way, the kinds of groups that W. B. Miller found in Boston and Short found in Chicago.

Cloward and Ohlin suggest that psychological predisposition

is irrelevant, or at least of secondary importance, in an explanation of delinquency. They state that pressures to delinquency cannot be said to determine the delinquency, when there are at least two conceivable deviant outcomes. In such instances, they say, the most that can be claimed for the strain toward deviance is that it limits the range of responses (pp. 38–39). They point out that the factors that channel pressure toward deviance in the direction of a specific outcome are the crucial ones. In their theory these determining variables are largely situational, with the possible exception of retreatist delinquency.

But one might also say that when at least one conceivable conforming outcome exists in a situation, the environmental factors cannot then be said to determine delinquent response. This is a restatement of a familiar criticism of sociological theories: Not all youths who undergo the particular situational conditions singled out become delinquent. In the widespread recognition of the prevalence of delinquency there is a tendency to overlook the fact that some youth conform even under the most adverse conditions. Empirical studies matching delinquent and non-delinquent youth on socio-environmental factors presume this fact. No study of incidence has failed to show that, however preponderant the majority of youth in a given area who are estimated to be delinquent, some proportion of that area's youth apparently manage to conform to legitimate norms.

Reckless and his colleagues and others (the Gluecks and Stott, for example) have been able to identify such youth in high-delinquency areas. The sociology of lower-class life has identified youth who were evidently committed to other subcultural tracks —upwardly aspirant "college boys" and those who seemed to be moving toward working-class respectability. If it is acknowledged that some similarly circumstanced adolescents reject delinquency (or are rejected by neighboring delinquents), then personal predisposition to deviance is as important in a deterministic scheme as are environmental factors: If personal pressures are absent, then situational variables may or may not be effective. In this sense personality factors do not just narrow the range of outcome; it would be more accurate to say that they may be logically prior and earlier steps (regarding sociocultural conditions found in adolescence) in a sequence of strategic determinants.

Summary Statement of Subcultural Pressures to Delinquency

It must be acknowledged that this model is largely, or more systematically, a theory of deviance, in the sense that it concentrates on strains toward deviant behavior. But an attempt will be made to relate psychological pressures to eventual delinquent outcomes. It is proposed that at least regarding the lower classes, where the most highly articulated and enduring forms of delinquent social organization are presumed to occur, the personality adaptations which have been suggested, and psychological processes involved in the attainment of these adaptations, codetermine, along with social and cultural processes, the emergence of characteristics in the adults' subculture that are relevant to delinquency. These characteristics narrow the range of choice among deviant behaviors available to youth growing up in these subcultures. The relevant subcultural characteristics are adult ideologies and practices that may be considered constraints which channel discontented youth toward delinquency.

In LL class subcultures and to a lesser degree in UL subcultures, ego modifications are part response, part stimulus, in a feedback fashion, to the emergence of deviant values and beliefs. Externalized ego deficiencies are invested in a series of disjunctive beliefs (perhaps oversimply, those that connote futility), which are a part of the distinctiveness of these subcultures as compared to the middle-class subculture. Among the ego deficiencies, and not mentioned in the previous discussion of ego limitations, is a certain simplification of ego structure. It has not been mentioned thus far because it is itself a function of the feedback system—initiated in part, that is, by the emergence of disjunctive beliefs, values, and practices among adults. Once this ego simplification is set in motion as a modal personality characteristic in these subcultures it blunts the learning capacities of the young, deflecting them from the legitimate opportunity structure, and limits the kinds and range of older identity models usable.

Ideological decisions are essential to identity formation, and the embodiment of ideals and ideology in functioning identity models is a prerequisite for these decisions (Erikson, 1959). Because younger and older adult models convey alienative (disjunctive) beliefs and values, it is maintained here that youth do not invent delinquency as a social form of deviance in vacuo (a tenet of Cohen's and in part of Cloward and Ohlin's theories) but rather, with W. B. Miller (1958), that organized delinquency is an adolescent variant on the adult subcultural milieus. Since in these milieus alienative beliefs and values support status criteria relevant to delinquency, there are real inducements for entry into illegitimate social systems to which psychological accounts of delinquency have heretofore not paid proper attention and which sociological accounts have described in very great detail. These beliefs and values are partial derivatives of externalized ego deficiencies prevalent in the subculture (or can function as vehicles for such externalizations). The beliefs and values are therefore consonant with the externalized self-discontent of youth, which predisposes them to delinquent behavior; the social and cultural inducements based on these values and beliefs thus synergize these action tendencies in youth.

Delinquent ideology becomes distinct from the more general alienative sentiments of surrounding adults, and delinquent behavior is differentiated from the diffuse or different deviance of the adults, because of the adolescent identity crisis and the nature of the adult ideologies presented to the adolescent. The disjunctive ideologies in these lower-class subcultures, adaptive though they may be to existing deprivations, also imply a sense of personal failure and disbarment from integrative activity; this defeat and disbarment is visible in the life-styles of available identity models. Thus while reality factors and predisposition press youth toward acceptance of adult outcaste status, they also recognize such adaptations (primarily in an unconscious way, perhaps) as surrenders of life chances. Adolescents in these subcultures are therefore caught in what amounts to a classic approach-avoidance conflict or, to put it another way, in a crisis within the identity crisis. They cannot renounce past compromises in their object relations without embracing a future that is no more worthy, or is indeed not very different in its psychological satisfactions. Their delinquency is thus a negative commitment, an attempt to foreclose their rather dismal prospects (see Erikson on negative identity, 1959), and an ineffectual effort to defy and overturn these prospects.

It is ineffectual because they are responding in old self-limiting ways to subcultural beliefs and values which they perceive as related to parental convictions which limited them. All adolescents, regardless of personality trends and subculture, are left open, by the psychosocial moratorium that our culture declares on adolescence, to reexperience infantile introjects and identifications (to regress), and in fact must explore these in order to refashion or repudiate them if they are to form a cohesive identity; this is one reason why Erikson characterizes identity formation in effect as a normal personality crisis. But most youth, or at least most privileged youth, are left free to risk exploring these old claims on their energies and consciences at their own pace and on terms most suitable to ego control of the consequences. Theirs is therefore a self-controlled regression in the service of ego development. (See Kris on the creative use of regression.)

The underprivileged youth we are considering here, however, are invited by some of the prevalent values and beliefs, and by reality factors based on these, such as status incentives, to regress and to maintain a regressed position. The unrelieved regressions prompt the use of externalizing as an ego defense, which these youths have already learned, and at the same time they are prompted to regress and to externalize in trying to find ways of resisting these very same beliefs and values, because they seem to beckon entry into adult blind alleys. Lower-class gang delinquency then, in this view, is a conjoint, *regressively bound effort at (ego) mastery* of the environment on the part of youth who are psychologically disadvantaged in similar ways. It is also a *living-through,* in the diffuse state of the ego during the identity crisis, *of subcultural sentiments* represented psychologically as regressive character trends in significant adults. Because they are resigned in their identities to their deprived conditon, adults express these trends only in episodic deviance, perhaps in anomic living patterns (which may be culturally deviant but not law-violative) and in shared and individual fantasy activity.

The rest of this chapter documents the above views regarding subcultural pressures to delinquency.

On Psychoanalytic Nativism

Social and cultural students of delinquency have roundly, and rightly, criticized psychological explanations for relying too heavily on instinctual bases for deviant behavior. While there are other threads in their work, many of the major psychoanalytic investigators of delinquency and crime—Alexander, Friedlander, the Healys, and Staub—have stressed the unconscious operation of psychosexual fixations as the primary pressure or motivation to deviance. They have tended to view the ego as a dam with a sluice for impulse expression; they have taken normative structure and traditions and resulting deprivations for granted, or have not sufficiently attended to the effect of these factors on ego and conscience. Perhaps because of their own historical necessities, growing out of the levels of conception in their discipline thirty and forty years ago (when all but Friedlander were writing), they have concentrated on problems of libidinal development; in taking for granted normative and cultural constraints they have tended to equate deviance with failure in drive maturation.

This is no more or less than their critics in the social sciences have said. In not paying due attention to what happens in the ego and in the conscience as a result of social and cultural factors, or to the organization of needs by these ego and superego factors, these psychoanalysts have tended implicitly to invoke Freud's premise (one which he modified in his later theorizing, according to Parsons, 1952, 1958, and psychoanalytic students of the ego) that behavior causing harm to others is fixed by an intrinsically asocial psychophysiological development which pits an original human nature against social control. As Merton (on anomie) points out, this nativism contradicts the fact that deviance is differentially distributed in the social structure and by environmental conditions. Their premises are thus questionable and their theories are cumbersome, because they skirt the social organization of deviant behavior and try to refer the behavior back to libidinal determinants.

Actually, the social scientists have somewhat overstated a legitimate case. The original psychoanalytic thinkers in delinquency were keenly aware that environmental obstruction of growth initiated immature or destructive behavior, not, as a reading of sociological comments would have one believe, a sheer neglect in taming antisocial impulses. Alexander and Healy, for instance, discuss an "early intimidation to the young child's narcissism," through the aggression and rejection of parents and siblings. Such one-sided interpretations of what psychoanalytic writers have said will be discussed in Chapter 4. Nevertheless these theories represented a refusal to drop what was really a superfluous premise: There are inborn destructive instincts, and so, by implication, all men have a natural tendency to "regress" to antisocial behavior in the face of stress. Friedlander, for example, says:

> Psycho-analytical research into criminal behavior is concentrated primarily on the fact that the same antisocial impulses which are unconscious in the law-abiding citizen lead to action in the criminal. . . . Charming though small children may be at certain times, at others . . . they give the impression of being little savages. . . . Many of [their] impulses are antisocial. . . . The modification of antisocial impulses leads to character formation (pp. 7–14).

The sociologists have been dissatisfied with this homunculus theory, and would rather have us understand exactly how stress initiates deviant impulses, rather than assuming simply that it does.

Cohen and Short (1961) say that "Delinquent and criminal behaviors [in psychoanalytic instinct theories] represent the eruption of . . . impulses from the cellars and caverns of personality. . . . In most psychoanalytical writings the Id is treated as a bundle of instincts. We are all, in this view, born criminal—or at least contain within ourselves a born criminal" (pp. 93, 94). They then point out that the treatment of misbehavior as a personality excrescence overlooks situational factors—group influence, local values, subcultural traditions, and institutions.

Over and over again, sociological sources reiterate the importance of this oversight. Cohen has suggested ways in which group processes provide delinquent solutions to discontent. W. B. Miller (1958) argues that a conventional psychiatric view leaves the integrity of lower-class culture entirely out of consideration. Cloward and Ohlin define the specific structural deprivations affecting lower-class youth. W. B. Miller again, and his colleagues in their empirical analysis of aggression in a street-corner group (1961), show that aggression serves group values and cohesion as much as the other way around. Becker, in his examination of non-delinquent forms of deviance, makes the plausible observation that deviants cannot be distinguished from conformists on the basis of the presence or absence of a deviant impulse, since it may be presumed that most individuals are deviant at least in fantasy; he reverses the usual psychological conception by suggesting that it is contact with a deviant group that produces the deviant motivation—Sutherland's differential association hypothesis updated and generalized.

Almost by default then, social scientists have accepted the exploration of situational factors in delinquency as their province, and, as the above glance through a fragment of their literature suggests, these factors comprise just about all of "external reality," excepting often the family context. But as I indicated in Chapter 1, "outer" and "inner" is no more real a distinction than that between mind and body; both definitions are methodological conventions by which an inquirer organizes his facts and logic; the difference between inner and external reality lies in the observer, who may choose to view an actor's relations with his environment either in environmental terms or subjectively.

It is people, therefore, and not "social factors" or "cultural factors," who make their own external realities, not just by evoking reactions, but also in the sense that every social and cultural circumstance has its inner, psychological aspects. The social scientist who forgets this divorces people from their sociocultural environment in what Spiro has called the error of sociological realism. Over ten years before Cohen presented his now-classic description of the "language of gestures," by which gang members formulate delinquent action—probably the first true social etiology of delinquency—Redl described the same phenomena in psychoanalytic terms (1942; 1945); we are dealing with viewpoints, not different realities.

Psychoanalytic Nativism as a Bugaboo

Because the realities involved—not necessarily the analyses—are intertwined, the social scientists who have been describing the controlling values and norms of delinquents have been doing the psychologists' work for them. They have been describing some of the ego and superego factors in delinquency; they have also, it must be said, been beating a dead horse.

They have been criticizing a psychology interested primarily in libidinal processes and seeing the ego mostly in its relation to these psychosexual forces. Psychoanalytic ego psychology has apparently long been developing the realization that an individual's psychosocial development and his psychocultural adaptation are as important as his libidinal organization in determining his action.

Hartmann offered the concept of semi-autonomous ego development (1958, originally presented in 1939): The ego is not wrung out of the id by the impact of reality, but develops independently from the same primal core from which the id develops, and is therefore an active agent in personality, in limited ways, from the beginning. Hartmann says that "the child is born with a certain degree of pre-adaptiveness; that is to say, the apparatus of perception, memory, motility, etc., which help us to deal with reality are, in a primitive form, already present at birth; later they will mature and develop in constant interaction, of course, with experience" (1956, pp. 34–35). The "demands of reality" presuppose "the existence of something in the individual that speaks out for reality" (p. 32). Merton must not have been aware of this theoretical development when he criticized psychoanalysis for proposing a human nature at war with social reality. As Hartmann suggests, criticism including that of other social scientists who have followed Merton's lead misrepresents Freud's later thinking on the subject; Freud asserted that the reality principle comes into effect to gain assured pleasure later by forgoing immediate momentary satisfaction. To assert that psychoanalysis maintains that people give up pleasure in the face of reality is an absurdity.

Freud's position, that the reality principle operates to assure pleasure, is a touchstone of Hartmann's contributions to psychoanalytic ego psychology (and those of his colleagues Kris and Loewenstein, as well as Erikson), to which he returns again and again in his writings. "Reality" is not "outside" of man, in contemporary psychoanalytic writings. Society has an inner ally almost from an individual's birth in patterning and elaborating primary drives: the organism's autonomous ego capacities (autonomous from the id, that is). It is an incorrect, or at least one-sided, interpretation, to say that current psychoanalytic theory imagines an unsocialized man who is a creature of blind instincts, or that it imagines an unsocialized man at all. (See Hartmann also on the difference between the id and animal instincts, 1948.)

The Personal Functions of Ideology Again

Hartmann makes some distinctions regarding rational and irrational action that are very useful for understanding some of the possible psychological functions of lower-class ideology and of the gang (1947). Behavior can be reality-syntonic, in accord with the "object structure," in an objective way and still be irrational subjectively, in that the actor does not calculate that the behavior will serve the aim that it does. Negro self-rejection is one such kind of socially functional and irrational behavior, in that it conforms with the prejudices of economically more powerful whites.

Ideological changes and different social institutions (such as, in our context, the divided marriages and female-based households among LLs, the male corner group and the adolescent gang) *may make regressive behavior subjectively rational,* i.e., calculated. Special institutions may provide ego support (through realistic gains and punishments); and ideological changes, superego support for the regressive behaviors. Hartmann suggests, for example, that totalitarian political regimes debase and oversimplify the superego values of their subjects and thereby lower their threshold for regressive behavior, in the sense that the individual becomes more pliable and is willing to surrender autonomy. Social institutions that emerge in relation to ideological changes tend to gratify ego interests, by distributing rewards and punishments for ideologically sanctioned behavior. An appeal may thus be made to the ego and the superego, and regressive behavior may become consciously purposive. If regressive trends exist in members of a subculture, subcultural sentiments and practices consonant with these trends may synergize their expression, much like the facilitative effect of the prospect of secondary gains in neurotic symptom formation.

Psychological Contributions of Social Scientists

If the above formulations (except for those about regression) accord well with sociological contributions on the function of belief, value, and normative systems, it may be, as remarked before, because social scientists have been students of ego psychology and superego processes in the area of delinquency. Cohen and Cloward and Ohlin talk about substitute delinquent values which support new, accessible status criteria. Cloward and Ohlin indicate a whole progression of ego and superego factors —ideals and institutionalized rewards and punishments—in the illegitimate opportunity system. Sykes and Matza discuss ways in which delinquents distort their perceptions of reality so that their delinquent behavior is acceptable to their consciences. The reason W. B. Miller's lower-class patterns (1958) are neatly termed "focal concerns," and why that term cannot be neatly equated with "values," "beliefs," "norms," or "culture patterns" as technically defined, is that each concern has richly subjective (psychological) as well as environmental (sociocultural) components in its definition.

Each focal concern, furthermore, implies the operation of one or several regressed behavior patterns that are socially approved (ego-supported) and consonant with particular beliefs and values. This connection between ideology and immature behavior was of course the reason for suggesting that the focal concerns may represent lower-class counteridealizations in the externalization of ego deficiencies.

Some of these modal lower-class psychocultural adaptations that Miller proposes are subjectively irrational, in Hartmann's (1947) sense, and socially functional, as in the case of those LLs who protest their "autonomy" so provocatively that they arrange for their support in a custodial institution. Others are not only objectively rational—conforming, that is, to the realities of LL constraints or to beliefs about constraints, which are functionally equivalent—but also mesh ideology and regressed behavior in the consciousness of the LL actor. For instance, the high valuation placed on "Excitement" idealizes behavior which is impulsive and occasionally self- or other-destructive, as in drunken bar fights; convictions about the inescapability of "Fate" permits many LLs to indulge in grandiose fantasies by giving their money to a numbers-runner. But whether subjectively rational or not, LLs' focal concerns as Miller describes them do offer at least partial basis for the presumption that immature behavior is realistically rewarded and is justified in the lower-class subculture.

In acknowledging the presumption—without, it is hoped, presumptuously "psychologizing" on social-scientific data—it might also be fair to indicate that Miller offers many plausible sociocultural explanations for LL ideology and customs, as do Cohen and Hodges in their paper on LL beliefs, that explicitly avoid any inferences about personal immaturity in the actors.

Immaturity and Ideology

Not only regressed trends but also externalizations of them are invested in some lower-class beliefs and values, because externalization is not simply a projective process. Blame for insecurity is attributed to an environment that was and may remain objectively inhospitable and disruptive of an actor's ego operations; this is the point of reconciliation between this theory and cultural and social accounts of anomie. The externalizer selectively perceives and sharpens those aspects of reality which support his justifications for taking counteractions. In a family of negatively deviant individuals, a depriving and coercive social reality emerges for all that reinforces their individual externalizations. One purpose in introducing the concept of externalization is that it may be a plausible way of explaining a predisposition in potential delinquents to attack normative constraints, a predisposition that will admit data regarding the relative immaturity of delinquents.

Cohen and Hodges' catalog of LL beliefs and values contain several items that, it seems to me, suggest this investment at a subcultural level. First, their list of features in the LL's life situation—simplification of the experience world, powerlessness, deprivation, and existential insecurity—contain many indications of an objectively inhospitable sociocultural environment. They make clear at the outset, furthermore, that though interested in examining situational factors which may underlie LL ideology, they implicitly accept the notion that childrearing practices and modal personality traits also participate in organizing these beliefs and values. Also, many of these ideological items refer to a larger "community" of potentially untrustworthy peers and status superiors.

LL misanthropy, for instance, refers to the theme that "people are no good" which pervaded responses to several items in the questionnaire used. Not only were UL appliance and car service people and middle-class people seen as untrustworthy, but also LL strangers were suspect in their intentions. "The LL's image of the world resembles a jungle" (p. 323). "The vulnerability to force, fraud and exploitation of all kinds *from members of their own stratum* is great" (p. 324). In discussing LL extrapunitiveness, these authors partly substantiate the suggestion here that many LL's externalize:

> LL subjects [frequently agree] with the statement: "When things go wrong at home or work I find it easy to blame others instead of myself." We have few items which go to the issue as straight-forwardly as this, but certainly our data as a whole strongly suggest that LL's find it easier to impute the fault for faulty outcomes to something outside the self (p. 325).

Their description of beliefs and values surrounding LL toughness indicate subcultural counteridealizations.

> There is "tough-mindedness" in the sense of subscribing to a "dog-eat-dog" ideology, expressed in agreement with this questionnaire item: "If a person hopes to get ahead in this world he can't help stepping on others' toes, and he can't let this bother him." . . . A second connotation [of toughness] is . . . an ability to "take it", whether "it" is physical pain, suffering, or a sea of troubles. . . . there is a third connotation . . . a general posture of truculent self-assertiveness, defiance, "don't-push-me-around" touchiness . . . apparently equivalent to [W. B.] Miller's "autonomy" (p. 328).

These are disjunctive beliefs and values in the sense that they indicate LLs' profound doubts about gaining security and satisfactions within the legitimate system. The Srole "anomie" items which Cohen and Hodges used in their questionnaire clearly defined LLs' pessimism and personal insecurity. To the extent that externalization enters into LL ideology, self-discontent is latently functional in alienation from the legitimate social system. Moreover, qualities like misanthropy, extrapunitiveness, and toughness involve antisocial values, encouraging the individual and his peer group to violate others' interests. Since the subjects were adult males, they comprised a significant segment of a subcultural context for many LL adolescents, and were identity models for the male adolescents. Their antisocial values operated as constraints on the kinds of deviance open to discontented youth. Their values, in short, constitute subcultural pressures toward delinquency.

I suggested before that to a lesser degree some similar UL psychocultural adaptations also constituted situational pressures toward delinquency. As indicated in the discussion of externalization in the working class in Chapter 2, Gans reports that his Urban Villagers were generally and continually preoccupied with thoughts that peers were imputing sexual and self-aggrandizing impulses to them. The men displayed a suspiciousness toward others' initiatives, and much the same kind of truculent assertiveness, it seemed to me, as that to which Cohen and Hodges referred in their description of LL toughness.

The subculture that Gans described was also alienated in important ways from participation in the legitimate system, even though it was a part of it. Adults mistrusted middle-class people and civic authorities; partly as a consequence these adults were inadequately represented politically and minimized their "dependence on the larger society" (p. 265). The men expressed some of their attitudes toward cultural and normative constraints when, in their adult peer groups, they nostalgically relived their moments of adolescent "action." "The[ir] stories reinforce the belief that one can fight back, outsmart, and even defeat the outside world" (p. 71). This also may suggest guideposts to delinquent behavior for those of their sons who may be discontented.

Gans indicates that alienation from legitimate ideology and norms may begin in the childrearing practices he observed. In what is a contribution to knowledge regarding the development of ego and superego in the UL subculture, he describes patterns of reward and punishment that teach a child the prevailing morality but not to internalize much of it. The differences between what adults say and how they act

> allow him to justify his own failure in terms of the ideal, and to develop a protective cynicism, especially toward the stated norms of the

outside world. In turn, this skepticism protects him from the deprivations and disappointments he encounters as a member of a low-income population. But it also blinds him to people's good intentions. . . . his failure to respond to them other than cynically often deprives him of the benefits offered by the outside world (pp. 60–61).

It is to be noted that Gans found no delinquency among the children of routine-seeking adults. However, he distinguishes between the living patterns of these people and those of the "action-seekers," who are lower-class by life style but working-class by job stability and job type. It is assumed that delinquency might be prevalent among the children of action-seekers; that what I have taken to be signs of alienation and externalizing among the routine-seekers would also be found among them, and that previous comments about lower-class subculture would apply as well.

Intrapsychic Processes in Culture Change

When we ask by what psychological processes people find and shape beliefs and values that allow and encourage them to live out their ego deficiencies instead of symbolizing them, psychoanalytic concepts may again be helpful. The operation may be the same as the one through which parents discover child-rearing practices that direct their children toward their own psychocultural adaptation. It is also proposed that adults and adolescents rely on the same process not only in establishing disjunctive subcultural beliefs and values but also in defining more individualized counteridealizations in their externalizing.

Pre-logical mental operations probably shape the beliefs and values people need to justify the direct expression of immature object attachments and to define their attitudes toward child-rearing issues. Whereas in psychoanalytic theory rational action is a function of the secondary process which is based on the reality principle—on attending to cause-effect relationships and to probable consequences of events—the primary process finds outlets for energies by displacing their original objects, aims, affects, and means of expression to others; by condensation of different needs into one act or symbol; and by finding symbols.

The magical thinking of preliterate societies and of our more imaginative fantasies are manifestations of the primary process.

Classically, psychoanalysis used the concept of the primary process to gain insight into the libido, as did Freud in his analysis of dreams and of the nature and function of psychiatric symptoms. But Kris (1952) has discovered that the ego may at times control and put to use the primary process in its task of mastering reality, of solving problems in the course of satisfying needs. There can be a "regression in the service of the ego," in which a person holds rationality and conventional ways of thinking about reality in abeyance and lets his potential responses represent themselves to his consciousness in new symbols, condensations, and displacements. This is a creative and adaptive act, a shortcut past logic, a use of visual imagery and symbolic elements that is found in productive scientific thinking, in every form of artistic activity, and even, I suppose, in minor acts like making figures of speech.

External objects—people and events—may become just as much overdetermined symbols—objects, that is, of condensed and displaced needs—as any image in the scientific or artistic imagination. Beliefs about the characteristics of others and valuations placed on their behavior, or on one's own, may be similarly overdetermined by the actor's needs. The "social dogma of the Southern white caste," as defined by Davis and Dollard, is such an ideological invention: the beliefs and values of whites involved structured perceptions of Negro behavior and characteristics which provided ego and superego support for white economic interests, which are, in turn, based on prior ideological considerations. Some members of one male corner group of Negro LLs, I have heard, said to a professional observer regarding their multiple sexual liaisons, "I have a lot of dog in me"—a remarkable figure of speech that combined a debonair justification for the sporting life with self-rejection. When one of Miller's corner boys yells "You suck!" at another accusingly, he is acting on his values regarding aggressive masculinity and proclaiming his beliefs about the kinds of negotiations that some males, especially those in out-groups, may have with each other; both of which, moreover, bear on his own preoccupations with receptive homosexuality (W. B. Miller, *c;* 1961).

There may be regression not only to pre-logical problem-solving processes, but also in the more familiar sense of reversion to satisfactions and relations characteristic of earlier levels of development, in the service of ego adaptation. The primary process rediscovers infantile introjections and relationships and puts them to use, in response to anomic sociocultural conditions and to the strains these conditions put on the achievement of a satisfying identity.

I agree with Szasz (pp. 184–89) that there is no such thing as a "natural" tendency to regress to a putative, uncivilized human condition, but that rather people's behavior becomes infantilized when others who exert power over them demand infantile behavior. When economically more powerful classes require the underprivileged to surrender latitude of personal action, some of the underprivileged may make an internal accommodation of the sort described in Chapter 2. Then they may discover, through the primary process, those modes and methods of child development which will establish a similar ego and libidinal adaptation in their child. They fixate their children.

The Negro matriarch again, for example, often has grown-up daughters who are vague, indecisive people, needing her to physically coddle and pet them (see Rohrer and Edmonson on the matriarchal family). She has probably perpetuated in them the need for passive, circumambient satisfactions—for "oral dependency"—by overstimulation and withdrawing love at the least sign of the girls' desire to separate themselves. The matriarch, for her part, has had to adopt a childlike submissiveness and a dependent loyalty to the white mistresses of the households in which she and her female forebears have had to work.

The matter is of course nowhere near this simple: There are reality factors involved in the matriarch's inculcation of dependency in her daughters, such as old-age insurance; also, her possible disappointment with Negro men causes her to abjure her daughters to rely on her rather than men; and perhaps also, the matriarch's externalized imputations of these men's untrustworthiness. But her patterning of her daughters' dependency after her own *functioning* dependency on higher-class whites is one possibility that should not be overlooked.

The daughters are therefore ready to regress to the (oral) psychosocial mode of "taking in" and being taken in by the men with whom they do eventually form relationships. The men usually belong to a male corner group (a complementary institution, according to Rohrer and Edmonson, to the matriarchy), have been themselves raised by matriarchs and are likely therefore to have similar introjections regarding infantile, enveloping love relationships. They are thus also ready to take in the women and be taken in, both in the sense of having bed and board provided (sometimes in their women's matriarchal homes) and in the exploitative sense of "taking" the women for all they can get.

There are so many unrealizable wishes and so much distrust built into these relationships that it is little wonder how often the affairs end with the women taking their babies home to the "Mammy," if indeed they ever left home. Or, at a later stage in the child's life, the mother may prompt him to enact her disappointment and distrust by expelling the man for her. The common contempt of LL Negro boys for their fathers and other male authorities may exemplify the possibility that infantile rivalries, possessive wishes, and other *regressive object relations, once established in childhood, may be reconstituted by the primary process in the adolescent's adaptations to his current conditions.*

Hartmann (1947) describes two processes, sometimes seen in the formation of political ideologies and arrived at, apparently, by regression in the service of the ego, that shed some light on the creation of the kinds of prejudicial views and values that have been discussed. He observes a tendency to relate as similar, or causally, or as part of a positively or negatively valued object, other similarly valued objects. He calls this process value agglutination. Thus, since an LL condemns art, intellectuality, effeminacy, and middle-class exploitativeness (Cohen and Hodges), he tends to see all characteristics present in the same middle-class person. Hartmann also describes what he calls irradiation of values: objects which *are* connected with a valued object tend to become similarly valued. An LL child may antagonize his school teachers in externalizing his ego limitations with them, or he may have relatively independent motivational and cognitive impediments to learning; in either case, he may come to reject both for the same ostensive reason. This connecting and severing of facts without due regard for their objective relationships, Hartmann notes, probably involves the operation of the primary process.

(The behavioral psychologist may already have noted, by the way, the similarity of value agglutination and irradiation to the learning theory constructs of stimulus and response generalization. He may also recognize a resemblance between regression in the service of the ego, especially when it reinstitutes old displacements, condensations, and symbols, and the concept of redintegration from classical habit psychology.)

Discontented lower-class youth who grew up in an age-graded subcultural track such as that defined by Miller's total "outlaw" organization (W. B. Miller, *et al.*, 1961) probably enact age-appropriate versions of adult ideologies as various social issues become important to them. Miller's observations (*c*) suggest that the one-sex peer group pattern, which many other writers have observed to continue throughout marriage, begins well back in the primary grades; his data on corner-group aggression (1961) imply the operations of adolescent versions of misanthropy (regarding out-groups and adults), pessimism (regarding the good will of parents and older youths), extrapunitiveness, and toughness.

It is proposed that each age grade adaptively refashions the ideologies brought down from the adult milieu by older age groups. Kobrin's analysis of value organization in delinquency areas, along with W. F. Whyte's observations on slum organization, indicate that anomie may not be directly expressed in a literal social disorganization. There obviously can be great consensus, within groups, on ideology and norms and a highly articulated social structure. But the structure may consist of a congeries of groups, each experiencing itself as somewhat isolated from other age-graded groups even within its own track, and certainly by sex; each group may consider the purposes of the others as alienated from or inimical to its own, even though substantively they share the same views.

Under such circumstances those individuals who readily assimilate, for their own benefit and that of their peer group, the traits of older identity models under these socially alienated conditions, will be rewarded with leadership status and prestige by their peers for showing the way. Cohen describes the values of lower-class delinquents as malicious, negativistic, and non-utilitarian; Miller has criticized such descriptions for reflecting a middle-class bias against lower-class values. The theoretical approach here would describe some lower-class delinquent values as malicious and negativistic, but utilitarian in the sense that they subserve counterideals and induce acts which obtain social approval. The delinquent may be following the dictates of his conscience and looking out for himself and his compeers when he vandalizes, steals from, or assaults those whom he views as enemies or victims; his wishes may be syntonic with his ego and superego.

Delinquency as Regression and Protest

The delinquent's wishes may contain the demands and the destructiveness that a deprived and an overly frustrated child might harbor, and the ego and superego may long since have been patterned to view people as enemies or victims. The disjunctive ideology and the alienated behavior of others in a lower-class milieu may exacerbate these trends and patterns in self-discontented youth, and they may respond and judge on the basis of childhood experience with externalizing families. Julia, the "frightened amazon" described by Davis and Dollard, was, in her membership in a fighting gang

> instigated to express her animosity against her mother and against life in revenge for the frightful "injustice" which had been done to her when she was incapable of protecting herself. . . . in lower-class modes of action she can shout her grudge, her unrequited claim against the world [p. 39]. . . . Julia is not a person to be controlled by force, or to accept rejection meekly. She fights back and returns hate for contempt. "I hate white people," she repeats many times. "I just like to beat on white people. I hate white people. They don't like us, so I don't see why we should like them" (p. 42).

Julia, Davis and Dollard suggest, responded to exploitation and injustice in terms of a conscience outraged to the extreme of sadism by the cruelties that her father and mother practiced on her. Erikson (1962) has suggested that the symbolizing adolescent expresses more in his symptoms than the regressive drag back to infantile objects, for example, restates more than his Oedipal embroilment with his parents. He also, through his symptoms, protests the conditions which originally intimidated his ego and blocked his psychosexual development, insisting symbolically that those conditions be recognized within a truthful reformulation of the realities of his own time and place. Erikson re-examines the case of Dora, one of Freud's classical cases of hysteria, and tries to show that it was just as important for Dora to establish the actual treachery of her father as it was for her to understand her own Oedipal feelings that father betrayed her for her mother. The cruel reality of Julia's adolescent time and place called for the same vengefulness she had felt toward her parents' cruelties, because the subcultural reality mirrored the familial, just as the familial, *mutatis mutandis*, mirrored the subcultural.

The self-discontented adolescent attempts to repudiate his harmful reality at those levels and in those ways which most offended him. If he is a lower-class externalizer, he makes preventive war with the same ideological weapons that harmful reality taught him, because he intuitively identifies, in his insightful and distorted way, the same threats to his ego that he has faced before. His occasional or regular delinquencies, imbedded among his other externalizations, are thus attempts to break the bonds of his subculture, but attempts which, by looking backward to old grievances and methods, bind him to others who see no future for themselves. Even as he refuses what is not good enough and demands what in all love and fairness should have been granted in the first place, he ties himself all the more firmly to the rack and wheel of a lower-class identity, one that evades its discontent with itself and is alienated from its own potentialities.

Following Erikson's hint, I have maintained the distinction throughout between symbolizing ("pathological") and externalizing ("lived-through") behavior to draw some comparisons between the meaning of psychiatric symptoms and deviance under certain conditions. Now (again in the light of my understanding of Erikson's insight—this time regarding the case of Dora) I have to complicate that distinction.

Regarding the delinquent adolescent's specific need to identify a uniquely valid and a valued position for himself in society as he finds it, his delinquency is symbolic. The distinction still holds for the delinquent activities themselves—they are still viewed as direct, behavioral regressions rather than as symbols for them. But just as a disturbed adolescent may express in *psychiatrically meaningful symbols* his relation to a familial environment which may objectively be depriving him of individuality, so too, the self-discontented delinquent lives out a frustrated child's defiance, aggression, tyranny, and violations as *socially meaningful symbols* of his thwarted struggle for a worthwhile identity in a constricting subcultural environment.

He lives out childish patterns of retaliation because they have been established in previous externalizations; they come easily to him. They come to him because his subcultural circumstances invite them: The subcultural arena reproduces some of the ideology and patterned relations of his childhood battlegrounds.

But the lived-out regressions are also displaced and condensed action-representations of dismay at his life chances. As there is a kernel of truth in every paranoid's system, there is a bushel of depriving realities on which an externalizing delinquent feeds his overdetermined sense of unjust deprivation. Paul Goodman predicates delinquency as social protest by assuming that our social system fails the potentialities of its youth. He asserts, for example, that delinquency "asks for" self-realizing work, money, esteem, living space; for loyalties and knowledge which would command the delinquent's attention; for a voice in a community of interests —all of which are signal lower-class deprivations (p. 50). Cohen is driving at the same thing, I think, when he describes delinquency as lower-class youths' malicious and negativistic reaction-formations to their status deprivations; on the specific issue under consideration right now, this theory agrees with his.

At a less theoretical level: A light-skinned, middle-class-oriented Negro correctional officer made reference to "black people" in addressing a dormitory of delinquent inmates. His comment was followed by several incidents in which Negro boys beat up or homosexually assaulted white boys. I have spoken with such assaulters, and they are usually indignant, interestingly, toward their victims; they consider them punks who "eat the man" (a figure of speech regarding ingratiation toward officers, similar to "sucking around"). In a subsequent confrontation some of these Negro boys denounced the officer for being just as prejudiced as white officers.

It seemed to me that the Negro boys were condensing and displacing, in these assaults, their outrage at the kind of degraded relationship to authority they thought the colored officer (and white adults) expected of them. They were defying his custodial control, and they were mocking his wishes, as they perceived these wishes, regarding them in sexualized terms which conveyed their introjections and fantasies of what parents and older children earlier wanted of them and wanted to do to them. They intuitively associated certain psychosexual issues (eating, punking) with psychosocial issues of degradation and exploitation.

Thus the self-discontented delinquent may do more than live out his hungry, angry, intimidated, and seduced earlier development. These developmental misfortunes become an action-language, interactional symbols, to express his demand for more equitable prospects. He insists on responsive recognition of his overwhelming disadvantages by those who might be able to do something—a correctional officer, a teacher, middle-class proprietors. He rejects what would mislead, cheat, ignore, and use him. He assaults violators of his interests and their accomplices, witting or otherwise. His inner and outer deprivations—his limited ego resources and the limitations of his subculture prevent more effective and self-realizing forms of dissidence and protest. In Camus' terms, subcultural delinquency is both rebellion and impotent vengeance, an affirmation of self against an unjust social order and a resentful negation of selfhood.

Simplification of the Ego

First things last: At the beginning of my summary statement of subcultural pressures toward delinquency (p. 87), a rather general and probably somewhat mysterious reference was made to a certain simplification in ego structure that may have an adverse effect on the learning capacities of many lower-class children. Many social accounts attribute lower-class educational underachievement, which is such an obvious deterrent to conforming socioeconomic aspirations, to conflict between these children and middle-class teachers, to the teachers' prejudices and discriminatory practices of school systems against these children. Underachievement is also attributed to an ideologically-based indifference to education on the part of the children and their parents. There is very likely something more to this than social conflict and differences in value emphases, having to do with a reduced capacity to form the skills needed for learning and to assimilate and retain what is taught. Strodtbeck and others have referred to these diminished capacities as "cognitive deficits;"

while his work suggests that there may be many theoretical approaches to the problem, I should like to outline one that fits into the ego-psychological basis of this theory.

The reality principle, according to Hartmann (1956), has two meanings: to think, perceive, and act in accord with the real features of an object or a situation; and to postpone the immediate discharge of an impulse. In adapting responses to reality, the ego has two general classes of function—its objectivating, cognitive tasks and its anticipatory and delaying operations. It may greatly oversimplify but perhaps also clarify matters somewhat to suggest that Erikson's theory of psychosocial development is an elaboration of changes in the anticipatory task of the ego; as the ego assimilates the different libidinal energies that become available in the course of organismic growth, it correlates their discharge to environmental conditions, which also alter with stages in growth. It is true that his theory relies on the development of certain objectivating functions, such as perceptual skills during the crises of trust and autonomy and the importance of memory in the crisis of industry, but he attends primarily to the ways in which and the reasons for which the child learns, or significantly refuses, to delay gratification.

In his original delineation of semi-autonomous ego development, Hartmann (1958) enumerates some of these objectivating functions of the ego. He refers "to the development *outside of conflict*" of motility, "perception, intention, object comprehension, thinking, language, recall phenomena, productivity . . . and to the maturation and learning processes implicit in all these and many others" (p. 8). He suggests that the organism makes conflict-free energies available for the development and exercise of those functions, that is, energies that are not wrested from the libido by socialization pressures. The organism is pre-adapted to put energies at the ego's disposal for these purposes given an "average acceptable environment"; but what specific environmental conditions conduce the ego to do so, or what conditions does the ego find so unacceptable that usually "surplus" energies are dissipated and absorbed into socialization conflicts?

Hartmann, Kris, and Loewenstein supply one answer (1946): In order to retain the mother's love the child must comply with her requirements of him, and she is therefore the prime instrument in learning and ego development. If the mother encourages him to pay attention to his environment, then his cognitive functions may be differentiated out of the primal core of his potentials; if she cares only that he accommodate himself to her needs and about little else, then his energies may be diverted into psychosocial issues related to delay of gratification, and the stimuli (not demands, let it be noted) for cognitive differentiation will be reduced.

There are several indications that many lower-class mothers do indeed overstress the anticipatory, psychosocial ego aspects and neglect to facilitate cognitive aspects in the child's growth. Kerr gives ample evidence that Ship Street mothers are almost completely preoccupied with organizing their children's attachments to themselves and in satisfying their own infantile needs in and through their children. They pay very little attention to the child's development apart from his direct relation to her. One result, Kerr suggests, is the relatively high incidence of very simple Lowenfeld mosaic patterns among these children and of Rorschach indices of intellectual impairment—findings comparable to those she made in a deprived Jamaican community. There is a hint in Gans' data that such an imbalance also occurs in UL childrearing practices. These practices, he indicates, tend to be impulsive and inconsistent, with possible extremes in reward and punishment, because parents are not interested in developing their children for later achievement. Again, development of the child as a separate person is not stressed as it is in the middle classes, because these parents have no clear goals for their children.

Strodtbeck's preliminary observations of Negro mothers and their small children from the deprived Woodlawn section of Chicago clearly indicate a similar trend. These mothers use little reasoning and frequently punish physically; are strict but inconsistent; and have low requirements for neatness, orderliness, and work of the child.

> The net effect is to reward keeping out of trouble rather than to reward positive goal-achievement. . . . (A) socialization atmosphere [is created] where attempts at control of young children are carried out by agents who believe the effort will inevitably fail. The resulting inconsistency creates an atmosphere in which the mother subtly encourages dependency (p. 24).

These mothers, according to Strodtbeck, essentially fail to support cognitive exploration by their children.

Why this neglect of cognitive development? In some instances it may be a by-product of maternal immaturity and aggrandizement which might siphon off the needed energy. But this cannot be an adequate explanation in view of the fact that some middle-class children perform well and even brilliantly in learning situations even though they may be disturbed, even profoundly, as a result of disruptive childhood experiences. I rather think that this particular form of maternal neglect is one aspect of a general simplification in ego structure that is a part of the psychocultural adaptations of the lower class. The term I should like to apply to this simplification is *ego syncretism* or *syncretization* (after Piaget), to differentiate it from other ego adaptations mentioned and from rudimentary cognitive development.

Ego syncretism is intended to refer to a fusing of elements that were previously differentiated in the ego, or to the absence of (internal) structural differentiations that may be found in individuals elsewhere in the same society. Syncretization is perhaps the internal accompaniment of the simplification of social experience that LLs undergo as a result of their relative isolation from the rest of our complex society (Cohen and Hodges). This impoverishment of experience is partly imposed by social-structural constraints and partly a response to them. It was previously suggested that blurring processes, like value agglutination and irradiation, which function in the service of the ego to produce disjunctive LL stereotypes and prejudices, may syncretize an LL's cognitions and his superego. Kerr has constructed a series of hypotheses that attempt to relate the socioeconomic immobility and the psychopathology of people in deprived subcultures to a simplification and an impoverishment of subcultural roles. She suggests, very briefly, that limitations, impairments, and uncertainties in available roles fail to create egos sufficiently differentiated to participate in a complex society and which are susceptible to fixations in infantile relationships.

Other forms of ego syncretism in lower-class people are indicated in some of the literature that has been used here. Cohen and Hodges suggest that LLs have simplified our society's complexities of subordination to authority to the single authoritarian dichotomy of command and obedience. Gans' description of the male sex role in the families he observed suggested to this reader that patriarchal Italian traditions have syncretized this aspect of the male's identity: He commands and he punishes. Cohen and Hodges' observations regarding particularistic LL criteria for evaluating others, as contrasted to middle-class universalistic criteria; Gans' highly similar distinction between the person-oriented individualism of his Urban Villagers and middle-class object-oriented individualism; and Langner and Michael's discussion of the middle-class person's self-conscious identity, all point to an ego differentiation lacking in lower-class people—a dualistic self, as Gans puts it, containing an "I" and a "me," the lack of which makes it hard for them to distinguish between their own and others' views of them and reduces their capacity for empathy.

All these syncretizations of conscious experience (as well as conscience), it seems to me, indicate that some of the objectivating ego capacities are less important to some lower-class people than are their skills for managing immediate interpersonal relationships. One might speculate as to the reasons for this, but, whatever the causes for human adaptations to structural deprivations, it would appear to follow that lower-class parents are no more likely to stress the cognitive capacities of their children's egos than they stress these capacities in themselves.

Their ego syncretisms put them at a disadvantage constantly in handling the technical, political, and bureaucratic machinery that runs our society. They suffer economic deprivation and sociopolitical dispossession as a consequence. Their children, deprived in their socialization of the inner machinery for upward mobility through education, bear witness to their parents' relinquishment of capacities and submergence in the legitimate system. From these adult limitations discontented youth seeks escape, not in the forms of deviance such as Bohemianism and political radicalism which may require a show of intellectual skills and achievements, but in delinquency, for which they are capable and psychoculturally fitted.

part two

critique

The following three chapters contain further criticisms of current social-scientific theories of delinquency. In the course of making these criticisms, theoretical positions and data will be introduced—those of other sociologists, anthropologists, and psychotherapists—to support some of the basic alternative views and concepts discussed in the psychocultural theory presented in Part One. These three chapters entertain some of the issues which have already been outlined, but go into more argumentative and technical detail. The reader who has no need for this more elaborate discussion may wish to proceed to Part Three, where data and inferences regarding the socialization experiences and the personality characteristics of delinquents are reviewed, and where additional data and hypotheses about psychocultural adaptations are advanced. Summaries are provided, at the beginning of each of the next three chapters, of their contents.

It is perhaps a reflection of the intellectual insecurity of social scientists that they spend an inordinate amount of time and energy defining the "boundaries" of their respective fields as if these were holy lands which had to be defended against expansive, barbaric, and heathen invaders. This need for a clear professional identity leads to a striving towards ideological purity, and often from their earliest student days those entering the field are carefully watched for signs of dangerous pantheistic belief. The discipline's name designates not so much a focus of setting or a mode of analysis as a banner around which the faithful rally. In sociology this tendency expresses itself in the attempt to analyze social phenomena with a method which strictly excludes psychological theory and data. . . . It may be that the only course open to [Durkheim] was . . . to insist on the exclusive relevance of social factors. Be that as it may, we are no longer living in Durkheim's time. Our criterion should be not disciplinary purity but, rather, the adequacy of our analysis.

. . . . .

Adequate sociological analysis of many problems is either impossible or severely limited unless we make explicit use of psychological theory and data in conjunction with sociological theory and data. Indeed, I would assert that very little sociological analysis is ever done without using at least an implicit psychological theory. It seems evident that in making this theory explicit and bringing psychological data to bear systematically on sociological problems we cannot fail but improve the scope and adequacy of sociological analysis. . . . The student of social structure seeks to explain the action consequences of a particular set of institutional arrangements. In order to do this, he must correctly estimate the meaning of those arrangements for their effect on the human personality. All institutional arrangements are ultimately mediated through individual human action. The consequences of any institutional arrangement, therefore, depend, at least in part, upon this effect on the human personality, broadly conceived. The human personality system thus becomes one of the main intervening variables in any estimate of the effects of one aspect of social structure on another. The need for a theory of personality is perhaps most evident in the study of those "rates" which represent the summary or end product of thousands or millions of individual decisions and acts, yet which are of distinctive size for different societies or cultures . . . suicide and delinquency rates (Inkeles, pp. 249–51).

chapter 4

the competition of etiologies

SOME psychiatric accounts of delinquent etiology do not stress uninhibited impulse factors to the exclusion of other formulations, as some sociological criticism suggests. A psychodynamic tradition views antisocial behavior as an intimidated ego's efforts to mount counterattacks against an external reality that is perceived to be cold and coercive. Arguments against psychoanalytic notions regarding arrested instincts miss possible theoretical reconciliations, because there must be sociocultural antecedents for abuses in socialization producing these antisocial maneuvers. Such reconciliations require the welding of personality processes and sociocultural analyses in a psychocultural approach.

Parsons (1950) remarks that the sociologist can get on with his job of analyzing the social structure only by holding individual variability in abeyance: He abstracts a modal personality pattern from idiosyncratic variability in order to focus on social processes. Parsons also observes that the psychoanalyst must adopt a similar convention, that of a modal environment, in order to refine his conceptions regarding personalities occurring within it. But personalities vary, as do environments. Conflicts among theoretical approaches to delinquency probably arise from these limitations of method and from these variations in facts, as much as from any other source.

Subjective Etiologies

Until Cohen's work (1955) sociological models centered on the concept of transmission of delinquency. Shaw and McKay and Sutherland offered accounts of acculturation in pre-existing delinquent and criminal traditions.

Psychiatric students of delinquency, on the other hand, have been developing ideas about individual etiology for forty years and more. These psychiatrists have been interested in remarkably more things about delinquency beside expressions of ensocialized aggression, even though some sociologists do not seem to think so. There has been a striking degree of agreement, for example, considering differences in setting, time, and theoretical emphasis that delinquency represents an expression of aggression because of early threats to security at least as much as to physical needs. Aggressiveness represents attempts to ward off, usually by provocation, any friendly overtures by others that would re-arouse this insecurity.

Aichhorn, who has been associated with an unsocialized impulse theory of delinquency, makes it quite clear in his description of his therapeutic management of aggressive boys (Chap. 8) that he was dealing with defensive maneuvers to antagonize him and his staff. When he gave his aggressive group its own destructive lead he points out that, far from "the children [being] very happy in this paradise where it is possible to live out their impulses without restraint," they became increasingly desperate in their provocation. He relates a confrontation in which, finally, he stood by while a boy threatened another with a knife; the boy abruptly threw down his knife in a helpless, howling, weeping rage. The boy's real interest seemed to be in getting Aichhorn to interfere.

Alexander and Healy elaborate on the effects of early deprivation on drives underlying criminality and on the lawbreaker's alienation from others. The failure of love and support by parents and siblings constitutes an early intimidation to the young child's narcissism; when developing active strivings are threatened the child's self-esteem is harmed lastingly, and he is driven back onto earlier, dependent ways of relating. They thus conclude that criminality is a type of pseudo-masculinity, an attempt to deny a sense of inner weakness and to restore inner prestige (pp. 285–86).

More recently, Donald Bloch and Kaufman and his associates (1955; 1958) have been interested in the intimidated and defensive ego operations of delinquents. Kaufman and his collaborators discuss an underlying "depressive nucleus," a profound sense of loss, which the delinquents whom they have observed initially deny and from which they try to divert themselves. In therapy, these youths eventually come to a phase of mourning and grief that reflects repeated physical or psychological separation from a mothering person. The sense of loss exists because the separation occurred so early in life that the child could not differentiate between himself and the other who had left him, and so feels that a vital part of himself has been taken away. The aggressive and self-destructive aspects of delinquency are attributed to "sado-masochistic" forms of relating, since injuring another and submitting to pain inflicted by another are the principal kinds of closeness with which the child has been familiar. Noshpitz has also described psychotherapy with delinquents in which grieving and depression have marked a phase of the relationship.

Donald Bloch's thinking is in the same line. The antisocial act, he says, is part of the specifically delinquent interpersonal integration: The delinquent means to stimulate rejection in the other partner to the integration. In his past the delinquent suffered when he sought tenderness and dependability. His delinquencies are provocations intended to destroy the possibility of intimacy, which induces intolerable anxiety in him. "He is, in fact, comfortable only when he is the recipient of harsh punitive action" (p. 302). Alexander and Healy give much the same reason for provocativeness and avoidance of relatedness when they say the delinquent "cannot endure being helped on account of overstrong but inwardly rejected dependence" (p. 288).

None of these formulations deals primarily with defects of conscience, which seem to be the only kind of "improper socialization" that Cloward and Ohlin consider (p. 39). It is true that these as well as other psychiatric formulations regarding the delinquent personality give ego and superego defects a significant place. Unless we are looking for straw men, it is just as easy to view "poor self-control" as an adaptive effort to control a frightening environment as it is to see it as reflecting a primitive human nature.

These writers seem to be in general agreement on the following: The family rejects, deprives, or abandons; there is injury to the precursors of self-esteem in the young child; he is blocked in some degree from the further maturation needed for growth of competence in his ego; and his way of seizing or letting go of initiative becomes brutalized. The delinquent's antisocial behavior, according to these observers, is an effort to live without mutuality, and this behavior renders us alternately anxious and angry toward him because he wants to have much less to do with us than we would wish. The delinquent provokes restrictions, revenge, or avoidance because he fears experiencing self-discontent—loss, shame, doubt, guilt, inferiority—in other kinds of relatedness. This thread of interpretation in psychiatric writings is tied to the concept of externalization as it was used earlier.

Environmental Etiologies

Cohen turns his attention to the social origins of delinquency, with consequences for thinking in this area that have been evident since the publication of his work. He asks, where in the social structure is delinquency most likely to occur? and attributes status discontent to disadvantaged lower-class youth as the motivational core for their rejection of legitimate norms. In his description of the conversation of interchanged exploratory gestures (p. 60) we may imagine the emergence of a delinquent subculture as a social form. We thus have a sociology of delinquency which locates pressures toward deviance in social processes and which relies relatively little on the concepts of a dynamic psychology.

There is another theoretical model, or rather the rudiments

of one, in Cohen's work. He hopes at the outset to contribute to a description of psychological and cultural factors "blending in a single causal process." The rudimentary model is a containment theory of deviance. He assumes that the position of the family in the social structure determines the experiences and problems that all family members encounter (Chap. 4); gang membership is therefore not a cause but rather a result of a breakdown of family controls. The breakdown in family controls facilitates gang recruitment. Toward the end of his presentation, he returns to his original hope of an ultimate blending, when he suggests that his theory does not render psychological theories obsolete. While he concedes that youth may join delinquent gangs for various reasons, some of which may be psychological, he finally concludes that status discontent is the "common core of motivation." He feels that the latter would explain, where psychological motivation might not, why the subculture has delinquent values. Even though he has thus conceded that psychodynamic considerations may be necessary to explain some of the relevant motivations, he evidently cannot link types of disturbed socialization with the social location of delinquency. He ends by throwing the baby out with the bath water in his concluding comment that psychological determinants and processes are vague and implausible (p. 132).

W. B. Miller's (1958; *c;* 1961) anthropological approach to delinquency greatly enriches our inventory of social and cultural influences on lower-class (and, therefore, more delinquency-vulnerable) youth. For Miller, delinquency is participation in subculturally prescribed acculturation into the lower class. He sees delinquent norms and behavior as all having some bearing on culturally shared values regarding getting into trouble, toughness, smartness, excitement, fate, and personal autonomy (1958).

Some of these lower-class concerns are extremely interesting from a psychological standpoint. Miller sees the concern about autonomy, for instance, as determined to some large extent by covert dependent needs and toughness as representing a subculturally shared fear of effeminacy. Miller's anthropological account, if viewed as a description of the nature of values and personality organization among lower-class individuals, would take us well beyond the behaviors that might be predicated, with any satisfactory specificity, on such concepts as status-striving and

-discontent or desires for material goods. Miller proposes psychological explanations, such as the sex-role anxiety of the child raised in a female-based household and predisposition toward receptive homosexuality and incest. These conceptions are quite compatible with the approach taken here.

Cloward and Ohlin go further than other sociologists in describing delinquency as a purely sociological phenomenon. They avoid allusions to a frustration-defensive-reaction image of delinquency; theirs is more properly a roadblock-rerouting concept. The whole society is committed to money and success; certain social levels, notably lower-class, are less favored in their access to these goals. Some lower-class youths want success, not in middle-class terms as Cohen argued, but in terms acceptable to their own class: They want money, clothes, and girls. They repudiate norms which prescribe striving toward these goals by legitimate means, which are less accessible to them. Instead, they enter into one or another type of organized delinquent activity to pursue generally accepted goals, such as money, by illegitimate means such as stealing; by substitution of new, illegitimate means and goals (*e.g.*, fighting to earn a "rep"); or by abandonment of both legitimate and illegitimate goals and withdrawal into fantasied gratifications that opiates provide (p. 15). They offer a germinal analysis of the dimensions of delinquency causation, and they go beyond Cohen in refining the steps by which pressures to deviance are transformed into delinquent norms.

Further Consideration of Merton's Environmentalism

A bulwark of opportunity-structure theory is Merton's description of the emergence of normlessness "as a symptom of dissociation between culturally prescribed aspirations and socially structured avenues for realizing these aspirations" (p. 128). According to Durkheim, an industrial society institutes unconditional or unlimited aspirations which rob men of the sense of fulfillment they might have achieved through activities prescribed by the norms of another society. The resulting dissatisfaction and restlessness bring about a chronic and pervasive questioning of, and pressure to repudiate, those values which regulate social behavior —a state of anomie. Merton has reanalyzed and refined this conception. In his view, anomie results from the *relative* unattainability of success goals. When the society does not have enough statuses symbolic of success to go around, then those social sectors, principally the lower classes, which feel most keenly the pinch of disadvantage, are most likely to withdraw their allegiance from conventional, and frustrating, norms.

Merton apparently considers any account of behavior based on a model of human needs that might exist independently of society an erroneous psychological realism.

This orientation is directed sharply against the fallacious premise, strongly entrenched in Freudian theory and found also in the writings of such Freudian revisionists as Fromm, that the structure of society primarily restrains the free expression of man's fixed native impulses and that, accordingly, man periodically breaks into open rebellion against these restraints to achieve freedom (p. 115).

It is equally clear, however, that Merton is not espousing an antithetical social and cultural realism. He is not taking the position that the process of rejecting conventional norms and of initiating substitute deviant norms is necessarily independent of personality changes or self-defeating adaptations as set out in the psychiatric literature. This is a very important consideration, because it is just this false dichotomy that I think has plagued theoretical writings on delinquency causation. It is still maintained to some extent by Cloward and Ohlin and Cohen.

Merton points out that what distinguishes him as a social scientist rather than a psychologist is that he approaches his data differently, and that he is observing only those shared behaviors described as social patterns (the same distinction, cited before, which Parsons makes between psychoanalysis and social science). He is interested in a *perspective* which abstracts social patterns from psychologically relevant behavior of individuals (p. 378, fn. 3).

Merton's types of norm deviation are not a psychological typology at all. He refers to descriptions by Horney, Kardiner, and Fromm of personality adaptations under cultural stress. He criticizes them, *not because he doubts that they occur as forms of personal adaptation to cultural stress,* but because they lack sociological specificity: The link between them as psychological types and the forces within the sociocultural order are not made clear by the respective authors, and the types of social and cultural influence to which they give rise are not precisely enough refined (pp. 379–80, fn. 12; in fn. 36, he comments approvingly on a speculation of Fromm's regarding anal character formation in the European lower middle class).

Merton's typology leaves the door open for linking distinctive social patterns of deviance with personality types. Cloward and Ohlin imply that these deviation types can stand as adequate descriptions of the psychological processes involved. Cloward and Ohlin have psychologized Merton's sociology of deviance.

Parsons has made another comment relevant to the psychologies and sociologies of delinquency:

> Freud and his followers, by concentrating on the single personality, have failed to consider adequately the individual's interaction with other personalities to *form a system*. On the other hand, Durkheim and the other sociologists have failed, in their concentration on the social system as a system, to consider systematically the implications of the fact that it is *the interaction of personalities* which constitutes the social system with which they have been dealing, and that, therefore, adequate analysis of motivational process in such a system must reckon with the problems of personality (1952, p. 17).

chapter 5

criticism of sociological theories

BOTH Cohen's and Cloward and Ohlin's concepts of personal pressures to deviance—"status discontent" and "position discontent"—are psychologically vague definitions of motivations to deviance. Their concepts only seem to explain the incentives involved and are primarily descriptive terms like "battle fatigue" and "dermatitis." Cohen's "status discontent" really refers in part to feelings of personal rejection, which is not exclusive to lower-class youths and which these youths are more likely to experience from within their subculture than from the middle-class agents of Cohen's theory.

Position discontent should, by definition and inference, prevail among lower-middle-class youth, so that opportunity theory is perhaps more applicable to middle-class than to lower-class delinquency. Cloward and Ohlin's data do not support their contentions that the economic aspirations of lower-class youth are strong enough to generate position discontent. Other data indicate that economic barriers to aspirations are not in fact the crucial determinants of lower-class delinquency, but rather that lack of family cohesion and school failures are. Opportunity theory accounts for violent, conflict-oriented delinquency not by reference to the social structure but by covertly invoking socialization factors.

Status Deprivation—Subjective or Structural State?

Cohen asserts that status discontent is the common core of disaffection with conventional norms. If one interprets this to mean that many lower-class youths have a variety of negative feelings related in some way to their status in the social system, such an assertion is hardly questionable. But an important consideration is that of the psychological validity, the usefulness as a personality construct, of status discontent.

"Status" is a social-structural concept. The term "status deprivation" makes most sense as the demonstrable denial or absence of some valued position; it makes less sense as the emotional or personalized consequences of this social occurrence.

It would seem scientifically more discreet to use a concept like "status deprivation" as a descriptive term referring to a general set of negative reactions to a given situation. It is probably in this sense that we use descriptive terms like "combat fatigue" or "dermatitis." To say that a delinquent engages in destructive or antisocial behavior because he has experienced status deprivation may be equivalent to saying that a soldier becomes catatonic because he is suffering from combat fatigue or that a person scratches because he has dermatitis. Nor is the substitution of the word "discontent" for "deprivation" helpful, because the impression may then be conveyed that the essential intervening variables within personality are being accounted for, when in fact they are not. The most that one might be able to say is that status discontent refers in a general, very indicative way to the fact that lower-class delinquents are discontented and that some of this discontent may derive purely from perception of low status, while other discontents may or may not overdetermine this perception.

When we try to transfer Cohen's status discontent or Cloward and Ohlin's discontent regarding economic aspirations to personal behavior, it becomes clear that we are bound to oversimplify matters. Miller informs us that the lower-class gang member has to be aggressively tough and is worried about being homosexual; that he is afraid of boredom and acquires prestige when he dupes or "cons" another; that his humor reveals preoccupation with "incestuous and perverted sexual relations with the mother" (1958, p. 10); and that while he brags in a rebellious way about his independence he arranges to have himself consoled and cared for. What do these characteristics have to do with status discontent or economic aspirations? We are confronted here with the realization that however valuable these terms may be for ordering sociologically relevant behavior, the need and reward constructs employed by the theoretical systems I am criticizing are, psychologically, instrumental acts and goals and denote nothing that is primary regarding the motives and gratifications around which personality is organized. These normatively defined needs for "clothes, girls, flashy cars," and so forth do not acquaint us with the kinds of satisfaction individuals may draw from these acquisitions.

The proponent of opportunity theory may argue that if individuals were enabled to earn the money, they would be able to satisfy themselves in whatever manner they chose without having to steal. The psychologist might rejoin, if the individual needs money to buy a series of dependent-exploitative relationships with women and to increase the number of his episodic drinking bouts, he does nothing for a new generation of children from mother-based, disrupted households. Further, if intervention efforts have gone thus far but no further, we may find such an individual, newly fired from one of the jobs that we have opened up for him, standing outside the candy store window again without two dimes to rub together and ready to smash the glass—which is where opportunity theory found him to begin with.

Personal Rejection—A Class or a Human Experience?

Cohen argues that lower-class youths internalize middle-class values from teachers and settlement house workers, and that their delinquency is a reaction-formation against the discontent they experience regarding their actual status. Critics have indicated that Cohen's own data indicate, not an acceptance of, but a resistance to middle-class values. Furthermore, this resistance is congruent with a variety of evidence that lower-class youths have had a rich and perhaps distinctive socialization of their own, replete with values that derogate middle-class imperatives (Davis; Gans; Miller). It is, as Kitsuse and Dietrich say, "difficult to comprehend . . . Cohen's image of the working class boy . . . standing alone to face humiliation at the hands of middle-class agents" (pp. 211–12).

The reference to "humiliation" deserves discussion. Actually Cohen advances two reasons for status discontent. One is the lower-class youth's perception that he is unable to achieve rewards related to internalized middle-class values. This is very close to Merton's and Cloward and Ohlin's formulations. A second argument seems to be that the middle-class agents continually reflect disparaging valuations of him, that he is a victim of constant "status punishment." This latter assertion is different from a means-end discrepancy argument, since it would appear from Merton that the simple knowledge or belief that opportunity is blocked is sufficient to generate pressures to renounce legitimate norms. I suggest that Cohen refers not only to a class-based and impersonal obstruction to normative behavior, but also to a personalized rejection of lower-class youth, to explain malicious and destructive delinquency. Even though he grounds this rejection in class differences, it is nonetheless of a kind that one intuitively concedes will breed insulted feelings and angry retaliation.

Cohen is clear about the personalized rejection in his original work and elsewhere: "In short, large numbers of working-class children are systematically disadvantaged in the competitive pursuit of status and are likely to find themselves repeatedly 'at the bottom of the heap' *and their self-respect damaged*" (quoted by Short, p. 368; my italics). Cohen is making an appeal here to human needs that have little to do with conforming to the Protestant ethic or striving toward middle-class goals. He turns to rejection by the delinquent's elders to explain the gravity and intensity of reaction. There are no class distinctions in the depression and bitterness a child feels when he is disregarded and derogated by adults. There is evidence that the lower-class youth is if anything perhaps less vulnerable than the middle-class boy to disapproval from middle-class authority figures. Who then *are* the adults who create these and other negative reactions in the child, if they are not the middle-class agents of Cohen's theory? Those in his own subculture, including his family.

In attempting this explanation of "non-utilitarian" delinquency, Cohen left his theory open to the observation that some delinquency is only incidentally malicious and is primarily utilitarian—criminalistic, organized for profit. Cloward and Ohlin account for this kind of delinquency by reminding us that the lower classes share a desire for material goods with the rest of our culture:

> It is our view that many discontented lower-class youths do not wish to adopt a middle-class way of life or to disrupt their present association and negotiate passage into middle-class groups. The solution they seek entails the acquisition of higher positions in terms of lower-class rather than middle-class criteria (p. 92).

According to their theory, a lower-class youth does not necessarily want middle-class membership; he is not motivated to acquire and to practice middle-class normative behavior. He wants only more money, which Cloward and Ohlin maintain is an aspiration that can be ascribed to lower-class acculturation. This aspiration for economic improvement is blocked in the opportunity structure. While this formulation eliminates the moot issue of humiliation by middle-class adults, it allows for a less intuitively persuasive version of social discontent. How much more money does the lower-class youth want than he can reasonably expect to have? How intense is his desire for money?

Position Discontent

Position discontent is a composite function of two variables: aspiration and access. Cloward and Ohlin offer what they seem to think is dependable evidence that aspiration is sufficiently high in the lower class to create discontent about lack of opportunity. Sections B and C below cast some doubt that their evidence means what they think it does, or that they have indeed offered data on those aspects of aspiration crucial for delinquency according to their own theory, particularly, the fact that felt disbarment must be relative to aspiration level. Before examining Cloward and Ohlin's data and inferences regarding level of aspiration in the lower class, let us consider other evidence that the class level in which the greatest discrepancy between opportunity and aspiration exists is not the lower class but rather the lower-middle class. (I am indebted to Dr. Roger Burton for bringing this point to my attention.)

A. *Type, Location.* If one assumes that almost all adolescents, across socioeconomic levels, want about the same amount of luxury goods and the money to obtain them, the relative economic disadvantages of the lower class would produce higher position discontent. This assumption may have a certain common-sense appeal, because it corresponds to certain homogeneous and ubiquitous tastes in the American youth culture ("clothes, cars, and girls"). But position discontent, like Cohen's status discontent, is psychologically non-specific. Its view of level of aspiration considers only economic aspects: individuals aspire toward more money and jobs that pay more. If one chooses (as Ohlin and Cloward obviously do not), one can consider level of aspiration in its relation to the psychological dimension of the achievement motive. But position discontent, as a frustration of the achievement motive, may be more prevalent in the lower-middle class than in the lower classes because of the high achievement need of the middle class in general.

Rosen makes a pointed comment about economic disadvantages when he remarks:

> Differential mobility is described as a function of the relative opportunities available to individuals in the social structure. This *structural* dimension of stratification is explicit in the "life chances" hypothesis in which it is argued that money, specialized training, and prestigeful contacts—factors which affect access to high position—are relatively inaccessible to individuals in the lower strata. Such an explanation lacks exhaustiveness, however, (since it does not take into account the possibility that) there may be *psychological* and *cultural factors which affect social mobility* by influencing the individual's willingness to develop and exploit his talents, intelligence and opportunities (pp. 495–96; my italics).

Sears and Levin assert a relation between level of aspiration and achievement need that is empirically supported by the correlation between level of occupational preference and achievement motivation in a group of veterans. (Minor and Neel; however, note that Rosen finds no significant relation between achievement need and educational aspiration level.) It seems clear that the achievement striving involves aspirations to meet standards of excellence and to outdo others in competition (McClelland, *et al.*, 1950; Atkinson). Rosen finds it correlated with school grades; Douvan and Hoffman, *et al.*, find the test-taking effort of adolescents with high achievement needs resistive to failure and non-reward.

Further, the last three studies mentioned show the achievement motive to be higher in middle-class than in lower-class high school students. Douvan, who presents evidence that her measure of achievement need is not seriously class-biased, concludes that "the pattern of achievement motivation a child develops depends on the class subculture in which he is trained" (p. 517). So does Rosen:

> Middle-class children are more likely to be taught not only to believe in success but also to take those steps that make achievement possible: in short, to embrace the achievement value system which states that given the willingness to work hard, plan and make the proper sacrifices, an individual should be able to manipulate his environment so as to ensure eventual success (p. 508).

The LM youth commits himself to this ideology in the hope of achieving vocational and economic goals appropriate to the middle class. His parents, however, are less capable of paying for or gaining his entry into the better universities; his father is less likely to have the money or contacts to finance the beginning of a professional or entrepreneurial career. If opportunity theory is correct, many LM youths who embrace the achievement values Rosen describes may blame themselves, but many other youths should blame the system. They should realize that they are still barred and that their values and attendant norms cannot bring them success and should be rejected. If position discontent results from the interaction of structural barriers and success motivation, then it is in the lower-middle, not the lower, class that one should expect to find the greatest severity and incidence of thwarted aspiration and, hence, the greatest pressure to deviance. If gang delinquency is, as Cloward and Ohlin maintain, primarily a function of position discontent, then opportunity theory should be a theory of lower-middle-class delinquency first and only second a theory of lower-class delinquency.

B. *Absolute Aspirations.* Cloward and Ohlin distinguish between relative and absolute economic aspirations. They offer data to the effect that, *in the first place*, *fewer* lower-class youths have high absolute aspirations—want to rise very high in the total occupational system—as compared to youths of higher classes. (And fewer still, judging by their own data, of the types of lower-class youths who might become involved in delinquency. One of the two studies they cite is of a high school senior population, which exempts the drop-outs and which must reflect a large proportion of upwardly mobile "college" boys, whom both Cohen and the two authors discussed here maintain are seldom delinquents.) However, they then assert that position discontent is evident if any substantial number of lower-class youths aspire very highly and "if it can also be demonstrated that these same persons contribute disproportionately to the ranks of delinquent subcultures" (p. 88). The demonstration they offer relates to the socioeconomic aspirations of, not gang delinquents in general, but narcotics addicts.

It is true that in Cloward and Ohlin's theory, these delinquents are different from others only in their failure to acquire status in either legitimate or illegitimate status systems; these authors might argue that what is true of the aspirations of drug users might be true of non-addicted delinquents as well. But there are other sociologists, notably Cohen and Short, who maintain that addicted youngsters are not like other gang delinquents in that they are personally less stable (perhaps because more frustrated) and hence more vulnerable to escapism. Judging from Cloward and Ohlin's evidence, one is obliged to conclude that the relatively low incidence of high aspirations argues as much against aspiration as a major source of pressure towards deviance peculiar to lower-class youths as it does for it.

C. *Relativity of Aspirations and Barriers.* Cloward and Ohlin cite evidence that the aspirations of lower-class students *relative* to their families' incomes or to the occupational statuses of their fathers are significantly higher than those of higher-class youths. (The cogency of this argument from base rates is blunted by a consideration of ceilings: the limits of realistic upward aspiration for higher-class children are foreshortened by their fathers' considerable attainment.)

Accepting the validity of these findings, we are still left with the question, Do lower-class individuals aspire toward jobs and income levels *beyond* those usually attained by their class? How frequently, for instance, are lower-class youths' aspirations directed toward semi-skilled and skilled jobs which are usual for their class? Cloward and Ohlin's information suggests that the level of lower-class youths' absolute aspirations, irrespective of present family status, is lower than for middle- and upper-class youths. In other words, since lack of legitimate opportunities is more meaningful to those aspiring to higher levels, the lower a person's aspirations, the less liable should he be to experience his economic prospects as disadvantageous.

It is true that there are fewer good lower-class jobs than there are youths who might aspire to them. But this is no different from the economic prospects of middle-class youths, since the educational prerequisites for the professions and the steeply graded avenues toward high-paying managerial positions create similar discrepancies between ambition and real opportunity. (See Parsons, 1962, on rising educational and work performance requirements throughout our society.) It may be that lower-class adolescents experience more position discontent than youth elsewhere in the social structure *specifically in relation to current status;* that is, more of them may be unhappy with their economic status than are higher-class youth. But we must recall that, according to opportunity structure theory, position discontent is only half the story of pressures toward deviance. Its exponents must also show that the aspirations of the population-at-risk meet significantly greater barriers to opportunity than is true for adolescents at other class levels. This they have not done.

Opportunity theory contends also that lower-class youths experience greater difficulty in acquiring an education; however, the importance of educational barriers should depend strictly on how high the level of aspiration really is. It is probably true that higher education is relatively inaccessible to the lower-class boy, but this barrier seems more important to the upwardly mobile lower-class "college boy" who does not contribute greatly to the ranks of delinquent subcultures.

There is a little more talmudic disputation in this section than suits even this writer's argumentative bent. It is obvious, after all, that lower-class youths do want money for the material goods that our culture extols, that work opportunities at the unskilled and semi-skilled levels are growing fewer, and that LLs suffer great relative impoverishment. Opportunity theory is an impressive effort to systematize these facts and their implications for lower-class delinquency; it will probably weather criticisms such as mine quite well and will also probably not lack for future defenders and developers.

What I have tried to show is that its definition of social discontent—economic and occupational aspirations against structural barriers—raises questions and contradicts other lines of thought. It seems doubtful that the most important effect of lower-class disadvantages on youth is that the disadvantages interfere with economic aspirations. In fact, Martin Gold's study of delinquent boys and their families in Flint, Michigan, indicates that delinquents' job aspirations are *lower* than those of non-delinquents who live in similar circumstances. His data suggest that delinquents have defensively lowered their sights as a result of school failure, and that they continue to feel discontented about their current and future prospects.

It should first be noted from Gold's study that it was school failure that differentiated the lower-class delinquents from the non-delinquents, and not poor earning expectations, which both share. Second, the delinquents were significantly more alienated from both parents. Status discontent was a function of a more individualized experience than lower-class deprivation, and this provocation to deviance, in Gold's analysis, was accompanied by a "pull" away from family contact and control—a containment approach to deviance which bears some similarity to Reckless' and to the premises of the theory presented here.

Opportunity vs. Socialization

When Cloward and Ohlin disclaim Cohen's rejection-distress hypothesis regarding pressures to destructive behavior, and when they substitute the presence or absence of illegitimate norms in the behavior of adults, they have freed themselves to extend their theory to criminalistic delinquency. Their substitute explanation for non-utilitarian, conflict delinquency generates its own difficulties.

Conflict gangs, they maintain, arise under two conditions: (1) In disorganized slums, the young are deprived of both conventional and criminal opportunities, and (2) *social control* in such communities is *weak*. They refer to Kobrin's assertion that

> the delinquencies of juveniles tend to acquire a wild, untrammelled character . . . the personality traits of the social type sometimes referred to as the hoodlum. Both individually and in groups, violent physical combat is engaged in for its own sake, almost as a form of recreation. . . . The escape from controls originating in any social structure . . . is here complete (Cloward and Ohlin, p. 174).

They are not talking about the presence of forces that would shape a boy toward violence or toward illegitimate (criminal) behavior, but a failure of control. They state specifically that an absence of illegitimate role models ("institutionalized channels") is a phenomenon related to, but distinct from, the absence of control. The reader is left with a suggestion that, when controls are lacking, something "wild and untrammelled" inevitably makes its appearance. This hypothesis is strangely like the Freudian premise that man has a presocial nature which is inherently aggressive. It is exactly the position that Merton opposes: he maintains that pressures arise in the social order, not in man, which create deviance and antisocial behavior in individuals. Thus, to the extent that they rely on aggression breaking through weak control, Cloward and Ohlin are deriving their formulation of non-utilitarian delinquency, not from Merton's theory of anomie nor from their own central theoretical position, but from a competing theory of deviant behavior.

Violence in the young of disorganized slums arises not only because of weak control but also because youngsters are acutely frustrated, Cloward and Ohlin further elaborate. Here, a frustration-aggression model, with gratification accruing from aggression, is employed and seems plausible. "These adolescents seize upon the manipulation of violence as a route to status not only because it provides a way of expressing pent-up angers and frustrations but also because *they are not cut off from violent means by vicissitudes of birth*" (p. 175; my italics).

It is not clear who, or what, exhibits these "violent means," but the "vicissitudes of birth" would seem to include the presence of demoralized and violent parents, among others. There is indeed ample evidence that the significant adult socializers of many slum children are asocial and aggressive. However, a socialization hypothesis of pressures toward deviance is not Cloward and Ohlin's central position. They have maintained throughout that the adolescent wants valued goods which he cannot have and becomes delinquent in search of them or their substitutes, and that his family experience is irrelevant to analysis of determinants.

The two positions are not necessarily mutually exclusive, but the point is that Cloward and Ohlin make an implicit appeal to a hypothesis which they have excluded. Further, they give no reason why this developmental model should not occupy a central rather than a supplemental position in relation to their blocked-means hypothesis.

Status discontent theory and opportunity structure theory derive a good deal of their force, and their relevance to delinquent acts, from two basic, self-evident truths: "Young people are hurt and angered by adult rejection," and "Almost everyone wants money; some get less than others and are more discontented about it."

chapter 6

psychological biases of social-scientific theories

I *INDICATED* in the last two chapters that the theories criticized, and indeed the whole Chicago Area tradition, including the work of Shaw and McKay and Sutherland, to which Cohen and Cloward and Ohlin are indebted, reduce too many events down to some few social and economic constructs. But this reductionism is not total, and it would be inaccurate to maintain that Cohen's and Cloward and Ohlin's works do not contain their own psychologies. Both theories have systems of personality implicit in them and do make estimates of the meaning of social arrangements for these systems. If we examine the viewpoints they seem to take about personality, we discover restrictions that preclude the use of powerful explanatory variables, such as the unconscious, and errors that contradict fact. What follows does not, of course, constitute a final or most accurate way of describing these sociologists' approaches to personality. Some of the examples employed, let it also be noted, might well belong in several rather than one of the four major categories below.

Rationalism

Over twenty-five years ago Alexander criticized sociological accounts of the effects of social pressures in a way that is highly pertinent to the sociological writings on delinquency of the past decade. He thought that these accounts were premised on a naive rationalistic psychology that said people act realistically according to their own interests. Alexander likened the conception of motivation that he was criticizing to the error of Marxian historical materialists who believe that the lower classes harbored a revolutionary ideology based on their economic self-interest.

Cloward and Ohlin's psychology exaggerates the importance of youth's rationality. For example, the authors reject the possibility of psychological disturbance as a general factor because, in their experience, most subcultural participants "are fully aware of the difference between right and wrong" (p. 37). The context of this passage is a rebuttal of the contention that delinquents have poor self-control, but what a lonely criterion for psychological normality this is. How curiously like the McNaughten test for "sanity" in a day when even the court begins to recognize other criteria for mental disorders!

Again, in their criticism of adolescent status anxiety as an explanation for delinquency, there is the same unheeding assumption of the rationality of youth:

> The problem of the transition to adulthood is obviously not a permanent one. Although the adolescent crisis is acute, *adult status is bound to come in time*. Given the temporary quality of this problem of adjustment, current theories of adolescent frustration as explanation of delinquent subculture do not seem convincing to us. (pp. 59–60; my italics).

One wonders what possible relation there might be between the objective duration of adolescence and the adolescent's perception of the passage of time. Indeed, writings on the psychology of adolescence, such as Erikson's, show that a *distinguishing feature* of the adolescent identity crisis is a sense of time diffusion, a profound vagueness about past, present, and future.

Alexander also asserted his own belief, in the same paper, that sociocultural pressures can create psychological disturbance; when there is a *discrepancy* between *social restrictions* and *per-*

sonal satisfaction, or where security is minimal, people may develop defects of conscience.

Alexander thus suggests that the superegos of people may undergo modification under the conditions which, Merton proposes, create anomie. It has already been shown that Merton does not exclude the possibility that psychological deviation may accompany normative deviation among deprived people. Kardiner and Linton also advance a hypothesis very similar to Alexander's regarding conscience changes under restrictive environmental conditions (pp. 414–15), which supports the theoretical possibility suggested at the end of Chapter 3: The superego as well as the ego may undergo syncretization under sociocultural constraints.

One may have reservations about Alexander's conception that the *kinds* of conscience changes that may occur are "conscience defects." Such a description suggests loss of control over aggressive instincts, and thus seems to presume a questionable nativism. Further, the notion of "defects" seems to adopt conventional morality as an implicit, and unquestioned, reference point, and assumes that something is missing in a different morality. Also, it is too crude a conceptual distinction, that is, that there can be only "more" or "less" conscience.

On the other hand, large numbers of people in a constricted subculture may lose flexibility and moderation in their consciences, and develop instead harsh, black-and-white judging tendencies, similar to those of young children. Such a superego adaptation may have a cause-and-effect relation to the authoritarian adaptations of some lower-class people, and it may also be functional in the kinds of blanket prejudices that Cohen and Hodges describe. It would not, however, be accurate to term these superego simplifications "defects."

Sociocultural Realism

Spiro has described a number of philosophical errors into which students of society and culture have fallen as a result of accepting the false dichotomies of individual and society and of culture and personality. Among those he enumerates is the fallacy of individualism, in which the individual is assumed to be chronologically and logically prior; this is the approach to which Merton takes exception in his paper on anomie. ("Individualism" is Spiro's term for the error of psychological nativism or realism). This approach, says Spiro, "is important in sociology and anthropology as a straw-man theory which can be replaced by some system of social or cultural determinism" (p. 20). A form of the latter determinisms is adopted by the cultural realists, who, according to Spiro, see culture as determined by its own laws which govern the behavior of the carriers, who have no effect in turn on the culture. The defect in the realists' position is that it can never account for the way in which culture can determine the behavior of an organism, since culture is defined as separate from the organism.

> What the realists fail to realize is that once something is learned it is no longer external to the organism, but is "inside" the organism; and once it is "inside," the organism becomes a biosocial organism, determining its own behavior as a consequence of the modification it has undergone in the process of learning (p. 31).

A. *The Sociology of Unjust Deprivation.* Cloward and Ohlin participate to some degree in this realist bias. In discussing the evolution of delinquent gangs they give an enlightening account of the suspension of belief in conventional norms as preparation for adopting antisocial norms, after youths experience a sense of unjust deprivation regarding success goals. Their realist bias is evident in their depiction of youths encountering deprivation: The goals and barriers seem to be transmitted to these youths as if these transmission processes had an existence of their own, separate from the socialization experiences and personalities of lower-class youth.

The sense of unjust deprivation, as these authors define it, begins with the individual who is likely to blame his failure to achieve success-goals on "a cultural and social system that encourages everyone to reach for success while differentially restricting access to the success-goals" (p. 111). This blaming may occur either when the individual has been led to expect more than he can achieve, or when the barriers to achievement are highly visible, as in the case of minority group membership (p. 113). The authors of opportunity theory believe that gang delinquents commonly feel unjustly deprived, and that this feeling results from the fact that they are potentially equal to others, non-delinquent children in capacities to achieve, but are barred from achievement. They cite evidence of equality between delinquent and non-delinquent youths in intelligence, physical strength, and agility. The potential delinquent then, according to their theory, repudiates law-abiding means to success, and begins to develop illegitimate norms.

Again it may be asked what connection there is between objective evidence of comparable capacity and the delinquent's own, private estimate of himself. His sense of unjust deprivation regarding racial discrimination or lack of "pull," no matter how cogently he expresses it, cannot be taken as a full statement of his sense of deprivation or anger. We are asked to believe that a lower-class adolescent has passed through childhood and pre-adolescence without having had any experience related to his disadvantaged status or any perception of disadvantage which would significantly contribute to deviance, and that he has not been touched in his feelings about himself by the level of achievement and the way of life of the adults surrounding him.

It is also implied that at the age of twelve or thirteen, the concern of a lower-class boy that is most crucial for delinquency is his doubt about making enough money to buy fancy clothes, girls, and cars; that he has enough objectivity or foresight to attach the blame where it should belong, in the social and cultural orders; and that again at the same age (*at the very latest*, because much school pre-delinquent misbehavior and actual law-violative delinquency starts earlier—see the Gluecks) he feels so unjustly deprived in his prospective earning opportunities five years thence that *for this reason* he begins school misbehavior and the development of delinquent beliefs and norms with his friends.

This is on face value an artificially direct connection between the individual and "society." What of the lower-class youth's parents, of their reaction to their own thwarted aspirations? Has he experienced nothing of their substitute norms, or of their own guilt, hostility, and personal dissolution in the event they have blamed themselves and not the social order? Have there been no preceding generations who have felt not only social discontent, but also discontent with parents, themselves, and perhaps a displaced sense of grievance against other LLs? One wonders what place opportunity theory makes for traditions of distrust or alienated exploitativeness in the family and neighborhood that might also condition a youth's definition of himself and his status.

It is as if Cloward and Ohlin, and Cohen also to the extent that he asserts that status discontent is the motivational core of deviance, assume that the lower-class child until adolescence knows a family and adult subculture that has had no proper relation of its own to a society with limited access to universally urged goals. Abruptly, at adolescence, that child has his first significant exposure to deprivation, and this deprivation, in Cloward and Ohlin's theory, is experienced solely as a lack of money. This sociocultural realism is unconvincing because it is unrealistic. Most gang delinquents can talk with eloquence and devastating accuracy about the importance of the "connection" for respectable citizens and about racial prejudice, especially if they are Negro. But these exercises in the withdrawal of legitimacy from conventional norms are the easiest rituals for them to perform.

The intense cynicism and suspicion which they express characterize personal experiences that distinctly antedate adolescence. It is often more disturbing and difficult for them to describe, not these general grievances, but the earlier gratuitous cruelties practiced on them as individuals by their elders and other children. When they come to describe these experiences, one can hear in their profound disillusionment the sources of their vehemently disrespectful and disappointed ideology. In a basic sense, Cloward and Ohlin are correct. One can detect in these personal disclosures a family and a subcultural history of disappointment with a culture that preaches what it does not practice, but in considerably more human and specific terms than those I have been criticizing.

B. *Another View of Unjust Deprivation.* I prefer Parsons' treatment of the sense of unjust deprivation, because it makes room for the inclusion of socialization factors where Cloward and Ohlin's derivation of the same sense of grievance does not. Parsons also sees what he calls the "sense of unfairness" as a condition for withdrawal of loyalty to conventional norms. He does not discuss this withdrawal process explicitly, but he makes the sense of unfairness an element in aggression, which he defines as "the disposition on the part of an individual or a collectivity to orient its action to goals which include a conscious or unconscious intention illegitimately to injure the interests of other individuals or collectivities in the same system" (1947, p. 167). Since he uses the term "conscious" and is explicit about using the term "illegitimately" with reference to a "moral order defining reciprocal rights and obligations," it seems clear that he is talking about acts which imply the repudiation of conventional norms.

He feels that the sense of unfairness is itself rooted in insecurity and anxiety, which are products of the level and consistency of maternal affection obtained by the young child. It appears that Parsons believes that the unusually aggressive individual suffered from attacks at a time in life when his ego was unable to withstand the threat to its security. Parsons maintains that structured patterns of aggression in childhood are crucial to later patterns of aggression in the social structure because "they are rooted in normal reactions to strain and frustration in human relations at the stages of development when the individual is particularly vulnerable, since he has not, as some psychologists say, yet attained a strong ego-development" (1947, p. 169).

Parsons' formulation of aggression allows him to approach psychiatric conceptions about the delinquent's fear of closeness (Chap. 4). He goes on to say that the child intimidated by closeness builds up defenses against re-experiencing loving situations and constructs rigid barriers against integration into normal human relationships. The child thus alienated is prompted toward uncontrolled, inappropriate aggression, or to inappropriate overreaction to frustration.

Parsons attributes the sense of unfairness not only to a denial of rewards or goals, as do Cloward and Ohlin in a larger socioeconomic context, but also to early intimidation, injury to personal development, and fixation of aggressive reactions to frustrations in childhood.

Alexander and Healy, dealing with the psychoanalytic verbalizations of criminals, also clearly saw the significance of social discontent in the etiology of criminality and tried to come to grips with the problem of relating socioeconomic disadvantages to a sense of personal deprivation.

They proposed that social discontent has a triggering function.

Emotional conflict and dependencies of childhood find a powerful ally in resentment against the social situation, which seeks a realistic expression in criminal acts. . . . If the social situation gives justification for discontent and expression of antisocial attitudes, if the earlier emotional dissatisfaction in the family situation is combined with social discontent, antisocial behavior rather than neurotic symptom-formation is likely to result (p. 288).

They found that the difference between the neurotic and the criminal lies in the emphasis that criminals put on "certain conscious and rational motives which are co-determinants of their behavior and which they utilize in covering up the underlying and usually more powerful unconscious motives" (p. 287). (Their analysis is highly analogous to the nature and function of externalization as proposed in Chapters 2 and 3.) So we find a social theorist and two psychoanalysts agreeing with Cloward and Ohlin about the importance of indignation as a prompter of antisocial acts, but who also attribute to it a much more individualized meaning and function.

C. *Subculture, Family, Personality*. An important outcome of the work of Parsons and his associates on a general theory of action (Parsons and Shils) has been a systematic effort to tie family into social structure and cultural order (Parsons and Bales). The theory of action is intended to provide a set of general concepts in terms of which any behavioral system, whether it be personality, family, or larger social systems, may be analyzed. The family is similar to other interactional systems for analytical purposes; but it also has a fundamental substantive relationship, in that the family conveys cultural imperatives and social means to the child. "Indeed, we have argued that the nuclear family not only *is* not, but *cannot* be, an independent society, but is always a differentiated sub-system of the society" (Parsons and Bales, p. 356).

The values that are institutionalized in the social system are also internalized in the personality system. Values conveyed by the parents and organized about their respective sex roles and role reciprocities are the values around which the need-disposition sequences of the child's personality structure themselves. These bundles of personal values in the theory of action are equated with the internalized objects of Freudian theory. Parsons and Bales assert unequivocally that the internalizations of personality and the values of society are not simply interdependent, but that they "interpenetrate."

> These are not merely the "same kind" of cultural values, they are literally *the same* values, looked at and analyzed in terms of different system-references. Neither of these system references (society, personality) is the "right" or the "real" system reference, both are equally real and stand on the same ontological level. This in essence is what Durkheim meant by his famous aphorism that "society exists only within the minds of individuals" (pp. 357–58).

The growing child is, these authors say, progressively fitted for participation in increasingly complex social systems, from the mother-child subsystem through the family system to the peer group and school system. Socialization is thus an orderly achievement of fitness for action in a "nesting series of social systems." It is important to stress that, according to Parsons and Bales, the foundation for these graded achievements is the way in which the sex-role dichotomy of the nuclear family schools the child in balancing his internal emotional economy (expressive function) and in establishing the desired relation between himself and external goal-objects (instrumental function) (p. 147, pp. 317–18).

It is equally important to stress, as has already been indicated, that Parsons and Bales conceive not only of a hierarchy of social systems and roles graduating the individual from infancy to adult participation in society, which is a familiar premise of socialization theory. There is as well an inward flow of shaping forces on the family and thence to the children. They state as a universal dynamic principle that where an action system of any level of complexity exists within a network of social-personal action systems, then each system in the network serves as a critical part of the total situation within which the given system must function.

> A leading example of this is the way in which the behavior of a socializing agent introduces changes into the situation in which the socializee has to adjust. This general order of relation is of the first importance as between social systems at various levels, between personalities and social systems, and even, we suspect, between different subsystems of the same personality (p. 358).

When we consider the implications of this assertion from the standpoint of anomie and psychocultural adaptations, we may imagine the ill effects of social disorganization transfusing into the rudimentary personality of the infant. This is precisely the connection that Erikson (1959) makes: "Widespread severe impoverishment of infantile narcissism (and thus of the basis of a strong ego) is . . . a breakdown of that collective synthesis which gives every newborn baby and his motherly surroundings a superindividual status as a trust of the community" (p. 39). Every mother-child relationship occurs within a social and cultural coordinate system. The self-regard of the child depends through the mother on whether the sociocultural coordinates support and protect the mother-child relationship. What devalues the mother may compel her to devalue the child.

Spiro offers a viewpoint very close to Parsons and Bales'. Acculturation must be understood in terms of psychodynamic processes; the child is learning his culture when he is identifying with his parents and while his superego is forming.

> It becomes apparent that the development of personality and the acquisition of culture are not different processes, but are one and the same learning process; and that the structuralization of culture and the structuralization of personality are not different processes, but are one and the same process of integration (p. 142).

The lower-class mother, occupying an apartment with her children in a transient disorganized slum, may be surrounded by people on whom the most elementary agreements about love, livelihood, and recognition are not binding from one day to the next (Hughes, pp. 410–18). This profound inconsistency and undependability of people exists under normless conditions, when there is no integrated culture. The predictability and dependability of others form the unconscious basis for the most basic decisions. This slum mother must experience considerable existential insecurity and a justified faithlessness. If she has grown up in these surroundings and in such a family, her character may be organized about aggression and impulsivity. In her alternate indulgence of aggression or impulsivity in her children, or her impulsive aggression in reaction to her children's self-indulgence, she is expressing a self-definition derived from her parents and her subculture. She is also defining her child's meaning to the culture and to himself. Through the definitional aspects of her socializing acts, the slum mother is stating the way in which one is human in that culture.

D. *Personality and Culture.* Some of the best evidence that sociocultural processes are indivisible from personality lies in the different ways in which various cultures affect their people's bodies. Where men's institutional arrangements work changes on their somatic processes, these changes must be accomplished through the symbolic processes of personality functioning. A person is, in his society, not in three pieces but in one, and that is as a human, bio-psycho-social experience.

Honigmann (1954, pp. 191–92) reviews and discusses cross-cultural psychosomatic patterning. The cultural shaping of personality may affect even gastrointestinal functioning: both the Iatmul and the Manus subsist on the same diet, yet the stools of the former are loose while those of the latter, who are prudish and rigid in their ways, are hard-formed (p. 193). Seward (1956) mentions Americans' high rate of angina pectoris and of hypertension and compares it to low Chinese rates for these diseases. She also indicates evidence that there is a significant reduction in incidence of hypertension among Americans who lived in China. She ascribes these differences to cultural effects on bodily processes. Opler cites evidence of shifts in incidence of diseases with variations in cultural stress (p. 82). Getting back to our own culture, Seward discusses the predilection among American Negroes for organic psychoses such as cerebral syphilis, general paresis, and alcoholic psychosis as a reflection of their anomic living patterns (1956, pp. 147–50). She notes further the incidence of hypertension, which has been related to hostility toward authority figures, and of peptic ulcers among upwardly mobile or immigrant American Negroes, both diseases being almost unknown among native Africans.

There is by now considerable evidence that cultural conditions can induce severe personality disruption. There are cross-cultural variations in incidence and type of mental illness (Opler, p. 25; Seward, 1956, p. 216; Linton; Miller and Swanson, p. 44), as well as among social classes within our own society. Hollingshead and Redlich's findings, and Langner and Michael's, that schizophrenia is higher in the lower classes than in other social levels in our society are confirmed by studies in several American cities (Miller and Swanson, p. 46, for references).

There is also a more direct line of evidence regarding personality as the product and proper vehicle for human institutions.

The work of Kardiner and his associates shows significant variations in personality patterns among preliterate societies, within an American community and as between American Negroes and other, more advantaged subgroups. Linton and Kardiner found a considerable correlation between the personality type that would be best suited to a given culture, and the personality type that would derive from that culture's childrearing practices; they concluded that these practices would produce a personality that would participate optimally in the type of culture having these practices. The adult personality which is modal for a given culture then becomes the keystone of cultural transmission and renewal; it determines what is retained and what new elements can develop and become effective within that culture.

Linton's conception of personality operating to accept and reshape or to reject and discard old and new ways according to whether they are suited to personality construction in that culture is very close in view to that of Whiting and Child:

> Members of a society are continually proposing and trying out minor changes and modifications in the customs by which they live. Thus, although culture is partly independent of the individual members of society, it is eventually and in the long run determined by them and represents an adjustment to their biological and psychological nature (p. 2).

Whiting and his associates provide sharp illustrations that *personality integrates culture*. Furthermore, their studies involve specific predictions and statistical treatment of data, a step in scientific processing of information beyond the observational material on which Linton bases his above formulation.

Some important differences in libidinal themes expressed by three New Orleans Negro subcultures might be mentioned, as further illustrations of what Parsons calls the "interpenetration" of personality and culture. Thematic analyses were undertaken for New Orleans jazz songs, Creole lyrics, and middle-class Negro newspaper editorials (Rohrer and Edmonson). Frequencies of expressions of personal sentiments were compared among the three types of verbal material. A level of 0.01 significance is reported for all the following differences: the newspaper editorials revealed significantly more frequent expressions of positive feelings, cooperation, achievement, and dominance; the jazz songs (which are taken to be the art forms of the gang and matriarchal subcultures) show greater incidences of rejection, negative feeling, and of genital, anal, and anxiety themes; the Creole lyrics contain these factors to an extent intermediate between the other two forms, and are high on oral, tactile, auditory, and visual themes. One may perhaps disagree with the selection of newspaper editorials as a means of assessing the personal concerns of the New Orleans Negro middle class, considered as a subculture, but the fact that themes of this type crop up sufficiently often in the jazz and Creole lyrics to produce the statistically significant differences noted argues strongly against the separability of personality and cultural behavior as phenomena.

Eclecticism

By eclecticism, I refer to a tendency on the part of Cohen, Cloward and Ohlin, and Miller as well, to pick and choose unsystematically and, on occasion arbitrarily, among the psychological concepts and data that they recognize, utilize, question, or ignore.

A. *Instinctualism and Shared Personality Patterns.* In presenting some of their basic views on the problems of adjustment which predispose to delinquency, for example, Cloward and Ohlin cite a source that implies that delinquents are more heavily loaded than others with pre-socialized, impulsive, egotistic, individualistic, and selfish personality traits (p. 37). They repudiate this view on the grounds that

> The capacities of participants to conform to the norms of their subcultures seems to be neither less nor greater than the abilities of other persons in our society to conform to the dictates of the groups to which they belong. The strategic difference lies, of course, in the nature of the norms to which these delinquents conform as opposed to the more conventional norms to which non-delinquents usually conform (p. 37).

We may detect here the touchstone of Merton's opposition to a Freudian nativism; but it is significant that a conception of the delinquent as psychopath, "the notion that deviance is . . . simply an asocial or primitive reaction," is the only kind of variant character development to which these authors pay attention. This does not adequately represent the major opinion and direction of psychiatry regarding delinquency during the past thirty-five years. The motivation and character formation to which Cloward and Ohlin are referring are much more specifically attributed to antisocial personality disorder (see Greenacre and Rabinovich for discussion of dynamics and character structure).

There is no reason to believe that modern American psychiatry finds an unmodified-impulse formulation to be a comprehensive account of delinquent dynamics. Sources can be found to support this contention, of course; there are at least as many theoretical differences within psychiatry as in other behavioral sciences. On the other hand, Leventhal and Sills, for example, advance ideas about impulsive acting-out that are compatible with my views. These therapists understand the self-control problems of "character problem adolescents" in terms of ego intimidation and externalization, and not in terms of raw hedonism and primitive needs. They treated youths, apparently successfully, by focusing on the boys' convictions that others were powerful enough to overwhelm their independence of action, and that they therefore had to pre-empt the initiative to protect their own integrity.

Nor is the argument that delinquents' aggressiveness and impulsivity is conforming to their norms and therefore no different from relatively mature, conforming youths, as final as Cloward and Ohlin and W. B. Miller, *et al.*) would seem to believe. There may be conformity here, but it is a conformity to norms that permit and prescribe impulsive, egoistic, individualistic, and selfish acts. The fact that *the total personality integrates institutions*—and this means that the consciousness and the conscience, as well as the libidinal needs, of the delinquent help organize his gang activity —should eliminate the oversimple and specious distinction between "symptoms" and "socially appropriate conforming behavior." If we accept the difference of delinquent *norms* from other norms, it does not follow from this that *delinquents* are the same as other children. While a delinquent is engaging in socially shared behavior when he yokes a passerby or rumbles with another gang, surely not *all* his motives and satisfactions are the same as those he experiences when he plays stickball in the street.

B. *On Adolescent Sexual Anxiety*. Another example of unwarranted eclecticism, in this case an ignoring of psychological insights, occurs in Cloward and Ohlin's assessment of anxiety regarding masculinity as a possible problem of adjustment for delinquents.

> Evidence is lacking as to the significance and the permanance of problems of masculinity. Plausible arguments may be advanced to support or reject the proposition that this problem intimately engages the major concerns of adolescents and strikes them as a permanent threat to the achievement of long-range personal goals (p. 53).

Leo Spiegel and Anna Freud (1958), on the other hand, in reviewing the writings of S. Freud, Ernest Jones, and Glover on adolescence and in stating their own viewpoints on psychoanalytic psychology, characterize this era as a period of great internal stress and disturbance. This is so, Spiegel and A. Freud say, principally because of the need to find a nonincestuous love object, and of the twin necessities for assimilating the sexual drive into the ego and for asserting the primacy of genital sexuality over all other libidinal needs. Spiegel indicates that a homosexual orientation is typical initially in adolescence, and that not until the age of seventeen or eighteen is heterosexuality established. All these are factors in the consolidation of a masculine identification. He speaks of the storm and stress accompanying the disruption of "psychological apparatus" (apparently the adolescent's ego), which is initially inadequate to cope with a revolution in growth, and of the upset of these major psychological systems.

Along the same lines, Anna Freud notes "the difficulty in adolescent cases to draw the line between normality and pathology. . . . Adolescence constitutes by definition an interruption of peaceful growth which resembles in appearance a variety of other emotional upsets and structural upheavals" (1958, p. 267). Evidence of a psychological nature is therefore *not* lacking as to the significance and permanence *during adolescence* of problems of masculinity. In view of this information, it might have been useful had Cloward and Ohlin presented plausible arguments rejecting the idea that the problem of masculinity is an intimate and major concern of male adolescents. It is true that the relation to lower-class delinquency of a problem ubiquitous in our culture is not immediately apparent, but that issue is not at stake here. What is questioned is the justification for the type of unqualified assertion quoted.

C. *On Regressive Tendencies in the Delinquent.* As another example of picking and choosing, I want to discuss a little further Cloward and Ohlin's and Cohen's neglect of the drive-discharging function of the delinquent act, a matter that was touched on at the beginning of Chapter 2, when I discussed the distinction these authors make between personality disorder and delinquency. Cohen and Cloward and Ohlin indicate that psychiatric symptoms and gang delinquency are different, in that the former represents a private solution, and the latter, a consensualized solution, to problems of adjustment. The difference seems to boil down to the presence or absence of controls. Cloward and Ohlin maintain a difference in internal controls: If the individual who fails accepts conventional norms, he may become, to all intents and purposes, neurotic (pp. 111–12); if he rejects these norms, that is, if they are not binding on his behavior, he is attracted to deviance. Cohen views the crucial distinction in terms of the presence or absence of external control; if the individual is surrounded by conforming peers, he has no one with whom to share his grievances, cannot develop a subcultural delinquent solution, and may therefore develop private, neurotic solutions (p. 71).

If these authors see no differences between the *needs* of neurotic and delinquent, why then do they overlook or reject the possibility that subcultural delinquents may also have infantile action tendencies and object relations? There is a character to needs which find substitute, symbolic expressions in neurosis. A disturbed individual in psychotherapy may indeed eventually excoriate his parents' arbitrary demands for achievement after an initial period of self-derogation in therapy, but typically this type of parental demand was allied with other threats which durably affected the child's developing needs. The resolution of repressed motives as it is observed clinically is not simply a matter of removing the repression—enabling the patient to alter his internalized normative structure, his conscience, with respect to the underlying need. If this were the case, psychotherapy would produce deviant behavior, which it does indeed sometimes, but only as a way-station on the path to a successful outcome.

In other words, if we consider the case of the neurotic who breaks into deviant acting-out, we may be witnessing the expression of early object attachments and their interpersonal aspects of dependency and defiance-submission. Cloward and

Ohlin's "absence of inner controls," then, may mean that the delinquent's immature needs are acceptable to his ego and superego, whereas those of the neurotic are not; and Cohen's "absence of external controls" may mean that the egos and consciences of some of the delinquents' peers are similarly integrated with their needs.

D. *Miller's Dilemma.* My final observation is on Miller's eclecticism of approach, which, because he does not follow through, leaves a reader with contradictory inferences regarding the meaning of his findings. Perhaps it might be better to describe the difficulty here as arising not from eclecticism but rather from a form of dualism between the individual and his culture. Briefly, Miller would seem to suggest that, on the one hand, most delinquents have normal character structures and almost all these "normal" delinquents are in the lower-class culture (*a*) and, on the other hand, that the lower-class culture leads the individual into disturbed personality development.

In the paper cited he reviews data that the majority of a large sample of delinquents were free of psychiatric symptoms. "Very frequently," he remarks elsewhere,

> personality characteristics or behavior patterns which are perceived as deviant or even pathological in the context of a treatment-oriented institutional milieu in fact represent customary and expected behavior in the context of lower-class community (*b*, p. 4).

One may infer from this that however disordered one may consider a particular set of culture patterns, the individual who conforms to them is himself normal.

Yet Miller seems to imply otherwise in his description of lower-class concerns and of the consequences of mother-based households. There is, for example, the difficulty of finding an adult male with whom to identify and the protraction of the primary identification with mother. "This produces inner fears over homosexuality which contribute, by a process of reaction formation [*sic*], to the strong emphasis on toughness and masculinity which dominates lower class male culture (*b*, p. 20)." In this paper and in others (1958, p. 9; *c*) he indicates the expression of a homosexual orientation in the work, play, and affectional relationships of boys and men who belong to street-corner groups.

> The role of homosexuality in lower-class culture is of great importance, and is far more complex and ramified [than a simple statement to the effect that lack of satisfactory male role model induces fears of homosexuality] would appear to indicate. Many aspects of lower-class culture may be seen as structured solutions to a dominant but implicit concern over this issue—and frequently functions for males to permit the expression of homosexual tendencies in such a form that they will not in any way be defined as effeminate (*b*, p. 20).

Again, with regard to the lower-class concern with "autonomy," he describes verbal assertions of defiance and independence which are then denied in non-verbal behavior. The individual means to provoke nurturance and support, whether it be from police, employers, or institutional authorities, when he breaks the rules.

> Since "being controlled" is equated with being cared for." . . . [Supporting environments] are rejected, ostensibly for being too strict, actually for not being strict enough. . . . The pose of tough rebellious independence often assumed by the lower class person frequently conceals powerful dependency cravings. . . . The periodicity observed in connection with the "excitement" (concern) is also relevant here; after involvement in trouble-producing behavior (assault, sexual adventure, a "drunk"), the individual will actively seek a locus of imposed control (1958, p. 13).

All the elements of a neurotic process are here—infantile needs, ego limitations, their indirect satisfaction, and mechanisms for removing the real intent from consciousness, such as rationalization and projection. The interesting consideration is that Miller is not describing an individual; he has transposed these constructions to an anthropological context. Miller is describing a series of cultural arrangements. The question arises, is it the individual or his culture which contains immature personality patterns? In the light of earlier remarks regarding sociocultural realism, it would be meaningless to assert either alone. The theoretical position in this book is that both individual and subcultural behavior define personally immature patterns; or, rather, that a range of modal personalities which might be found to comprise the traits and behavior of lower-classs culture as Miller describes it must be immature to the extent that such sequences of motive and behavior occur.

I shall conclude this excursion into exegetics with a further consideration of one horn of Miller's dilemma, the relativity of personality to culture.

Sociocultural Relativism

Jackson Toby has said, regarding Cloward and Ohlin's theory, "What they probably mean is that youngsters with personality disturbances do not predominate in the delinquent gangs they have known" (p. 5). "I suspect that gang delinquency as defined by Cloward and Ohlin does not amount to 10% of the cases handled by American juvenile courts" (p. 4). It has been suggested that just because the behavior at issue is socially shared and socially and culturally describable, it does *not* logically follow that it is also psychologically normal. To reach this conclusion, one must take the relativistic view that a modal individual of a given culture cannot be compared against any standard; one can therefore conclude only that he is psychologically normal for that culture.

A. *The Integration of Adjustment Problems and Institutions.* Man everywhere varies with the nature of his social and cultural forms. To assert that he is normal in his culture misses some of the significance of his variation, just as, with regard to delinquency, an adjustment definition of normality misses the psychological point of gang aggressiveness and of alienated attitudes and behaviors in relation to the community.

This extreme relativism is opposed by the view that cultural forms may be outlets for culturally induced intrapsychic tensions. Honigmann maintains that ". . . Culture may induce stress in the individual . . . cultural pathways . . . may also be utilized as mechanisms for relieving stress" (1950, p. 25). He quotes Margaret Mead in the following:

> What appears to be a valid generalization derived from the study of many individual social systems is the following: "The way in which parent-child relationships are patterned in respect to such behaviors as: succoring-dependency, dominance-submission, and exhibitionism-spectatorship, provide a learning situation for the child which patterns his subsequent behavior in situations where these behaviors are involved" (p. 26).

(See Parsons and Bales' thesis and beginning comments on family transmission processes in Chapter 3.) Honigmann goes on to propose the concept of *dyscrasic cultural outlets for tension reduction;* such cultural forms discharge tensions but also create "an atmosphere of suspicion intensified by anxiety, and promote a breakdown of cooperation within the group thus adding to the problem of adaptation and adjustment" (p. 32). (The concept of disjunctive ideologies proposed in Chapter 3, subserving ego externalizations, and seen as adaptive and self-defeating, is intended to convey the same set of functions.

Honigmann, by the way, makes the general observation, fascinating and dismaying to the student of delinquency intervention, that:

> Stressful patterns may be entirely crucial integrative positions. It follows that patterns in strategic positions cannot usually be altered without a fundamental reorganization of a people's way of life, a process of change which the group might not welcome and which might be accompanied by an increase in tension (p. 32).

One is immediately reminded of Bromberg's statement that:

> Since each member of society is unconsciously identified with aggressive, rebellious, or asocial impulses released overtly by the psychopath, the former defends himself against encroachment of his own aggressive impulses by projection to the person already in trouble with society . . . The congealed hostility . . . is an expression of society's unconscious preoccupation with widespread and persistent conflicts over acted-out behavior (604 ff.).

Cloward and Ohlin, Kai Erikson, and Merton have all made significant, and related, sociological observations on the usefulness of the deviant to the conformist.

Kardiner and Linton support the identical position, regarding the institutionalized release of personal conflicts. A culture, they say, may provide institutional outlets for motivational consequences of experience; for example, the Marquesan male's hostility to women follows from his childhood deprivation and frustration at their hands. This culturally permitted expression thus saves the individual from developing a neurotic expression in a personalized disorder; but, these authors maintain, *the pattern of perception and motivation may be the same for normal and neurotic alike* (p. 418). (Note the clear parallel they draw, based on their anthropological data, between what I have called symbolic and externalized expressions of ego limitations.)

B. *Why Impersonalized Sociology?* Aside from the different interests of diciplines, there are several possible reasons why social scientists are reluctant to fit certain psychological elements into their theories regarding any large number of delinquents. One such reason may be the reservation that concepts derived to explain behavior of the individual and of the family, as a very small social unit, have no place in the description of behavior so widely practiced that it may be called a culture pattern. From a logical standpoint, such concepts need not be so restrictively used, if it can be shown that the socializers of a cultural group or subgroup commonly create conditions similar to those described in the background of the various personality disorders.

A second possibility is that the long-range consequences of primary drive patterning and of secondary drive induction are not uncoverable by the analytical tools available to the sociologist and anthropologist (tools in the broadest sense, including not only research methods, but also the bodies of concepts by which the scientist orients his inquiry). If these motivating consequences are not laid open, it may be that they are assumed either not to exist or not to be related to what is uncoverable. Cohen and Short seem to assume the latter when they remark that everyone has personal adjustment problems. It is true, for example, that the sexual anxieties of adolescents may be partly observed in group-relevant behavior. It is also true that the referents for the clinical concepts by which these anxieties might be described are often found by attending to certain kinds of verbal content—slips, omissions, repetitions, associations, fantasies, and dream materials—and to body language which may or may not be observable in a gang context, or meaningful to the gang observer. W. B. Miller bases much of his discussion of lower-class preoccupation with incest and homosexuality on just this kind of verbal material (*c*). Such verbal content is likely to be attended to by the psychodynamically oriented observer. A considerable amount of careful empirical observation lies behind psychoanalytic formulations. No one has yet established that inferences drawn about psychological development are any less reliable for adolescent delinquents than for the psychiatric patient.

Even after one has said all there is to say about the gang controls exerted over gang "debs," the social limits on "respectable" status for a lower-class girl, the weakness of social control over her behavior, etc., we still cannot reasonably ignore (unless it is our explicit purpose only to describe these structural characteristics) the psychological implications of "gang bangs" and other sadistic and impersonalized sexual behaviors that occur among some delinquents. The sociologist may take note of various sexual behaviors in lower-class as against middle-class adolescents, and may conclude that the lower-class boy has greater "sexual freedom," and is indeed less deprived and even more normal than the middle-class boy. The psychologist looks at the incidence of certain other characteristics of these sexual behaviors and may end up with quite different inferences.

Closely related to this second possibility is the tendency to discuss socialization experience as if the *specific* organic needs—the fulcrums on which rewards, extinction, and punishment sequences lever role induction—are irrelevant or interchangeable. On the matter of the induction of aggressiveness, for example, we have seen that Cloward and Ohlin's only reference is the rather obtuse statement that certain delinquents are "not cut off from violent means by vicissitudes of birth." Cohen also indicates that the lower-class child is encouraged to develop aggressive qualities. It seems doubtful that either status discontent theory or opportunity theory can make much distinction between aggressiveness induced as part of latency-age peer play or as alternate frustration and indulgence of an infant or toddler. Again, the matter of relevance to social-structural description is probably involved in this possible indifference. A proponent of opportunity theory, for instance, might say that since his theory shows that conflict delinquency is functional in the absence of any means to conventional or illicit success goals, information about how angry this type of delinquent can get or about the motivational basis of his anger is relatively unimportant.

Still a fourth possibility for reluctance stems from the misleading nature of the distinction between "normal" and "pathological." This distinction leads to the position that if an individual has experienced stressful socialization in any area, he should have clinically observable and definable symptoms; that is, he should be either neurotic, psychotic, or character-disordered in some way. Otherwise, he is normal; that is, not crucially different psychologically from anyone else who is integrated into another subgroup that is a part of the total social structure. This overlooks the point that where culture provides, the individual personality need not devise; symptomatic expression is obviated by cultural values serviceable to the individual's ego and by culturally patterned emphases on certain developmental levels and types of object relations. *A tangential and misleading distinction in delinquency is that between health and disease;* the crucial distinction, between the completion or failure of maturation, as maturation is defined in a general culture.

C. *Theories as Status Symbols.* Szasz has pointed out that "the myth of mental illness" is perpetuated, at least in part, by those who preserve vested economic, status, and moral interests by defining psychiatric problems and social problems as sickness. He clearly defines psychiatric symptoms as symbolic expressions of discontent with self and others. Medical terminology, the professional self-concepts of some experts on personality, and their power-and-status interests have very little to do with identifying the fundamental problems of adaptation involved in delinquency.

No one brand of expertise seems sufficient to solve these riddles. It is a great mistake, I believe, to think that distinctions among areas of professional practice—questions of who does what—and questions of political-economic control describe substantive differences in the realities of the people upon whom the professionals practice their skills. One is reminded of the song, "Gee, Officer Krupke!" that the "Jets" sing in *West Side Story*—a hilarious parody, that the lyricist Stephen Sondheim puts in the mouths of delinquents, on the pet theories and spheres of caretaking influence with which legal and social agencies preoccupy themselves. After the Jets run through all their sins and burdens as defined by willing caretakers, the gang boys cry, "We got troubles of our own!"

The sick-healthy continuum is misleading because it directs attention away from the central fact that character structure varies with the type of socialization undergone, whether good, bad, or indifferent. It follows that character structure will vary in relation to the socialization practices common in a particular culture.

part three

bases for a psychocultural theory

It is hoped that the extended criticisms of sociological theories in the last three chapters have indicated why it seemed to this writer that a broader approach to explaining delinquency-in-society was in order. In the following three chapters, an effort will be made to organize and summarize some of the fundamental aspects of the theory as it was outlined in Part One.

Chapter 7 reviews psychological data regarding delinquents for assimilation into a theoretical model. In Chapter 8, the underlying premises of the theory are restated and summarized. Chapter 9 presents a discussion, in greater depth than the purposes of Part One allowed, of a process of psychocultural adaptation to adversity—an adaptation that would lend itself to personal disorder and normative deviation.

chapter 7

the facts of delinquent life

IT would be well to review some of the accumulated information regarding the personalities of delinquents and their personal experiences in family and community, which find no place in the significant theories of delinquency as they are presently stated. All that follows is legitimate scientific information, in the sense that it is based on observed behavior. In certain instances, we have quantitative, statistically treated data; in others, consensualized clinical inference.

Psychological disturbance is prevalent among both delinquent and non-delinquent youth in disadvantaged urban areas, which would indicate that disturbance is an accompaniment of economic deprivation. School failure and misbehavior among pre-delinquent children occurs well before adolescence (and, presumably, before these children get economic aspirations), and may be related to emotional instability and immaturity. Training in aggressive and other antisocial conduct is an inevitable part of the enculturation of many lower-class children.

Economically disadvantaged groups have shown significant differences in crime rates; my theory would explain low rates in such a group as indicating normative collaboration with accompanying opportunities for consolidation of ego strengths. Such an explanation is partly supported by the finding that high-delinquency neighborhoods are commonly anomic.

It has been found that families of delinquents are sometimes more disruptive and disorganized than those of non-delinquents; that a delinquent boy may have experienced considerable paternal deprivation and rejection; and that he may have been in league with his mother against his father. Reckless' data on the "insulating" strengths in the personalities and family lives of some lower-class non-delinquents are also reviewed.

A Decisive Test?

In an English study, Stott (1960) directly tests hypotheses derived from a strict sociological explanation of delinquency against those of an etiology that takes personal processes into account. In criticizing the approach that thinks of delinquency only as subcultural conformity, he adopts a view similar to that in the section on sociocultural realism in Chapter 6:

> That delinquency is a response to unfavourable ecology cannot be doubted. What needs to be determined is to what extent delinquency is induced by *direct cultural suggestion*—as the theory of the delinquent subculture implies—and to what extent the adverse factors in the ecology produce a *general behavior disturbance*, of which delinquency is only a part—one might say the small part of the iceberg which is visible (p. 157; my italics).

He makes two predictions: If urban delinquency is a function of direct cultural influence, then comparable samples of delinquent and non-delinquent youths should show no significant differences in personal maladjustment. And second, if a process of "social infection" is hypothesized, separate from mediation by personality processes, to explain subcultural delinquency, one would expect a lower incidence of personal disturbance among delinquents from urban areas where social infection is strong, and a significantly higher incidence of disturbance among delinquents from non-urban areas. (The test of this second hypothesis is highly relevant to the degree of importance one should attach to the concept of the psychologically "normal" delinquent; see Miller *a.*)

Eighty-two percent of all probationers under age fifteen in Glasgow during 1957 were rated by teachers on Stott's own social adjustment instrument, as well as were a sample of control boys drawn from the same schools. There were about six times as many maladjusted boys in the probation sample as in the control sample. He then rank-ordered the school zones by prevalence of delinquency to obtain some classification of high- and low-delinquency areas. None of the differences in the probationers' mean maladjustment scores among these school-based subcultural units were significant. He grouped all the probationers who came from areas of relatively high concentration of probationers, as an alternate way of checking on the effects of subcultural conditions. Their mean maladjustment score was very close to that of the lowest-delinquency area, as grouped by school zones. "Among this group one would surely have expected to find a significant tendency to normality among delinquents if it be true that within certain environmental settings delinquency is a phase of normal development."

(P)robationers . . . are equally maladjusted in whatever locality or cultural grouping they live. Since only a proportion of the maladjusted boys would be expected to become delinquents within any given locality, it is reasonable to infer that there must be a larger volume of non-delinquent maladjusts, as well as delinquents, within the high-delinquency areas. This would also be consistent with the hypothesis of an unfavourable ecology responsible for behavior-disturbance, of which delinquency is the presenting symptom (p. 162).

He tested this last possibility by comparing the mean maladjustment scores of non-delinquent boys from the high- and low-delinquency school zones. In contrast to finding no significant differences in maladjustment among delinquents from the various school zones, he found statistically significant differences among the non-delinquents.

Kerr's and Spinley's data support Stott's finding. Their participant observations with and projective test results from English slum children indicate that a childhood in deprived conditions entails great psychological risks to well-being. Both researches paint the modal personality characteristics of such children in dark colors: They tend to be immature, impulsive, and personally uncertain youngsters who may feel depressed and estranged from those around them. (The reader may find a summary of Kerr's projective test data on pp. 151–54 of her work, and Spinley's summary of probable basic personality characteristics on p. 79 of her book.)

Stott rejects a position of strict sociocultural determinism and entertains in its place the alternative general hypothesis that socioeconomically depressed areas predispose individuals to a wide variety of physical and psychological disturbance. This viewpoint lies at the heart of the psychocultural model offered here.

A methodological fly in the ointment is the fact that, in Stott's study, teachers made the ratings. Assuming the reliability of his Bristol Social Adjustment Guides (Stott, 1956) as measures of a child's personal stability, one might wonder whether teachers' attitudes to delinquents' school misbehavior might bias their ratings. It might have been better, although obviously more difficult, had Stott obtained ratings from non-participant observers of in-school behavior.

On the other hand, the items rated seemed to have been largely behavioral, and therefore less subject to interpretation; and non-delinquents in high-delinquency areas also tended to receive high disturbance ratings, which would seem to eliminate teachers' disapproval of delinquent acts as one possible source of bias. It would appear that the alternative predictions that Stott checked are such clean and direct tests of strictly "sociological" against social-psychological premises that his study is probably worth replicating, perhaps with different raters.

The Delinquent and School

It will be recalled that Cloward and Ohlin indicate that the potentially delinquent lower-class boy is indifferent to school or rejects it because he is oriented toward materialistic success-goals only—money for clothes, cars, and girls—and is not interested in attaining middle class respectability, of which educational achievement is a part (pp. 96–97). I pointed out earlier that this purely economic motive has to be functional no later than age twelve or thirteen if it is to explain school rejection. Drop-outs represent a culmination of school difficulties which often reach well back into the primary grades. The Gluecks found that twice as many delinquents as non-delinquents in their sample had not yet gone beyond the sixth grade, while the mean age for both groups was roughly fourteen and a half. Again, twice as many delinquents as non-delinquents were two or more years behind the appropriate grade for their age. Of even more significance for us here is the age of earliest maladaptive behavior in school. *Almost a third of the delinquents, but only a twelfth of the non-delinquents, markedly misbehaved before the age of eight.* The fact that school truancy and other misbehavior starts in the middle of the latency period or earlier, a good five years before the modal onset of adolescence, is supported by the findings of Kvaraceus, Healy and Bronner, and others (see Bloch and Flynn, pp. 198–202, for a brief review and references). Andry's comparison of interview information from delinquent boys in English remand homes and a matched sample of non-delinquents bears out the other findings regarding age of onset of misbehavior. He indicates that 64 percent of the delinquents (vs. 26 percent of their controls) reported having first truanted before they were twelve, and 72 percent of the delinquents (vs. 53 percent of the non-delinquents) reported having committed their first theft before they were twelve.

Hollingshead observes,

> school withdrawal is a complex process which begins well down in the primary grades. The *effects* of the factors which *condition* it *come into focus* in the *upper* elementary grades as the child becomes aware of the way in which he is regarded by his peers, teachers and the community in general; from then on the process is intensified (p. 331; my italics).

We must ask ourselves how useful for understanding pressures toward deviance in lower-class children of latency age the notion of economic aspiration is. How much money does a latency-age child of any class level of our society want, how much does he want it, for what purpose does he want it, and what relation might he experience, at that age, between being a have-not and "behaving" in school?

One might take the point of view, as do Cloward and Ohlin, that the child's particular acculturation devalues or discourages educational achievement (pp. 99–101). Why, then, does not the delinquent express his estrangement from school simply by truancy? The earliest misbehavior of 25 percent of the delinquents in the Glueck sample consisted of defiance and other forms of in-school deviance. Further, the Gluecks note that the delinquents were consistently higher in both attacking as well as withdrawing behavior in the school situation.

Why indeed is the potentially delinquent lower-class child often disruptive and aggressive in his primary grades? In view of the contradictions between assumption and evidence which have just been reviewed, an alternative explanation is entertained. It does not deny the possibility that the lower-class child may acquire success-goals discrepant with those held by his teachers, through an undisturbed socialization. But it does imply Stott's assumption that the child of a lower-class subculture runs a greater risk of disturbed socialization, and hence of personal instability, as a result of the numerous relative disadvantages pressing in on his socializers, *and*, one might add, on *their* socializers before them.

This alternate hypothesis is the psychoanalytic proposition that latency is the age for development of means for mastering the environment, through the growth of ego functions involving perceptual skills, object comprehension, thinking, language, etc. (Erikson, 1959; Hartmann, 1958, pp. 3–21). It is the age during which Kardiner and Ovesey call "learned systems," such as the multiplication table, are mastered, and during which capacities for manipulating symbols mature. Accomplishment of these stage-specific developmental tasks depends, according to psychoanalytic theory, on the successful socialization of drives and on the resolution of crises in ego development in the earlier stages of babyhood and childhood. If disturbed family relationships have arrested the child's prior psychological growth, his major energies will be invested in earlier object-strivings. Furthermore, his family may have failed to cultivate his cognitive skills, so that these functions may have remained undifferentiated out of his basic potentialities (as suggested in the discussion of ego syncretisms at the end of Chapter 3). He will not want to be enabled to learn, and he will not be able to learn, without special techniques; he will be seeking entirely different gratifications from his teachers than those they intend (Friedlander, *passim*).

Bloch and Flynn's summary of reasons for delinquents' school difficulties is worth quoting here:

> [Truancy] unquestionably arises mainly from [the child's] inability to countenance frustrating classroom situations, and, because of emotional shortcomings, to develop a sense of responsible self-control in [his] relations to the school; the development of such an attitude of self-responsibility with regard to school functions is characteristic even of those children whose response to a normal school routine is considerably less than enthusiastic. . . . Additional light is shed on delinquents' maladjustment to school and their generally unstable mental state by their marked distaste for subject matter that demands strict logical reasoning, persistency of effort, and good memory. Although both delinquents and non-delinquents coming from similar environments show preference for manual training and a dislike for verbal discipline, delinquents' distaste for such studies as arithmetic, social studies, foreign languages, science, and commercial subjects were fairly well marked in the Glueck study. . . . It has not been determined to what degree the school situation creates frustrations that render socially and economically deprived children, although otherwise balanced and integrated, susceptible to delinquency. Evidence indicates, however, that this is likely in a small percentage [*sic*] of cases (pp. 200–2).

It is not a really adequate explanation of the LL child's school frustrations, in the final analysis, to characterize what is taught in the primary grades and how it is learned simply as expressions of middle-class values. Subject matter and study do, after all, represent the accumulated functions, in our culture, of abilities to manipulate verbal, numerical, and spatial symbols. It is proposed here that a considerable number of future lower-class gang delinquents cannot listen, obey, and delay long enough, and are not able to grasp the content in the early grades, to acquire the secondary drives and rewards necessary to motivate ongoing school effort, because their personal development has been neglected and disrupted by poor family conditions.

Socialization

What follows is a review of some of the more salient facts concerning personal experience in lower-class delinquent and aggressive children:

A. *By Class*. Davis sees six class sectors in American society, three two-layered classes, as subculturally distinct:

Within each of these participation levels, with their cultural environments, a child learns characteristic behavior and values concerning family members, sexual and aggressive acts, work, education, and a career. . . . Thus, well-defined cultures are developed and maintained by means of restricted social participation between groups or between individuals of different social status (p. 523).

Davis clearly describes the sharp class differences in induction of aggressive as well as other behaviors;

Lower-class culture, white or Negro, organizes adolescent behavior with regard to aggression, sexual relations, age roles, and family roles, to mention only a few of the basic types of relationships, into patterns which differ radically from those of middle-class adolescents. . . . With regard to a great many goals, what is rewarding to a middle-class adolescent is not at all so to a lower-class adolescent. What they fear, what they abhor, what they desire, what they crave, what they will work for, or fight for, what they consider valuable or sacred differ in almost every basic area of human relationships (pp. 527–28).

The following passage is quoted almost in its entirety because it points to the lower-class family as the specific medium for the socialization of aggression, as well as for the violence of that socialization:

In general, middle-class aggression is taught to adolescents in the form of social and economic skills which will enable them to compete effectively at that level. It may be full of personal hostility and insecurity, or it may be realistic and socially directed. The lower classes not uncommonly teach their children and adolescents to strike out with fist or knife and to be certain to hit first. Both girls and boys at adolescence may curse their father to his face or even attack him with fist, sticks, or axes in free-for-all family encounters. Husbands and wives sometimes stage pitched battles in the home; wives have their husbands arrested, and husbands try to break in or burn down their own homes when locked out. Such fights with fists or weapons, and the whipping of wives occur sooner or later in many lower-class families. They may not appear today, or tomorrow, but they *will* appear if the observer remains long enough to see them.

The important consideration with regard to aggression in lower-class adolescents is that it is learned as an *approved and socially rewarded* form of behavior in their culture. An interviewer recently observed two nursery-school boys from lower-class families; they were boasting about the length of their fathers' clasp knives! The parents themselves have taught their children to fight not only children of either sex, but also adults who "make trouble" for them. If the child or adolescent cannot whip a grown opponent, the mother or father will join the fight. In such lower-class groups an adolescent who does not try to be a good fighter will not receive the approval of the father, nor will he be acceptable to his play group or gang. The result of these cultural sanctions is that he learns to fight and admire fighters. The conception that aggression and "hostility" are neurotic or maladaptive symptoms of a chronically frustrated adolescent is an ethnocentric view of middle-class individuals [almost exactly the position taken by Miller (1958) pp. 18–19]. In lower-class families in many areas, physical aggression is as much a normal, socially approved and inculcated type of behavior as it is in frontier communities and in war (p. 528).

Davis goes on to attach much the same kind of importance, for the subsequent sexual behavior of the children, to the sexual instability and promiscuity of parents and older sibs.

Cavan, in reviewing the work of Davis and others, reaches similar conclusions regarding the determining influence of family patterns on lower-class Negro youths. Rohrer and Edmonson and Kardiner and Ovesey also provide evidence which would support Davis' conclusions. Miller (1958; *b; c*) sees such lower-class cultural concerns as toughness, smartness, excitement, and autonomy as expressed so prevalently in norm- and law-violative ways that he views lower-class gang delinquency as merely an age-grade variant on a total cultural orientation. Gans suggests that "many elements of [LL] life are not merely culturally different from other ways of life, but . . . are in fact pathological" (p. 269). These observations support the earlier proposal that there are many antisocial elements in the social context of lower-class delinquency, and that gang behavior is a living-through of regressive trends implied by the behavior and the shared sentiments of LL adults.

One might raise the argument that since these socialization influences are attributed to a whole class, or, as specifically as possible, to the lowest class, one cannot explain why these influences find a delinquent expression among only some lower-class youths. Cloward and Ohlin adopt this type of argument in rejecting Miller's attribution of male role anxiety as a pressure to deviance among lower-class youths. One can easily imagine differences, not only across the total social structure but also within the lower class, of extent and types of aggressive and other impulsive family patterns. Some LL family systems may proscribe almost all but symptomatic expressions of aggression and regressive wishes; others may permit or prescribe externalizing; others, mixtures of both forms of expression. These differences in patterning might account for differences among LL youth in predisposition to act out inner experiences in delinquency, and for differences as well in delinquent character types.

B. *By Ethnic Subculture.* Ethnically definable subcultures in our society vary significantly in rates of delinquent and criminal activity, and this variation is not entirely accountable to differential access to success-goals.

There were great variations in the rates of crime among respective European immigrant groups, apparently independent of allegiance to the American success ideology (Wood). The crime rates for Yugoslavs and Hungarians were less than the average for the South and East European countries, and less than half that of the native-born white population in general. On the other hand, Italian and Austrian rates were about half again as high as that of the "later" immigrants taken as a whole. These rates cannot be attributed to a rejection on the part of the Yugoslavs and Hungarians of the ethic of success; Wood reports that both these groups, as well as a third "new" immigrant group he personally studied, the Bohemians, apparently came to this country determined to work hard and succeed by American standards.

A proponent of opportunity theory might reason that it was just because success was already valued by them that they worked hard to escape lower-class economic disadvantages. But this begs an interesting question. Presumably, no recent European immigrant group was able entirely to escape the economic deterioration that usually befell the peasant in industrial America. (Indeed, it would seem that the studies cited by Wood and conducted by him were made at a time when the bulk of these European groups still belonged to the working class.) Why, then, did not the Yugoslavs, Hungarians, Bohemians, and other groups with low rates experience extremely acute frustrations when they were economically disadvantaged, in view of their presumably high economic aspirations, and so be even more quick to repudiate conventional norms? These groups should have produced high, not low, rates of crime and delinquency.

Wood reasons that cultural and social integration among the Italians could not withstand economic deterioration, while the ethnic groups with low rates retained and even augmented their family and social affiliations under adverse economic circumstances and through these social institutions kept alive their subculturally valued ends. In the terms of the theory offered in this book, the social and cultural integration that, according to Wood, persisted in the low-crime subcultures meant the relative absence of ideologies and norms that would have subserved externalizations in these groups. Their cleaving to their indigenous values, beliefs, and institutions suggests that these ethnic groups sustained their original internalizations—their own consciences. They insulated themselves from self-evaluations in terms of normative restrictions existing in American society, and permitted self-discontent only symbolic expression. In this theory, *externalization is considered a psychosocial correlate of anomie* (but not identical with it), and the degree of *normative collaboration*—the degree of eunomie—in a subculture is considered *the social-structural basis for acquiring ego strength.*

C. *By Neighborhood.* Relative economic impoverishment is only one characteristic of a delinquency area, and perhaps not the most significant one at that. Lander's study of Baltimore finds no significant correlations between economic level and housing conditions and delinquency, but does suggest a relation between indices of social disorganization and delinquency rates. (Opportunity structure theory would predict a difference in type, but not in rates, of delinquency between disorganized and integrated lower-class areas.) Lander's findings are partially supported by those of Bordua and Polk.

Kobrin's analysis of values in delinquency areas (1951) suggests that "disorganization" usually means conflicting organizations of values and of social institutions embodying them, but no depletion of ideology and institutions. Although some communities may approach states of literal normlessness, as in some of the Stirling County depressed areas (Hughes, *et al.*), ordinarily anomie means disagreement among, not the absence of, norms. Weakened social control is thus an effect, not an accompaniment, of disorganization, because an individual has alternative ideologies and normative systems readily accessible to him.

Which groups are identified as "outcasts" and outsiders depends on the group to which an individual who is making such an evaluation belongs—an interesting point that Becker makes in his work on deviance. From the standpoint of group psychology, an individual who can contribute to his group's responses to its strangers and enemies may obtain social rewards from his group. This theory, then, would explain higher delinquency rates in disorganized neighborhoods by suggesting that anomic situations—anomic in the sense of displaying normative dissensus—facilitate externalizing adaptations to subjective insecurity.

Maccoby, Johnson, and Church describe some of the ways in which a disorganized neighborhood fails to exert adequate social control over delinquency. Comparing two areas of Cambridge, Massachusetts, of similar socioeconomic level, occupation, and education, they found one area had three times as much delinquency. They do not specify the socioeconomic status of the two neighborhoods, but it appears that both were lower class.

A word here regarding the importance of ascertaining socioeconomic comparability: The student of individual differences in delinquency may fairly question, I think, this need to reconcile, justify, and qualify the comparison of data derived from the same or different class levels.

It may be methodologically proper to control for extraneously determined environmental differences, as Maccoby, *et al.*, did, when one is comparing *environmental* characteristics. But a restriction is often put on comparisons of personality data drawn from different class levels. This type of restriction, viewed from the premises of this book, may be meaningless, because it seems based sometimes on the error of sociological realism. That is, the researcher may fear that personality differences are artifacts of class differences, expressing themselves in differing family patterns. Personality differences are not side-effects of anything, at least no more than are class differences. Family organization and other human action are themselves products of personality factors. Society, as Durkheim said, exists within the "minds"—in the personalities—of people.

For instance, findings from Bandura and Walters' study of aggressive boys and their families will be introduced as pertinent to the socialization of delinquents; a student of social structure may, however, criticize the inclusion of this research on the grounds that the subjects were from intact families and came from low-delinquency neighborhoods. The Glueck study has been criticized in this vein; it has been claimed that their samples of delinquents and non-delinquents are not really of the same socioeconomic level; hence the differences they found between family conditions in the two samples are ultimately attributable to class differences.

An assertion that family and personality organization "really reflect" structural conditions is always of course justified by the purposes of the inquirer if he is explicitly interested in the sociological aspects of these phenomena. However, the problem of the direction of the flow of causation constantly arises to plague the behavioral scientist because of the very nature of his subject matter. Since he is not usually in a position to manipulate the complex behaviors that are our concern here, let alone social and cultural events, he must rely on empirical correlational methods, which almost always make it impossible to determine, without adducing outside information, which correlated factor is cause and which is effect. In the absence of suitable principles and methods by which to weigh the relative importance of psychological and structural variables in the determination of culture patterns, we must remind ourselves that personality binds and integrates culture, as Whiting and Child point out, and that sociocultural conditions *absorb personalities*, to use Arnold Green's phrase. Subcultural behavior may reflect pertinent socioeconomic conditions, but it is certainly just as true that particular personality configurations organize these distinctively stable behaviors. It may also be true that modal subcultural personalities, in their reactions, modify or significantly fail to modify, the socioeconomic conditions themselves. The criticisms of the Glueck study and those anticipated in connection with Bandura and Walters' research ignore the point that certain patterns of family and parent-child relationship *are* associated with aggressive and delinquent children, class distinctions notwithstanding.

The Cambridge study, which prompted the above digression, found families and neighbors to be more estranged in the higher delinquency area than in the other. Even though both areas had fairly stable residence patterns, the members of the "high" area did not like their neighborhood or know them well, and their points of view and interests were different. In addition, they were more reluctant to interfere when they saw a child involved in deviant behavior in which they were not directly involved. While the authors do not see a causal relation between this absence of social control and delinquency itself, their findings, as well as Lander's, suggest that it is important to separate normative dissensus and its subjective aspects, of isolation, indifference, or distrust, from socioeconomic factors.

D. *By Family*. One may quarrel with the Gluecks for calling the findings of postdictive research "prediction tables"; but it is a remarkable commentary on the importance of family socialization that they compute the chances for delinquency as 98 out of 100 if a child in their sample had unfavorable experience in four areas of family life—discipline by the father, supervision by the mother, affection of both parents for the child, and family cohesiveness. The relationship between broken, disrupted, demoralized, and antisocial families and delinquency has been repeatedly documented in many studies over many years (Bloch and Flynn, pp. 181–88). We may be currently turning our backs on these data while we are all, students of personality and society alike, caught up in the exploration of socioeconomic inequities introduced by Cohen in 1955. This body of research on families is a basic reference point for the definition of the problem of delinquency.

The significance of the multiproblem family for delinquency theory may not be fully appreciated as yet. Such families may teach us a good deal about factors underlying variation in mobility within ethnic groups undergoing assimilation. It is probably to such families that a concept like the pile-up of pathology in the slums (Opler), or a concept such as mobility arrest, would be most applicable. There is also the possibility that the link between these families and psychopathology has already been forged. The chronically catastrophic state of affairs in the multiproblem family may cause indigence and self- and other-destructiveness, as in the character-disordered families reported by Reiner and Kaufman. (Here is perhaps a perfect example of the difficulty in determining the priority of psychological or sociocultural determinants. Does the multiproblem family result from unfavorable lower-lower-class pressures? Or, do the action consequences of certain personality configurations in one of these families, multiplied, abstracted, and generalized into institutional arrangements and ideological agreements, constitute a sociological description of the LL class?)

Among 310 children of the 150 multiproblem families studied by the New York City Board, almost 60 percent of them were referred for study and treatment because of aggressive acts. Noteworthy is the fact that 72 percent of the children were under age thirteen at the time of referral (New York City Youth Board Monograph No. 2). Over 90 percent of the families were experiencing "moderate" to "severe" social and emotional disorganization, and in only 22 percent of the most seriously disorganized families were both parents in the home. "More than half of the total number of families were found to be failing in their marital adjustment when factors such as severe marital discord, promiscuity, and out-of-wedlock children were rated" (New York City Youth Board Monograph No. 5). In a related study the 150 families were examined for functional failure of the mother, the father, or of siblings; in marital adjustment; and economic deprivation; 87 percent were found to be failing in three or more counts. Apparently not one of these families was known to less than five different agencies, while some were known to as many as twenty.

The lower-class delinquent grows up in a family of estranged and conflicting relations: Family routine is disorganized; family members have little self-respect; the parents get along poorly and the family is not cohesive (Glueck and Glueck, pp. 108–16). The parents and siblings are sometimes aggressive or antisocial, and thus provide delinquent models (Bandura and Walters; Glueck and Glueck; Shaw). Another important finding has been that of parental neglect and rejection of the future delinquent, with some indications that it begins early in childhood (Hewitt and Jenkins; Jenkins and Hewitt; Glueck and Glueck). This is probably related to other findings of deprived or thwarted dependency needs in delinquent boys (Bandura and Walters; Bender; Bowlby; Healy and Bronner). The reader is reminded of the psychiatric formulations based on aggression as a defense against anxieties surrounding these thwarted wishes (Alexander and Healy; D. Bloch; Kaufman, *et al.*)

The delinquent's paternal relationship has come under study. Nye and Wattenburg have found a closeness to mother and an avoidance of father on the part of delinquent boys. Bandura and

Walters studied this relationship in some detail, and concluded that there was a disruption of affectional relationship between aggressive boys and their fathers. They found the fathers to be rejecting or indifferent toward their sons, and the boys were hostile toward their fathers.

Andry also concludes, on the basis of his interview data with delinquents, non-delinquents, and the parents of both, that "paternal deprivation" is a much more significant etiologic element in delinquency than has heretofore been credited, at least by those adherents of Bowlby's concepts regarding maternal deprivation and its effects on the personalities of delinquents. The delinquents whom Andry interviewed and their parents agreed that they were less likely to go to their fathers first, when in trouble. These boys also felt better understood by mother than by father, and they had generally weak and unsatisfying relationships with their fathers.

Gold's data, from survey interviews like Andry's, tend to support that researcher's findings. Both the delinquent's parents were less attractive to him than the non-delinquent's; he was less attracted to his father as a model; had less to do with him; and, if he had repeated delinquencies, may have had a physically more punitive father.

Other of Bandura and Walters' findings are pertinent to the question of the role of the female-based household in the production of male sex-role anxiety in the adolescent boy. (Cohen and Hodges' paper contains a series of bibliographical references to the extensiveness of this kind of household among LL families.) Miller has suggested that a resulting feminine identification among LL boys makes them turn to the gang for sex-role definition. Cloward and Ohlin point out that the middle class may have its own type of female-based household, Parsons' "suburban matriarchy," and discard this structural factor in the production of lower-class delinquency (p. 52). "Female-based households" of different classes may be similar in name only; other factors may be decisive in the contribution of the female-based household to delinquency, for example the status of husband-father and wife's derogation of husband. It may make a crucial difference in the identities of the children if the father is respected, whether or not he is a suburban commuter, or if the father is disparaged, whether or not he is present in the family.

It is interesting that both Bandura and Walters and the Gluecks report significantly greater hostility between the parents of deviant boys. Bandura and Walters report that "Since both the mother and the boys showed relatively little warmth for the fathers and were also hostile toward them, the fathers were unlikely to serve as important models for imitation" (p. 310). These authors also found apparently greater doubt among these fathers about their masculinity. They had sexual anxieties, and part of their distance from their sons may have been based on an avoidance of their sons' burgeoning masculinity. The fathers made fewer demands for masculine behavior and failed to encourage male-appropriate behavior.

In addition to Gold, McQueen reports that lower-class Detroit delinquents also find their fathers significantly less attractive than do non-delinquent controls. McQueen reports a rejection of school by his more intelligent Negro delinquent subjects whose fathers held unrealistically high educational aspirations for them. He indicates that only 18 percent of boys with I.Q.s of 100 to 119 made average or better grades in school, as compared to 50 percent of delinquent boys with I.Q.s ranging from 90 to 99 and as compared to 50 percent of a control group with the same relatively high intelligence levels. This striking reversal of educational achievement is attributed by McQueen to a rebellion against fathers who were both demanding and weak.

Bandura and Walters' findings regarding aggressive children point up a factor that is fairly common in lower-class female-based households and even in intact, relatively privileged families. (Judging by Andry's, Gold's, and McQueen's data, this factor seems common in the family relationships of lower-class delinquents as well.) Mother and son share a mutual antagonism toward father. It was indicated earlier that plausible social and cultural reasons have been advanced by others for the estrangement between lower-class fathers and their families, such as job instability. Another factor, however, has probably not been given adequate consideration: the maternal dependency of the fathers themselves.

The men are very likely to have had similarly strong ties with their own mothers in their own childhood and youth; they were also products of female-based households in which their fathers were similarly disparaged and without influence. These men may be preoccupied with obtaining personal security and satisfaction from their wives, or equally absorbed in not getting them. They may be willing to suffer disparagement and surrender of family authority to their wives in order to maintain an overly dependent relationship. Indeed, these men may feel that this is the way things should be, an accommodation in their consciences to formative experience and to current needs. Even the English fathers observed by Kerr and Spinley were characteristically submissive to the Mum's prerogatives, and these men exercised a greater measure of family authority, and had considerably more status, than American men in female-based LL households, judging from most accounts.

On the other hand, these men may also view their growing sons, or rather mothers' growing sons, as competitors for mothers' attentions. Studies of the interactions of such families give every indication that these dominant mothers bind their children to themselves. The boy's direction of his will and initiative toward her would only threaten his father's possessiveness regarding mother. If mother is antagonistic toward father, she may actually put off his claims on her more than she does her son's. The realities of the mother-son relationship, and of the marital relationship, may create an Oedipal encounter that is in neither the father's nor the son's unconscious: Both the father and the son provide targets and provocations for externalizing their respective ego insecurities. It may be, then, that in such families the father's dependency plays into the mother-son relationship and perpetuates the maternal dependency of the son—who is thus readied for the same role with his wife and her sons.

Whiting, Kluckhohn, and Anthony (1958) have provided cross-cultural evidence that a strong primary identification with mother, if it finds no transfer to father, will create a persisting estrangement between fathers and sons. They also indicate that this early strong attachment to mother will produce sexual insecurity in the males in general. In cultures where this attachment to mother occurs, certain kinds of institutional arrangements are found which seem intended to allay male sexual anxieties.

In a comparison of preliterate societies they found a strong correlation between propinquity of mother and baby and harsh, sometimes brutal adolescent initiation rites. Their original explanation of this finding was that the living arrangements in these societies protracted and intensified the Oedipal rivalry of the male child, and that the initiation rites forced a resolution of the conflict. Burton and Whiting (1960) subsequently refined this initial hypothesis. They predicted that under conditions where the child establishes conflicting identifications, such as in early sleeping arrangements with mother followed by living with father's people, painful rites of passage would ensue to compel a masculine identification. Where female identification is culturally instituted through both sleeping with mother early as well as in matrilocal residence, the culture would provide some symbolic means to act out the female role. The researchers selected the custom of the couvade, in which the husband goes to bed and undergoes the same taboos as his wife during her labor, as the cultural vehicle for feminine identification. Their data strongly confirm the occurrence of initiation rites and couvade in relation to their respective antecedent cultural conditions. Both Miller's and Rohrer and Edmonson's studies of lower-class and Negro youths have observed highly analogous compulsive masculinity and sexual anxiety in the gang behavior of boys from female-based households.

Unsound discipline has been regarded as a prime factor in the production of aggressive behavior disorders and predisposition to delinquency. Lax, erratic, and overly severe punishment have all been associated with the socialization of delinquent and aggressive children (Burt, Bandura and Walters, Glueck and Glueck). Burt found defective discipline almost seven times more frequently in the homes of English delinquents than in the homes of nondelinquents. He also concluded that poor discipline is four times more important than poverty in the background of delinquency. The effects have been variously explained in terms of the child's failure to internalize standards imposed loosely or unpredictably; his rejection of controls which are harshly inflicted; and the inadvertent example of parents which teaches the child to do as they do and not as they say. When one imagines, from a psychoanalytic frame of reference, a young child learning to requite his parents' wishes by submitting to their brutality, and witnessing the brutal ways in which they may discharge their frustrations on one another, one can see why Kaufman (1955) observes that a sadomasochistic orientation may be a cornerstone of pre-delinquent character.

The Self-Concept and Vulnerability

Reckless and his collaborators (Dinitz, Kay, Murray, Scarpitti, Simpson) have drawn certain distinctions between potentially delinquent and non-delinquent boys which empirically support Reckless' containment theory of delinquency (1961). Central to containment theory is the self-concept; several differences that he and his collaborators find between potentially delinquent and non-delinquent children in this dimension suggest differently organized personalities. The non-delinquent child, they report, is insulated from delinquent temptations because he has been dealt with and regarded favorably by his family and others and so comes to have a high self-regard. Presumably this positive self-concept is based on favorable socialization and the expectation of present and future success in conventional actions. The delinquent who has experienced failure comes to believe that he will fail and to anticipate it in aggressive and deviant acts.

All the subjects came from high-delinquency census tracts in Columbus, Ohio. All were white and were selected by their sixth-grade teachers on their prospects for future police contact or conforming adjustments. There were no significant differences between the two groups on relevant socioeconomic indices. The potentially non-delinquent group indicated a desire to stay out of trouble at any cost, did not expect trouble with the law, and had few friends who had been in trouble; they more often liked school, and pictured themselves as obedient sons living in a harmonious family. They did not feel that their parents were either overly strict or lax.

The potentially delinquent boys' mothers much more frequently disliked their sons' choice of friends, but paid less attention to their whereabouts and associates; they indicated more family conflict and less family cohesiveness. Parents of the non-delinquents punished less frequently and more often said that they were "quiet." Parental supervision and interest in the latter group's welfare and activities were pronounced, yet these boys did not feel unduly restricted. Many of the family differences found by the Gluecks seemed to be suggested in this study; it is further noted that the potential delinquents were not drawn from an institutional population, as were the delinquents in the Glueck study, nor had they undergone any other selection process than that mentioned.

Scarpitti, *et al.*, and Dinitz, *et al.* (1962), compared the delinquent and non-delinquent boys four years after the original studies, when both groups were about sixteen. Their differences remained. The delinquent boys had more court contacts, a higher frequency of delinquent acts, were more pessimistic about prospective trouble with the law, and on a questionnaire displayed attitudes that indicated an antisocial adjustment.

Reckless' (1961) and Dinitz, *et al.*'s (1962), conclusion regarding the follow-up of their original findings is that the less favorable self-concepts of the delinquent boys at twelve years governed and selected their responses to inner and outer stimulation during the ensuing four years, and would probably continue to do so in the future. These researchers are not precise about the personality factors indicated by their self-concept data and inferences, but the factors seem to refer to resources for ego control and negotiation, and to the content and structure of conscience. The boy whose ego skills are limited and whose internalizations do not support conformity and collaboration will be more vulnerable to deviant social systems and to inner pressures to deviance—a conclusion which is a central premise of this theory.

These findings of personality strengths in a group of non-delinquents have to be reconciled with some of the Gluecks' and Stott's data, which seem to show just the reverse—that is, that there are significant indications of personality disturbance among non-delinquents from the same urban areas. Stott found non-delinquent boys from high-delinquency school zones to be significantly more maladjusted than non-delinquent boys from zones with lower rates. The Gluecks found several characteristics occurred with extreme frequency in both delinquents and controls (p. 241), among which were vague insecurity and anxiety, feelings of not being wanted or loved, an absence of self-assertion and of kindly or trusting attitudes. In addition, 35.8 percent of their non-delinquent sample showed some degree of neuroticism, compared to 24.6 percent of the delinquents.

If delinquency is a legal and a sociological word, so is conformity. Just as there can be psychological types of delinquents, so may there be psychologically different ways of conforming. The teachers in Columbus probably chose, for Reckless' studies, a rather select group of non-delinquent boys who demonstrated considerable personal competence and relative maturity. Stott's and the Gluecks' non-delinquent samples, on the other hand, probably more nearly reflected a cross-section of non-delinquents in the neighborhoods from which they were drawn. Restrictions on the Glueck sample, for instance, consisted only of similarity in neighborhood, absence of serious police and court contact, and some ethnic limitations. It seems reasonable to assume, therefore, that the inner containment of the Columbus non-delinquents was qualitatively different from that of some boys in the other two studies: The control subjects in the Columbus research had conforming internalizations and considerable ego strength, while some of those in the two other studies—a very large number in Stott's—had conforming consciences that militated against lived-out rather than symbolic, e.g., neurotic, forms of expressing ego insecurity.

chapter 8

a review of premises

THIS chapter brings together and restates the major assumptions underlying the theory of delinquency in this book. This review of premises is offered here, rather than earlier or later, after the reader has had the chance, along with the writer, to consider some of the doctrinal issues that come up in any general attempt to explain delinquent behavior, so that we both may understand more fully the reasons for making the particular ground-assumptions that follow.

I recognize that the following assumptions are really decisions for and against certain opinions about human realities, and as such some of them may be open to scientific test while others may simply be unprovable assertions, at least at this stage. But all are open to agreement or disagreement. They are offered in the hope of making critical examination and modification easier.

Personality and Society

Cultural values and personal values interpenetrate. Little distinction can be made between the conduct standards, beliefs, and ideals held by an individual and the norms, ideology, and goals represented in his culture, except for purposes of analysis and abstraction. Schilder observed that a system of ideas or convictions that determine the course of life may be complexly constructed out of the character of a person's relationships and childhood experiences (pp. 134–37). Ideologies peculiar to a subculture may imply a common core of socialization experience. It is further assumed that sociocultural events can produce a greater risk, in a given subculture, of particular kinds of personality disorder. It has already been indicated that Kardiner and Whiting with their respective collaborators have provided considerable evidence, both observational and quantitative, that different child-training practices are related to differing adult traits and personalities. What is further meant here closely resembles Whiting and Child's concept of cultural fixation, for which they have provided cross-cultural validation: needs which were commonly deprived or indulged in childhood may result in elements of modal personalities in a subculture out of which culture patterns may derive. Examples of such elements may be the focal concerns that Miller observes in lower-class culture, and lower-class gang delinquency as he sees it may be an example of derivative culture patterns.

Epigenesis

The approach to personality taken here is not that of a role-patterning theory in which development is almost totally determined by available behavior models and only secondarily by motivation, by internal psychic organization, and by inner objects. It is assumed that not only availability and types of models, but the fate of specific phases of ego development, the channeling of primary drives in early periods, and the nature of internalizations will have genetic consequences for the adult personality. Further, it is assumed that there is an orderly maturation, a phasic development of these three intrapsychic systems, with disturbance at particular developmental levels having differential genetic effects; and lastly, that motivation and coping cannot be reduced to a general pain avoidance-reward adience propensity without losing refinement in description.

This position assumes an epigenetic development in the individual, and also states personal issues in terms of the three major intrapsychic systems of psychoanalytic theory. The epigenetic principle means, among other things, that all the elements in personality functioning—basic needs, incentives, and coping skills—are phased on the basis of physical and intellectual preparedness, the expectancies of socializers, and culturally determined conceptions of how and when a child expresses his humanness; and that the particular organization that is given to a function, when inner and outer stimulations call for its emergence, will lastingly affect subsequent development in ways that no other part-function preceding or following, no matter how it is organized, will.

This generalization will be left as it is because it would be far outside the scope of delinquency issues to fill the statement in systematically. But its importance should not be underestimated; it refers to matters of psychological development that mark some of the real differences between psychodynamic theories of personality and what was referred to above as the role-taking, role-modeling, and imitation theories popular among social scientists. It follows from an epigenetic approach, for example, that "aggressiveness" in children, that is, its presence or absence, is a limited distinction. It may be essential to know also whether the aggressiveness is one aspect of an "affectionless character" that has resulted from early extreme emotional deprivation, or whether it is a street-corner toughness, learned in latency and adolescence, after a child may have acquired feelings that people are reachable by other means as well. Different sources and aims of aggressiveness suggest different life histories.

On Psychoanalytic Vocabulary

Regarding the use of personality concepts based on id, ego, and superego, a psychoanalyst might raise no question about this choice of vocabulary, but a social scientist who is a proponent of role theory, and modern students of socialization and of culture, have their own alternatives. The latter group, particularly during the past decade, have been developing a general theory of behavior which is based on principles of academic psychology and of learning theory. General behavior theory utilizes some of the insights of psychoanalysis but rejects others, notably drive epigenesis (Child; Miller and Swanson; Sears, Maccoby, and Levin; Whiting and Child).

Behavior theory's operational definitions are probably more applicable to research than are psychoanalytic terms, which are usually defined from subjective experience and in relation to other subjectively based concepts. But psychoanalytic concepts and inner experience are still the language and the data of many clinicians, and the concepts seem to be implicit in virtually every way of describing personality dynamics. It is hoped that, even though the delinquency theory here may lose something in the way of verifiability because of the language in which it is stated, it may also stimulate more thinking about delinquency and and society among students of personality.

Intrapsychic Systems and the Environment

If psychoanalytic formulations about drives, consciousness, and conscience are to be used, it is incumbent on the writer employing them to be equally cognizant of the importance of all three systems; he should not rely on "psychoanalytic theory" as it was usually applied a generation ago and as it is often understood by behavioral scientists still—that is, as libido theory, as a theory of drives. Hartmann has cautioned that "human behavior is essentially overdetermined; and that in every cross-section of behavior (upward of a certain age) we can trace the influence of all three psychic systems" (1947, p. 364).

The original psychoanalytic absorption in understanding libidinal development, both Erikson and Kardiner have noted, limited the usefulness of psychoanalytic theory for understanding social processes. Erikson has observed that cultures, through their organization of the ego, make distinctive life-styles and self-abandonment to different kinds of activity possible. Freud did not observe this, since he studied rather the ways that cultural repressions affected sexuality. As a result of this viewpoint, all cultures became suspect, unwarrantedly, as suppressors rather than organizers of sexuality (Erikson, 1950, pp. 237–43).

Kardiner and Linton offer a very clear discussion of the inadequacy of libido theory by itself as a way of explaining the consequences of socialization. Instinct theory, they assert, cannot account for the process by which certain kinds of pleasures may be transformed into character traits. For example, the classic traits of the anal character cannot be derived, in these writers' view, from the pleasures of anal activity, unless one makes some quite special assumptions that all children instinctively enjoy being stubborn, withholding, and messy with their excreta, and that what socialization chiefly accomplishes, when it is successful in our terms, is the suppression of these "given" pleasures and acts. This is the kind of very rigid libidinal determinism that not only social scientists reject, but also apparently Erikson, Kardiner, and most other recent personality theorists. Kardiner says that anal character traits can be explained in terms of socialization, however. Thus orderliness represents extreme compliance to adult cleanliness demands; and obstinacy, rejection of these same demands. Stinginess can be equated with anxiety over loss of something valuable and may result from a variety of unfortunate socialization experiences (Kardiner and Linton, pp. 390–93).

Elsewhere Erikson states that

> psychoanalysis first studied (as if it could be isolated) man's *enslavement by the id,* i.e., by the excessive demands on ego and society of frustrated organisms, upset in the inner economy of their life cycle. Next the focus of study shifted to man's *enslavement by seemingly autonomous ego (and superego) strivings*—defensive mechanisms which curtail and distort the ego's power of experiencing and planning beyond the limits of what is workable in the individual organisms and in social organization. Psychoanalysis completes its basic studies of neurosis by investigating more explicitly man's *enslavement by historical conditions which claim autonomy* by precedent and exploit archaic mechanisms within him to deny him health and ego strength (1959, p. 49).

It would appear that psychoanalysis, confusing basic discoveries with first principles, set up a conceptual hierarchy of its own that was as erroneous as the social determinism of some social scientists. Psychoanalysis, or rather libidinal determinism, extrapolated from the imprisoned, clamorous private experience of culturally (and ontogenically) misused people. It imagined imperious instincts extracting service from the ego and requiring the conscience of a prison keeper. Further, this extrapolation was in only one direction: It was imagined that thwarted strivings possessed people, but not that men's environment might have first tyrannized and brutalized their wishes.

Drives are not prior to anything in a child's real experience of himself and his surrounding reality. They are partly dependent on inner, physiological stimuli, it is true; however, each time that a child's maturation triggers a new erotic, motor, or cognitive activity, the child simultaneously experiences, as far as the consequences for him are concerned, the conceptions of those about him regarding how he is to live with, and what he should do with the newly aroused function. Furthermore, these adult (and older sib) expectancies are all integrally chained together in some coherent variant on a functioning life-style—all are aspects of one definition of the human life cycle—that is given in a culture. This would seem to be the meaning of Erikson's repeated observations to the effect that culture reaches down from the furthermost sectors of the life cycle to affect the personal organization of the very young.

We can also see how culture lays claim to man "by precedent," as Erikson puts it: Parental transactions may take hold of a very young child's introjections and fantasies, while his inner experience still has the power to engulf and possess him, and can apparently shape or mute the energy bases of his needs in some fundamental and lasting ways. The observations of Ribble and Rene Spitz indicate that a lack of certain kinds of stimulation in infancy will produce a profound dampening effect on a person's later responsiveness. It probably oversimplifies matters only a little to say that in this sense cultural values may be prior to libido in an individual.

Somewhere in his writings Erikson offers an illustration of how this may at times be literally true, in a chronological sense. His clinical experience with a certain type of youth, of white Anglo-Saxon background, who display a paradoxical mixture of quiet reserve and vague inner disquiet, led him to believe that these boys' mothers overemphasized the importance of training for dependability and self-constraint; they toilet-trained their sons too early and too well, before they could come into an awareness that they might choose to control—or not control—their bowels on their own. These mothers thus launched a pre-emptive sphincter war under conditions—the infant's helplessness—favorable to their own values, and they deprived the child of his struggle for self-assertion before he had the sense to know what he was losing. On reaching adolescence these boys were dissatisfied with the ways in which their constancy limited their exploration of experience, but could not summon the strength of will and the spontaneity to rebel against it. In these ways then, the ego and the superego, as products of the original ground-conditions for satisfying needs and of primary object-attachments, may influence the fundamental structure of drives just as they are themselves influenced by drives; the three intrapsychic systems interdetermine each other, and all are in part products of culture in the individual.

Ego and Environment

Psychoanalytic theory has evolved away from nativism to environmentalism, a change that has come with the development of ego theory. Freud's first, and consistently more explicit, bridge between personal disorder and culture was the war between civilization's agents, the parents, and the child's instincts. Freud couched his formulations regarding libidinal unfolding, and the nature of these libidinal needs, in the terms of the phylogenetic model available to him at that time, as Hartmann and Kris (1945) point out. It was this formulation that made psychoanalytic theory appear useless to students of society and culture. They were confronted with the fact of social and cultural diversity and its effects, and with stressful pressures in the social and cultural orders and not in man's instincts; hence there came social-structural analyses such as Merton's on anomie. Some psychoanalytical students, such as Horney, Fromm, and Sullivan, in trying to state the ill effects of the environment on personality development, had to depart from the mainstream of psychoanalytic thought to convey their points of view (Gill, p. 3). There have been efforts, primarily within the psychoanalytic movement, but significantly from outside it as well, to show that another, implicit thread in Freud's theory of object relations could tie together sociocultural forces, personality disorder, and the psychoanalytic findings and theories regarding disorder.

Parsons, the social theorist who has made contributions of his own to this development, has said:

> Perhaps for reasons connected with the ideological needs of the intellectual classes, the primary emphasis in interpreting Freud's work—at least in the United States—has tended to be on the power of the individual's instinctual needs—the deleterious effect of their frustrations. . . . The consequence of such a trend is to interpret Freud as a psychologist who brought psychology closer to the biological sciences, and to suggest the relative unimportance of society and culture, except as these constitute agencies of the undesirable frustrations of man's instinctual needs. There is, however, another side to Freud's thinking, which became, I think, progressively more prominent in . . . his theoretical scheme. . . . This trend concerned two main themes: the *organization* of the personality as a system; and the relation of the individual to his social milieu, especially in the process of personality development. . . . It will be my main thesis that there is, in the structure of Freud's own theoretical scheme, a set of propositions which can, with relatively little reinterpretation, be very directly integrated, first with the sociological analysis of the family as a small-scale social system, and, further, with the problems of the child's transition from membership mainly in his own family to participation in wider circles which are not, in Western societies, mainly organized in terms of kinship (1958, pp. 321–22).

Parsons then proceeds with an analysis which reconciles libidinal stages, object-choice, and introjection with the socialization of the child in family, school, peer group, and youth culture. Following this, he offers a summary statement of his views:

> I emphasize this continuity from the objects of identification in childhood to the role and collectivity structures of the adult society in order to bring out what is to me the central point of the whole analysis. This is that Freud's theory of object relations is essentially an analysis of the relation of the individual to the *structure of the society* in which he lives. . . . Had Freud lived long enough to enter more deeply into the technical analysis of the object-systems to which the individual becomes related, he would inevitably have had to become, in part, a sociologist, for the structure of these object-systems *is—not merely influenced by—the structure of the society* itself.

He quotes Freud's statement that "the character of the ego is a precipitate of the abandoned object-cathexes and that it contains a record of past object-choices" (pp. 338, 339; my italics). These *constitute*, according to Parsons, the structure of the ego.

Within psychoanalytic theory, this more recent emphasis on the importance of relations with other people has produced several fundamental changes (see Gill's and Rapaport's brief reviews of these developments). In the first place, there has been a wide-ranging reexamination of the origins, structure, and processes of the ego. The ego is seen not as developing from the id, but rather both structures are seen to differentiate from a common matrix. The ego has independent origin, and its apparatuses for perceiving, thinking, remembering, concept formation, etc., are autonomous of the id and develop free from conflict (Hartmann, 1958). Hartmann indicates that these same independent apparatuses afford the organism a phylogenetically based guarantee, a readiness to adapt to an average acceptable environment. This state of adaptedness exists before conflict and does not result from conflict solution; it is not squeezed out of the instincts by socializing influences. Erikson's whole theory of psychosocial development is based on these ideas of ego psychology. It is his theory which, more than any other psychoanalytic effort thus far, places man's fate in the hands of his socializers. (See Erikson's comments on these advances in ego theory and on the "pseudobiology" in the traditional psychoanalytic conception of the mother-child relationship, 1959, pp. 150–51.)

(One wonders, in passing, whether the proponents of the developing general theory of behavior, for example, Whiting and Child, have taken these theoretical modifications into account in their opposition to drive epigenesis. It would seem that any disagreement would rest mainly on the degree of fixity in nature of the emerging drive, and these recent theoretical changes allow much greater room for conceiving of fundamental organization of these drives by experience. How much difference truly exists between Parsons' conception of the developing organism as a nonspecific base structured by cultural values and object meanings, and the adaptability of drives? Certainly the ego theorists imply that the id itself becomes structured by internalized object relations, that it undergoes drastic reorganization by the residues of the earliest object relations, as Parsons [1958] maintains.)

Thus it is argued that the use of psychoanalytic theory need not lead inevitably to an image of man as a wild animal who is tamed by society. It is theoretically possible to describe the adverse effect of culture and society on man in psychoanalytic terms *as these effects modify, or disrupt, his development.*

Symptom as Symbol

The basic distinction between psychiatric disorders as symbolic expressions of discontent with self and delinquency as an externalization of similar dissatisfactions owes something to the ideas of two other therapists and theorists besides Erikson. Szasz uses concepts from symbolic logic to argue that traditional analogies of neurosis to physical symptoms and illness misconstrue the fact that psychiatric conditions are symbolic protestations. The neurotic feigns illness "unconsciously." He conveys his resistance to living a life-style that he feels has been foisted on him and which would injure his interests, not in the more readily translatable and reproducible language of consciousness—words and thoughts—but in the much more secretive, "non-iterative" language of somatizations. Thus, a patient who complains of a hysterical paresthesia in his cheek may be communicating, in language almost too private for another to understand, that the way he feels compelled to relate to others and the way he feels they treat him are as insulting to him as a slap in the face. "My thesis," Szasz says,

> is simply that it is as possible for a person to use intrapersonal conflicts to avoid facing up to interpersonal and sociopolitical difficulties as it is for him to use the latter difficulties to avoid facing up to the former. It is in this connection that mental illness plays an important role as a concept that claims to explain, whereas it only explains away (p. 71).

Szasz also suggests that what are called the secondary gains of neurosis provide the neurotic with ample opportunity to gain retribution from his malefactors: He gets concern and attention; others may remove inequities from his situation or remove him from them; and in the name of his illness he can punish and control others.

In a rather moving paper on the importance of self-affirmation in psychotherapy, Colm very clearly describes the character-neurotic problems of patients she has had as symbolic assertions of desires to exert power over others, to gain equality and intimacy with them, to punish them for mistreatment or unfair demands, real and anticipated—thus symbolizing both collaborative and antisocial wishes which a more self-accepting person would allow himself to experience and on which he might act in self-realizing rather than self-defeating ways. She says that definitions of neurosis which

> refer to a life that has failed to integrate its resources, shying away from them and taking refuge in protection and defenses . . . are misleading. . . . A neurosis is stifling insofar as it makes the patient unable to affirm himself as a worthwhile person in relation to other persons because he is not able to accept, and is threatened by, the negative in himself, in others, in life itself (pp. 280, 281).

Colm urges and challenges each patient to set aside his guilt and consternation with his symptoms and to acknowledge and understand the personal satisfactions he obtains from his neurotic behavior. The childhoods of these patients justify the domineering, sadistic, self-isolating, or demanding purposes of their behavior; each had family experiences that initiated ego limitations which could easily be described in Erikson's terms. Each had little faith that they could make their way, except by coercion and deprivation of others, indirectly enough to escape the vigilance of oppressive consciences. These people had no faith that there could be a saving reality for them beyond the existential causes for distrust, shame, doubt and guilt that more secure people can surmount, or with which others can at least live. Partly in the light, then, of Colm's ideas about the nature of neurosis, it has been suggested that psychopathology covertly seeks restitution for damages done to the person who shows it.

It has also been proposed that externalization is the other side of the coin of personal insecurity and disorder, that it is a functional equivalent among the discontented to individual neurosis. In Chapter 6, similar conclusions drawn by Honigmann (1950) and Kardiner and Linton from their anthropological observations, regarding institutionalized release of personal tensions, were noted in support of this contention. Honigmann proposed the concept of dyscrasic cultural outlets for tension reduction, and Kardiner and Linton observed that neurotic and culturally conforming people may share similar patterns of perception and motivation, even though their acts differ. The concept of externalization is also close to Fromm's conception of the socially patterned defect:

> Spinoza formulated the problem of the socially patterned defect very clearly. He says: "Many people are seized by one and the same affect with great consistency. All his senses are so strongly affected by one object that he believes this object to be present even if it is not. If this happens while the person is awake, the person is believed to be insane. . . . But if the *greedy* person thinks only of money and possessions, the *ambitious* one only of fame, one does not think of them as being insane, but only as annoying; generally one has contempt for them. But *factually* greediness, ambition, and so forth are forms of insanity, although usually one does not think of them as illness."*
>
> These words were written a few hundred years ago; they still hold true, although the defects have been culturally patterned to *such* an extent now that they are not even generally thought any more to be annoying or contemptible. . . . For most of [those millions who are alienated from their individual potentialities], the culture provides patterns which enable them *to live with a defect without becoming ill.* It is as if each culture provided the remedy against the outbreak of manifest neurotic symptoms which would result from the defects produced by it (Fromm, p. 16).
>
> * Spinoza, *Ethics*, Prop. 44 Schol.

Integrative Activity as Means and Ends

In Chapter 2, a distinction was made between developmental and integrative capacities in Erikson's compilation of basic ego functions. The first four, achieved during childhood, progressively fit an individual for increasing social and cultural participation. The four ego capacities which are realized during adolescence and adulthood—identity, intimacy, generativity, and integrity (seeing an accrued meaning in one's experiences and values)—subsume the first four and are built out of them; if they are experienced by an adult, they signify that he is operating effectively in his adult roles, in terms of opportunities for effectiveness.

These ego capacities are called integrative because through them an adult integrates himself, or harmonizes his functions, and is integrated into his culture, that is, he harmonizes his personal interests and sentiments with the larger interests of his group. It was suggested that, while all of the ego functions which Erikson has represented may be thought of as means to the attainment of social ends and the performance of normative behavior, these latter four, the integrative functions, may also be viewed as psychological ends: Being in a state of culture means to engage in actions that define one's value to the whole, that establish one's connectedness, that recreate one's inheritance and heritage, and that lend coherence to a lifetime. It is not assumed that these are inborn needs, but rather that it is in the nature of participation in society and culture that these capacities be realized. Cultural continuity and collaborative behavior require and determine integrative action, and adults are enculturated to strive to experience these states of integration. It is assumed therefore that these end-states are socialized incentives and goals. Actions which would provide integrating experiences may vary between and within cultures, but an adult binds his energies together and directs them, sublimates them, toward fulfillment of self in these ways.

Leighton and Fromm offer their own lists of adult psychosocial functions. If we divest their lists of any implications regarding innate human needs and view them simply as two theorists' summary descriptions of what men generally seek, they bear interesting resemblances to Erikson's later ego stages.

For instance, Leighton constructs a list of ten striving sentiments. Of the first six—strivings for physical security, sexual satisfaction, expression of hostility, expression of love, and the securing of love and recognition—Parsons states that

> The first two are closest to the organic level of integration. The third, fourth, fifth and sixth belong together with reference to deep-rooted motivational systems taking origin in child-parent relationships. . . . The last four are more differentiated relational needs, the products of later phases of socialization. They come very close to what I have been calling 'structurally generalized goals'. Those I consider post-oedipal as contrasted to primary need dispositions which are pre-oedipal (quoted in Leighton, p. 184).

Leighton's final four striving sentiments are:

7. The expression of spontaneity (called variously positive force, creativity, volition).
8. Orientation in terms of one's place in society and the places of others.
9. The securing and maintaining of membership in a definite human group.

10. A sense of belonging to a moral order and being right in what one does, being in and of a system of values (p. 148).

There is a very close similarity between these latter strivings and, first, the psychosocial crises which, according to Erikson, must be negotiated by the adolescent and the adult, and second, the needs which, Fromm maintains, men resolve for good or bad, through their sociocultural participation. Compare strivings for spontaneity with Erikson's crisis of generativity, and with Fromm's need for transcendence; the striving for orientation, with the crisis of identity (Erikson) and with the need for a sense of identity (Fromm); the striving for group membership, with the crisis of intimacy, and with the need for rootedness; and the striving toward morality and a values system, with the achievement of personal integrity and with Fromm's need for a frame of orientation and devotion.

chapter 9

psychocultural propositions

A tenet of the psychocultural theory of delinquency offered in this book is that adversity, whether material or sociocultural, may produce enduring psychological disturbance in people as individuals and in groups. Certainly this is not a new proposal; it has been treated at some theoretical length by others, most recently by Leighton; and there is a wealth of empirical evidence that it is true, particularly from studies of psychiatric disorder among the economically deprived.

Where environmental conditions are favorable, eunomie or normative collaboration exists. Eunomie synergizes the personal achievements of adults, their realization of the integrative capacities of their egos. Norms calling for adult collaboration are the social-structural basis for ego strength. They constitute the environmental conditions for sublimation of adult energies into self-realizing action. Collaborative norms in the adult are supported by personal values and beliefs, regarding self and others, which in turn govern their guidance of their children toward personal maturation.

However, ideologies and the normative systems that attend them make a common and a collective response to environmental conditions possible. Ideology inventively justifies productive *and* destructive innovations in normative conduct. If environmental conditions—material, structural, cultural—have been enduringly hostile, adults cannot realize themselves. They make a series of cumulative sacrifices to adverse circumstances, which may be psychologically represented as changes in adult character. These personality changes were referred to in Chapter 2 as an erosion of characterological achievement over generations. It is given the destructive connotation of erosion because adult character is equated with self-realization; in ego terms, the latter refers to the exercise of adult integrative capacities—hence the damage to character, in this sense, when integrative capacities are sacrificed.

If conditions are hostile, men are at war with them or in bondage to them. People's values and beliefs will convey the character traits that have proved adaptive and that they have commonly adopted. (See discussion of Cohen and Hodges' data in Chapter 3.) Character traits and ideology determine each other: Traits summon up ideological inventions to justify their existence and expression; values and beliefs facilitate the development and spread of adaptive character traits.

When men in a group have been undergoing environmental stress—stress experienced as deprivation and suppression—their ideology will support disunity and conflict within their group as well as rebellious attitudes toward their suppressors. Alienation and divisiveness release expressions of individual struggle and rebellion against adversity. Since character change is a response to adversity, externalizations of the way a person experiences himself and others may be a psychosocial correlate of anomie. People's personal frustrations, expressed in anomie and externalizations, are reflected also in conflict relations with their children, whose strivings are also treated as those of adversaries. The subjection of children results in weakening of their egos and disharmony within their personalities. When, in short, the parents' lights go out, their children stumble and fall.

The psychocultural adaptations that have just been summarized will be presented in the form of a series of ordered propositions, somewhat after the fashion of Leighton's theoretical work. This method is used because it emphasizes what I imagine to be a sequential, historical process—an evolution in the face of adversity, or, from a psychological standpoint, an involution of capacities to make the environment serve and to assert individual interests effectively in interaction.

Propositions

PROPOSITION ONE

Being in a state of culture involves the induction, in individuals, of integrative strivings, since the state of culture is itself a product of energies invested in these needs. Division of labor, invention of tools and technology, provision for mutual survival and protection, etc., are products of integrative efforts toward self-definition, regeneration, community. These products that a culture creates also constitute its own particular channels for the attainment of end-states of integrative activity. The father, in a state of culture, wants the son to have what he values in his own identity, and so may teach the son the manly arts appropriate to that culture; these arts and skills, age-graded peer societies, and institutionalized rewards for particular achievements are examples of such channels.

PROPOSITION TWO

Adult members of a culture participate in utilizing these channels, and in doing so they not only exercise their developmental ego capacities but also achieve integrative ends which guarantee the maintenance and development of their culture. The psychological attainment of integrative end-states thus both accompanies and is an incentive to social cohesion, to what Benedict called a state of social synergy: the condition that exists when an individual perceives that he advances his own welfare and also contributes to the well-being of his community. Social synergy appears where people allocate prestige generously, where they expect to be helped by their neighbors, and where the community is seen as a friendly place (Honigmann, 1954, pp. 281–82). Normative collaboration, "eunomie," is another expression of the reciprocal relation within a culture between end-state attainment and social synergy.

PROPOSITION THREE

A. *Socialization.* A condition for the attainment of integrative end-states is the socialization of the young. Erikson has said:

> I have characterized the psychosocial gains of adult ego development with the terms of Intimacy, Generativity, and Integrity. They denote a postadolescent development of libidinal cathexis in *intimate engagements;* in parenthood or other *forms of "generating"*; and, finally, in the most *integrative experiences* and values accrued from a lifetime. All of these developments have ego aspects and social aspects; in fact their very alternatives (Isolation, Self-absorption, and Despair) can be held in check only by the individual's fitting participation in social endeavors which "invite opportunities for ego functions in spheres free from conflict." The older generation thus needs the younger one as much as the younger one depends on the older [*sic*]; and it would seem that it is in this mutuality of the development of the older and younger generation that certain basic and universal values such as love, faith, truth, justice, order, work, etc., in all of their defensive strengths, compensatory power, and independent creativity become and remain important joint achievements of individual ego development and of the social process (1959, pp. 154–55).

B. *End-States.* A related proposition is that only by their own attainment of end-states are the adults enabled to socialize the young without disordering them; the attainment of end-states is thus also a precondition for adequate socialization. For as Erikson goes on to say:

> In fact, as our clinical histories began to reveal, these values provide indispensable support for the ego development of the growing generations, in that they give some specific superindividual consistency to parental conduct (although *kinds* of consistency—including consistent kinds of being inconsistent—vary with value systems and personality types) (1959, p. 155).

Elsewhere Erikson makes the same point. "The growing child must, at every step, derive a vitalizing sense of reality from the awareness that his individual way of mastering experience is a successful variant of the way other people around him master experience and recognize such mastery" (p. 89).

In a paper on the conflict between generations, Bettelheim (1962) makes the same comments: Adulthood realizes itself when it shows youth the way toward worthwhile achievement, and it must be committed to the pursuit of goals which are out of its reach to show youth the way. Adults, he says, create the causes that only youth can win; adults cannot give meaning to youth's work in any way other than to strive for deeper meaning in their own, an example which youth may then freely choose to follow. Thus, when parents and other socializers are approximating, in action, the meanings they find in living; when they are feeling and being productive; when they find themselves in these meanings, and find each other familiar, then they lead and attract their children to the sense and coherence of parental values. They can respond freely and inventively to the emerging, and separate, interests of their children, and therefore be led by their children into self-realization as parents.

PROPOSITION FOUR

The inaccessibility of the particular integrative channels evolved in a culture destroys the conditions for end-state activity. This inaccessibility might be defined in terms of the blocking of large population segments from entry into the role systems and social organizations, and from practicing the attendant norms, which a given society has evolved to institutionalize approaches to end-states. Examples of such massive blocking might be the condition of the European peasant during the past three centuries; the status of the English, French and German industrial worker in the last century; the status of the American, particularly the immigrant, laborer in the last century and the early part of this century; and the continuing degradation of large segments of the American Negro population.

Several sources of inaccessibility may be described:

A. *Socioeconomic Deprivation.* The most visible source of inaccessibility, and the one which all observers of lower-class delinquency recognize, is poverty and exclusion from economic opportunities. Our economic system is responsive mainly to those who already have political and economic leverage in it, by means of salable skills, corporate influence, and bloc pressures on government and other economic interests. (I think this may be a fair statement without regard for any particular economic-political ideology. To be plain about my own preconceptions in this area —if they have not already become plain enough—I favor economic planning and a mixed economy within democratic political processes.)

Economic deprivation in our culture means human exploitation, rejection, suppression, and/or indifference by the privileged, and it is *experienced as such* by the deprived. There must be very great degrees of self-rejection and despair among the very poor; otherwise there would be no way of accounting for the chaotic life-styles that many of them have and their pessimistic and frustrated outlooks, unless, of course, one wants to resort to an argument about some kind of inborn depravity. There have always been poor people who have lived in true communities with one another, whose personal and family lives demonstrated their self-respect (Lewis). The fact that such people have usually been among the working poor is very much to the point: Whether because deeply ingrained caste or religious beliefs helped a man reconcile himself to his station, or because a general level of poverty was evident everywhere and seemed inescapable, such people felt that what they might reasonably strive for justified their being alive; they had a sense of attainable worthiness.

As Merton indicates in his paper on anomie, the legitimate values and norms of our culture equate worthiness with economic success. Adult integrative activity, within conventional norms, consists of some form of economically profitable activity and the multiform patterns of consumption of profits, or wages, from that activity. The poor are more or less prevented from experiencing the kinds of self-realization that are possible through (but by no means guaranteed by) these patterns of productivity and consumption. The poor have nowhere else to go, culturally speaking, except to generate goals and norms of their own, as best they can. What is valued in the general culture is out of their reach, and they are driven to define their powerlessness in the varied terms of personal despair. Even if we assume that there are some among the very poor who are strong enough to resist the ideological attributions of inferiority and reprehensibility that the privileged use to rationalize their grip on the goods and benefits that flow from the economy, the poor cannot help but experience abandonment, and with it mistrust and insignificance.

Oscar Lewis has said, regarding their psychological traits:

> The people in the culture of poverty have a strong feeling of marginality, of helplessness, of dependency, of not belonging. They are like aliens in their own country, convinced that the existing in-

stitutions do not serve their interests or needs. Along with this feeling of powerlessness, is a widespread feeling of inferiority, of personal unworthiness (1963, p. 2).

There may be about 29 million Americans whose yearly income is $2,500 or less (S. M. Miller). For these people, and for perhaps an additional 16 million whose economic marginality is only slightly less grievous (*ibid.*), the grinding necessities of sheer physical survival must be all-absorbing, and wishes to realize some kind of personal dignity and value must have the quality of unrealistic fantasy.

As I said at the beginning, this is not a book about what to do regarding delinquency and the problems that give rise to it, and programmatic suggestions about alleviating poverty are beyond my competence. But on the issue of poverty particularly, it seems to me crucial that behavioral scientists, and especially personality experts, should know quite precisely what they can and cannot hope to achieve with their professional skills. The personality expert who is working out of or consulting with a welfare agency, for example, and who fails to recognize the fact and effect of economic starvation may be inclined to reduce his understanding of styles of life among deprived people to expressions of "maladjustment" and "psychopathology." If he treats these human conditions as if they are the chief obstacles in the way of the poor, he is being used, and is using himself, wittingly or otherwise, to contain and pacify the demands of the deprived. (This, as it has been explained to me by a veteran of the labor movement, is a reason for a contempt that some union professionals feel for industrial psychologists; the latter are viewed, rightly or wrongly, as company men, kept technicians who manipulate labor to get greater productivity with little or no benefit to the worker himself.)

This is not to say that widespread normative deviation, antisocial behavior, and psychological disturbance are not significant features in a portrait of poverty. Indeed, the theory here is intended to inventory some of the psychological damages that result from and that may help perpetuate economic deprivation. One of the action implications of this theory is that experts in personality change are needed to program methods for eliminating personal adaptations which would subvert opportunities opened to the underprivileged. But this theory remains nothing more than an inventory of some of poverty's consequences, and serious attempts to change psychocultural adaptations among the poor must be accompanied by commitment to break open the closed circle of economic privilege.

B. *Cultural (or Subcultural) Inadequacy*. There may be a problem of culturally obsolete identities: The socialization of a child may not fit him for assimilating the roles and instrumentalities (the integrative channels) for experiencing end-states as they have been formed by the dominant culture. This imprisonment in an identity that has validity only for a past "ego space-time," to use Erikson's term, may occur among the very rich (Erikson, 1959, pp. 33–37), among the very old or very new ethnic subgroups in a culture, or among the suppressed and poor. Opler (1956) observes that newspaper and agency accounts of crises in immigrant Puerto Rican families point clearly to the effects, in family disorganization and in childrearing practices, of changed opportunities for the exercise of indigenous age- and sex-roles. Handlin indicates that the mobility of the European peasant immigrant in industrial America was encompassed by his own traditional humility. "The idea of success itself was strange; to thrust oneself above one's station in life called for harsh competitive qualities the peasant had always despised" (p. 80).

The inadequacy of a subculture is complicated by the dominant culture absorbing it. For instance, Seward gives examples of Africans who undergo personality disorganization when they move, in a process of detribalization, from a simple context, in which ample rewards are made to individuals who achieve a dependent adjustment, to complex urban areas (1956, pp. 16–9). Reckless (1943) indicates that studies of Negro crime bring attention to the maladjustment of the former Negro sharecropper in a complex urban culture; as his urban adjustment continues, his family and personal disorganization decline, as does his crime rate. Reckless indicates similar data regarding Mexicans and Poles.

> The common denominator in all these citations appears to be the increased liabilities and maladjustments due to the change from a simple and backward to a more complex and advanced environment. Furthermore, these migrants do not possess a community organization which is equal to the change (1943, p. 45).

Kerr tries to explain the socioeconomic immobility of Liverpool slum people in terms of an inadequate subcultural preparation for greater participation in the general culture. These people, she suggests, are not prepared to make complex discriminations among roles; they make only simple and gross role distinctions among themselves, and cannot perform all of the required aspects of roles which are functional in the larger society. As a result they cling rigidly and uncertainly to the roles they do have. As indicated in an earlier reference to Kerr's theoretical model, she equates a gradual enrichment of a person's role repertoire with increase in his ego strength. She therefore thinks that limitations on roles available to a group of people lead both to their subcultural fixation and to personal immaturity, and that the latter two conditions are correlated—a position with which this theory agrees.

Erikson's observations on the cultural anachronisms of the Dakota Sioux represent exactly what is meant here by a problem of obsolete identities. Erikson disagrees with the contention of MacGregor, *et al.*, that the "repressive forces" in Sioux family life cause the apathy, withdrawal, delinquency, and projected hostility of the Indian adolescent. Erikson maintains that the Sioux child has in fact a rich socialization in the family, directed toward non-existent cultural roles. The absence of suitable identity models, for example, men who actually live the lives of hunters and warriors, causes failure in this stage of ego development. Infantile rage and initiative, also products of distinctive Sioux socialization, have no functional outlets; there is therefore a projection rather than a direct use of these energies (Erikson, 1950, pp. 381–88).

C. *Cultural Assimilation.* The condition of transition itself may be described separately as an obstacle to access. A subculture may have identity formations available, important elements of which may be entirely compatible with requirements of integrating roles in the dominant culture, as for instance the emphases on education and financial success among the Jews and on respect for male authority among Chinese and Japanese immigrants. Yet individuals undergoing culture conflict may not be able to avail themselves effectively of either set of channels, indigenous or American. The process of assimilating the dominant culture requires by definition relinquishment of old identifications. The individual may give up a sure grasp on identity fragments which might have stood him in good stead before he has accomplished the work of shaping a view of himself which would allow him to participate in the prospective achievements which the dominant culture offers. Thus Wood offers several examples of increasing crime rates among people who divorced themselves from the kinship and community affiliations of their original subcultural group, from "the folkways of a group [which] enable people to attain their culturally defined ends" (p. 509). Furthermore, this transition may go on for several generations with adverse effects; one group of the "old" immigration, the French, although it has a relatively low crime rate, is still higher than the rate for the "old" immigration as a whole, a fact which Wood attributes to its urban location and to the consequent greater impact of American culture.

D. *Ostracism.* By ostracism, I mean the withdrawal of eligibility, the degradation of an ethnic group to an outcaste. The wider society defines a particular group as unfit to accede to the integrating channels evolved in the culture. The classic case is that of the American Negro. However, many other ethnic categories are endowed with varying degrees of unfavorable status, as social distance studies suggest. To the extent that minority group members divest themselves of their indigenous institutions which might protect them from this ostracism, and to the extent that they underwrite the new goals of the dominant culture, they will be cut off from the conditions necessary for a sense of personal integrity. In American culture a value that binds ego energies and groups may be what Erikson describes as the equality of industrial association: the equality of all those who work hard together (1959, p. 91). Many latency-age Negro children may realize, however, that no matter how hard they work they will never be granted equality by some white children and some teachers. This may have damaging consequences, as Erikson points out, in a sense of inferiority born at a critical stage of their development.

Wood states as succinctly as any the consequences for the Negro of denial of access and denial of integrity:

(T)he Negro has no strong ideologically distinct culture. What remains of an African or a plantation slave culture does not represent values of which the Negro is proud. To an overwhelming extent, the

Negro, especially the Northern Negro, has thrown his lot in with the white man's social and economic system, and he has failed according to its standards [*sic*]. Whatever social integration the Negro has, it is insufficient to combat the impact of his low economic status. His unequal treatment in all activities has been a felt persecution so deflating to his ego that crime, particularly crimes of violence, has been a common form of adjustment (pp. 504–5).

It may be worth our while to reexamine just what some of the other destructive effects of prejudice are. It may be, as Ehrlich suggests, that stereotyping and prejudices are inevitable in human affairs, because stereotyping is a natural consequence of the distinctly human capacity to abstract qualities which are common to categories of objects, including categories of people. But inevitable or not, prejudice has such insidious and debilitating consequences that it is like a cultural cancer. Prejudice is also analagous to neurotic, self-defeating behavior in the individual: Both may have served effectively in the situations in which they originated, but both end by sapping the ego resources of their possessors and of those on whom they are inflicted.

As an ideological instrument, prejudice serves at least two functions. It permits a more powerful group to advance its interests over and against another's, and it maintains the cultural integrity of a group when it is in contact with another. The culture contacts of the white American with the Negro, and of the white South African with the native, for example, exposed certain of the white men's cultural inhibitions to consciousness. The spontaneity and sensuality of preliterate African societies, carried over by the Negro to America, ran counter to the ascetic ideologies of these Northern Europeans. The personal conflicts which may then have occurred in many whites perhaps also made it necessary for them to add further controls over their impulses, by labeling the other group inferior. (Much of this discussion is drawn from Simpson and Yinger.)

Attributions of inferiority and of moral reprehensibility sanction roughshod suppression and exploitation which might otherwise be condemned by the prejudiced person himself. There was an economic basis for antisemitism in medieval Europe; the pogroms, levies, and occupational restrictions against the Jews were aimed as much against them as business competitors as for any other reason. Similarly, discrimination in the South was furthered by competition for work during the Reconstruction between the poor white and the Negro. Rather than turning their class discontent on the economic system, white laborers turned on their class competitors.

The social dogma of the Southern white caste (Davis and Dollard) is highly functional economically. The dogma asserts that Negroes are inherently childish and primitive, that they lie and steal impulsively like children, that they are unable to control their sexual urges, and have no complex social and economic ambitions similar to those of whites. Since they are primitive and childlike, they accept restricted opportunities. Consequently, they feel no pain or deprivation in performing the heaviest, dirtiest work or undergoing the severest discriminations (p. 237).

Simpson and Yinger remark that

> Many studies have shown . . . that a ruling group which has exhibited violent aggression against a racial minority and has exploited it sexually is likely to be firmly convinced that members of the racial minority are uniformly violent and sexually unrestrained (p. 79).

These authors suggest other reasons for this type of projection, beyond the justification it provides for transgression. The dominant group frees itself, through its prejudices, to believe that what it gives, perhaps in the way of government or religion, is much more than what it takes, or that there is at least a fair trade. Thus, nineteenth century colonialists nobly assumed their "white man's burden," slaveholders brought the blessings of Christianity into their slave quarters, and racists today may shout indignantly at demonstrators, "If it's so bad here, go back to Africa!" Similar beliefs, that they deserve worse and are better off being free Americans though destitute, may support middle-class indifference to the poverty and squalor of 45 million fellow citizens.

A second reason is that prejudice begets more prejudice—a collective repetition compulsion that binds over the denied guilt and conscious fears of retaliation to continued projection and aggression. "It is very difficult not to hate someone whom you have harmed," as Simpson and Yinger put it (p. 293). The maintenance of such systems of hostility-projection-degradation is as wasteful of a nation's resources as it is of an individual's talents. German antisemitism may have been an important element in the chauvinism that revitalized that country between the wars, but beyond this immediate gain and gain from the seizure of Jews' property, it served no useful purpose in solving Germany's economic problems. Furthermore, there was the macabre destruction of human and material resources and of industrial inventiveness in genocide. In the South, racial prejudice has, if anything, obstructed steps toward economic development needed since the Reconstruction; the lack of which has sustained the obstruction, in a vicious circle. Simpson and Yinger indicate that antisemitism in France during the Third Republic obscured and confounded the complicated political, social, and economic issues and interests that divided that country then (pp. 306–9).

The individual who is prejudiced dissipates his personal resources in his defensive preoccupations with his scapegoats. The really profoundly prejudiced person is the one with an authoritarian personality. It makes little difference whether he needs his prejudices to hold his personality together, or whether his personality is an adaptation to prejudice, first against authority and then against scapegoats; he is so much opposed to his inner experience and to the richness of outer reality that he is bound to defeat his most promising interpersonal opportunities and his own most creative inclinations.

The target of prejudice may displace his hostility toward the dominant group with counter-prejudices which may become as fixed and embittered as those of the dominant group. Black nationalism, in Garveyism and in its contemporary, the Black Muslim movement, relies on such profound hatred and disparagement of whites. Julia, one of Davis and Dollard's adolescent subjects, belonged to a fighting gang who despised whites; I have known delinquent Negro boys whose antisocial ideology consisted in large part of sadistic and vengeful attitudes toward whites.

I think there is not only this revengist element in the "nonutilitarian" norms of lower-class delinquents, but there may also be a commitment to a negative identity (Erikson, 1959) that actually is a living-out of a polar racial (or minority) stereotype. Julia's father, as he is described in Davis and Dollard, was a sadistic bully who brought his identity in his adult social context into the house with him. His exchanges with his wife and children were largely sadomasochistic; his libidinal characteristics meant being a "free-hearted" male in his own view of himself. His ego integrity seemed to be achieved only at the price of relating his libidinal energies and his ego values to being a "bad nigger." He was deeply alienated from ego values and forms of successful identity that were esteemed in the white caste.

Prejudice is a tool that uses up and finally enslaves its masters, and that confirms the worst in both aggressor and victim.

E. *Cultural Instability*. Cultural instability refers not to any subculture, but to the proliferating character of the dominant culture itself. Leighton makes an arresting comparison between an old farmer who clings forlornly to his old inappropriate ways while a strange new way of life grows up about him, and the plight of the immigrant who stands on the shores of an alien culture. If Leighton observes this much cultural change in the rural areas and small towns of the Stirling County Study during one lifespan, how much more rapid the transition is likely to be in the industrial cities. Bronfenbrenner reviews evidence of important changes in child-rearing methods within social classes, and of reversals of differences in methods between classes within a twenty-five year period. The constant rationalization of roles and the continuing reordering of work and symbolic systems to fit a changing technology (Parsons, 1947; 1962) represent an unceasing adaptive challenge to urban middle and lower classes alike. While Erikson decries "our child-training customs [which] have begun to standardize modern man so that he may become a reliable mechanism prepared to 'adjust' to the competitive exploitation of the machine world" (1959, p. 46), he recognizes elsewhere that, just because socialization must ready the child for the changing culture, this rationalization of child-training customs is a matter of survival.

Linton states culture change as a problem of imbalance between what one is trained to cope with and what one must finally encounter: "(T)he differences between the personality-shaping influences experienced in childhood as contrasted with those experienced in adulthood, as a result of cultural change, can be an appreciably disorganizing factor, as all acculturation studies tend to show (1956, p. 14)." In other words, a dynamic industrial society such as ours may render channels to end-state attainment obsolete before new ones, coordinated with the changed technology, become widely available; the middle-class individual, precisely because he *is* integrated into the dominant culture, may fall victim to this type of deprivation, and to the disorganizing personal consequences which may follow from it. The sacrifice of the familiar in adapting to culture change, as discussed in Chapter 2, is an example.

It is proposed, then, that at least five sociocultural events block access to end-state activity as it is currently defined in a given culture: poverty; cultural inadequacy; cultural assimilation; ostracism and discrimination; and cultural instability. These obstructions prevent an individual, and his group, from living out an adulthood that is valued, and from experiencing the validity of values and beliefs. The institutions that lend direction and offer incentives to integrating capacities and energies are, in effect, withdrawn or, for practical purposes, cease to exist.

In Chapter 2, several kinds of constraints on ego activity, emanating from the social structure, were discussed, as well as certain cultural anachronisms which may also constrict ego functioning. The five sociocultural obstructions discussed above may be related to these constraints in the following ways:

Poverty and prejudice result in the exclusion, the psychosocial distance, and the economic and political dispossession that were said to affect LL's. Assimilation of an ethnic subgroup produces the culture conflict that was attributed to some ULs and LMs. Centralization of authority and work bureaucratization may be attributed to cultural instability. Parsons (1962) describes an unceasing differentiation of work roles as an accompaniment of change in our culture, which would bring about a constant narrowing of areas of competence (bureaucratization); the rationalizing of production processes that he describes in an earlier paper (1947), as well as differentiation of functions, may promote a concentration of decision-making in the hands of a relatively few managers. Technological and culture change are also related to cultural instability, not in the sense of breakdown of function, but rather in the sense of rapid and disorienting change. Subcultural inadequacies are equivalent to the anachronistic traditions discussed earlier. Work subordination and routinization may also be part-functions of cultural instability, again by way of work role differentiations and the rationalization of production; but to some important extent these particular social-structural constraints may not be products of any of the forms of blockage discussed. They may simply be built-in hazards, inherent flaws in our particular social system.

PROPOSITION FIVE

The blocking of approaches to integrative end-states exercises a centrifugal force on cultural and social integration in the group that is obstructed. This is a reworking of Durkheim and Merton's conception that norms which are conduct standards for the individual are also the governing rules for his group, and that repudiation of the standards means also disruption of the group. But here it is also asserted that men sustain their social and cultural relations in order to meet integrative ends, and that the blocking of these ends destroys the incentive for collaboration. This disintegration will be reflected in a diffusion of what is prescribed, preferred, permitted, and proscribed in a state of normative dissensus. The cultural forms and social organizations which were fitted to one economy and polity are often given up in another. So, the European extended family falls apart; craftsmanship and the master-apprentice relation lose their value; informal communal social controls weaken, and so forth.

Gans reviews data regarding the social alienation and the absence of community sentiments and institutions which existed among the peasants and landless laboring castes in southern Italy at the turn of the century, at the time of the great migrations to the United States (pp. 199–204). Great poverty existed among these two lowest castes, a condition which had probably existed for centuries. (This fact is relevant to the possibility that self-limiting personal adaptations to chronic adversity may accrue over generations, a process that is discussed in detail in the next proposition.) People in these castes were traditionally hostile not only to clerics, the government, and the police, but also, within the community itself, treated members of higher castes as aliens and oppressors—which they no doubt were, in significant ways. People from other communities, even if from the same caste, were considered criminals. More specific to this proposition is the traditional distance between family and community in southern Italian society. Gans (p. 203) cites Banfield's concept of "amoral familism" to indicate the near-total estrangement of family sentiments and interests from what might be for the good of a whole village. The resulting distrust of village organization and leadership was of exactly the same kind that Gans observed among his contemporary American "urban villagers"—an anomic and anachronistic subcultural constraint that must have psychosocial correlates and consequences.

Thus also, for example, the Depressed Areas of the Stirling County Study were found to resemble closely the authors' theoretical pole of a "collection," a totally disintegrated community.

> Although these areas are not completely lacking in the functional prerequisites [of a society], they are, by comparison, markedly deficient. The properties of being a system and the "density of interaction" are exceedingly low, and inaction and noncommunication prevail over collaboration and synthesis. There is, moveover, more diversity than consensus among those sentiments which do exist and which bear on system maintenance and group preservation. The tendency is toward isolated behavior and unpredictability. There is a lack of clear goals for striving and a consequent failure in agreement on institutionalized means for their achievement (Hughes, *et al.*, pp. 394–95).

The authors relate this state of disorganization in these communities directly to a lack of political and economic power among the individuals living within them. Such power would be viewed here as an expression of participation in integrating means.

Further evidence for this proposition may be found in the congruence between attitudes prevailing in the Stirling County Depressed Areas and the five subjective indicators of anomie introduced by Srole. The five criteria are: the perception that community leaders are indifferent to one's needs; that little can be accomplished in a society seen as basically unpredictable and lacking order; that life-goals are receding rather than being realized; a sense of futility; and the conviction that one cannot count on personal associates for support. Both the antecedent and the consequent of this fifth proposition are conveyed in Depressed Area attitudes. The first and third of these indicators, indifferent community leaders and receding life-goals, would reflect withdrawal of access; while the other three would express social and cultural disintegration among disadvantaged individuals (see Hughes, *et al.*, p. 400).

It is pertinent also to recall the conditions which Kardiner and Linton lay down for the emergence of hostility as a common response in a culture. Hostility, they say, is generated by (1) a shifting economy, with no sense of control over its change, with no dependability on skill and hardiness, and in which a record of achievement may become meaningless; (2) a social organization with low mutual responsibility and helping; and (3) the lack of reward for self-control. While it has not been asserted here that hostility is the sole or inevitable consequence of the thwarting of integrative activity, it may be assumed that in a culture where hostility is common there may often be an accompanying disruption of social and cultural forms. These three sources of hostility may well be taken as accompaniments of blocked access.

The state of affairs that eventuated among the Dakota Sioux, after their subjugation, very closely matches all three of the conditions for the emergence of general intra-cultural hostility that Kardiner and Linton set down, and resulted in the social disorganization proposed here as a consequence of end-state blockage. The Dakota Sioux lost three different economies in the space of four or five generations; the whites exploited their lands and destroyed their economic independence. Dakota self-control and cooperation was based on a system of very tightly knit external controls. Indian custom and authority was suppressed by enforced education of their children in white schools, and culminated in the forbidding of their annual Sun Dance festival, which symbolized, MacGregor, *et al.*, say, the destruction of Dakota culture. The result was social disorganization, in terms of numerous cleavages within the group, and a common aggressive adaptation toward others and self.

Other studies of what happened to aboriginal Indian cultures when they underwent contact with representatives of white culture also bear out the relation between loss of indigenous approaches to end-state activity and social disorganization. Indian leaders lost the confidence and the respect of their people when they were subjected to white authority. "They felt themselves to be in a cultural vacuum *without incentives and objectives*" (Simpson and Yinger, p. 208; my italics). Faith in the native religions was lost before Christianity was imposed, "with resulting personal and social disorganization." It is most interesting that there seemed to be a correlation between their loss of an integrated values system and the emergence of brutality: the Iroquois League tribes were much less warlike before the whites attacked them. "Then the decline of cultural cohesion expressed itself in increased personal aggressiveness and organized violence" (*ibid.*, p. 208).

The point of this proposition is that a group which is barred from normative access to cultural ends, their own and other, does not just find new, deviant means and/or define new goals, as Merton's treatment of anomie indicates. First the group undergoes a period of dissolution, which seems to arise from a sense that their values and beliefs are unraveling and from the accompanying disorientation and ego insecurity. Anomie, at least initially, is not simply a search for new solutions but is also a disordered reaction to the threat of cultural (or subcultural) extinction and a fear of personal extinction.

PROPOSITION SIX

People who are socioculturally blocked and confronted with integrative failure cast about, in their ego insecurity, for ways of transacting reliably with their depriving circumstances. They define the meaning of the disadvantages imposed on them and they organize modal responses to these disadvantages; they negotiate institutionalized relations between themselves and their depriving realities, and with each other. In these relations, they salvage and modify integrative activity within the limits imposed on them; they also establish, as modal responses, ego operations which are based on the absence of their integration into a viable culture (with its integrative channels), but which are nevertheless adaptive. Some of these ego adaptations pertain to their relations with those who are "in," those more advantaged people who keep them "out"; the ego defines disadvantage in terms of a losing personal struggle.

Indigenous integrative channels are no longer functional when a disadvantaged group withdraws from them, because they require collective adherence for validity. For example, an old-style patriarch needs respectful obedience to validate his style of life. If his children defect, so to speak, to the autonomous values of our culture, as most did during the last several generations of our history, the patriarch is bereft and set adrift. His identity, many of his opportunities for intimacy, the achievement of generativity through the new generation, and the integrity of the values by which he has oriented himself—almost all of his integrating experiences, as Erikson defines them—are violated.

When men cannot live their potentiality as human beings, they become what their environments demand—beasts of burden, predators, wanderers. The more the environment constricts, and the less meaning a man can attach to ritual, hierarchy, faith and communion, both sacred and secular, to husbanding, cherishing, invention, and adornment, the likelier it is that men will be driven to state issues of survival and mastery in new terms. The old culture and forms of socialization are undone, and individuals in a suppressed subculture strive to possess, to surrender themselves, to rebel, dominate, destroy. They assume these relations not only toward one another, but also toward those representatives of the dominant culture who control and bar access to integrity—priest, boss, teacher, official, cop. (In this we may see another clue to the riddle which Cohen and Miller pose for us: How can a lower-class subculture be, at one and the same time, in opposition and in conformity? Its members conform to a value system that evolved to convey their deprived and alienated relationships to a society that has degraded them. They live, as Yinger puts it, in a contraculture.)

Erikson indicates that the deepest personal energies are put at the disposal of the goals and values of a culture, principally through its child-training system (1950, p. 121). Basic personality traits are made in the image of ideology; a person lives out his culture's conception of being, at all levels and in all systems of his personality. Erikson gives two examples of how ego- and superego-values are assimilated to cultural values and beliefs. Among the Dakota Sioux, the self-torture of the Sun Dance was atonement for a sense of sin, an expiation and a salvation through suffering for the "badness" surviving from a crisis of trust, resulting from the Sioux mother's socialization of her infant's orality. The atoners in the Sun Dance symbolically destroyed themselves in order to achieve a mystic reunion with the tribe, as did the tribe vicariously, one supposes, through watching them.

Yurok mothers knew it was "bad" for their babies to have complete oral gratification; their men had to yearn to catch fish. It was bad for the man to be too readily or quickly satisfied with the size of his catch. He had to supplicate the food-sending powers; he could not be too eager; he had to concentrate fervently. In short, Yurok culture made use of an oral puritanism and dedication to dramatize a nostalgic need for intake. It emphasized, in libidinal and ego terms, the ugliness of lack of restraint in acquiring food.

So too, it is proposed, members of a disadvantaged subculture experience their oppression and deprivation as defeats in their egos. They reorient their libidinal and limited ego energies by resisting, exerting counterpressures against, and subordinating themselves to their environment. The ideologies of their subculture bracket the range of life-styles and activities within which individuals may maintain security and satisfaction. Perhaps through the process of regression in the service of the ego, as suggested in Chapter 3—through the intuition of similarities between libidinal and ego issues and the particular social and cultural constraints imposed on them—they adapt personality to restriction, and adopt an ideology to suit both.

References to Plant's concept of personality "hardening," a process in which an extremely harsh environment, whether physical or psychosocial, reduces affective sensitivity and brutalizes its victim, are scattered through the literature. Seward, for example, reviews Frazier's observation that the lower-class Negro male, for whom existence is bitter and hostile, learns to fight, cut, and shoot as "manly arts" (Seward, 1956, p. 122). Honigmann (1954) discusses the brutalizing, isolating nature of the Tepoztlan farmer's work, resulting in a grim individualism and a reluctance to receive or give help.

These references to hardening suggest a withering of collaborative ego skills, and the centering of object relations on traits of stubbornness, irascibility, implacability, and suspicion. We might assume that hardening occurs when the environment, whether physically inhospitable or socially alienated, stands in the stead of the parent whose mismanagement of his child's maturation obstructs the satisfactory resolution of a given level of development.

The importance of such a process may be overlooked, because it is precisely these kinds of personalities that one would expect to raise disturbed children. They would engage their children destructively at their own levels of ego failure and fixation; they would provide the child with an oppressive conscience and an aggressive and intimidated ego. In a psychosocial sense, these personalities would be incapable of welcoming the child into an identity formation which would promise him continuing fulfillment.

The need for a psychological rendering of the hardened personality is great in delinquency theory. Here we must take into account the effects of adult criminal models on the young in certain urban areas. That criminal models, "rackets," and high delinquency rates are associated in some inner-city areas has been the basis for one of the oldest environmental explanations of delinquency, traceable in a direct line through the writings of Shaw and McKay, Sutherland, and Cloward and Ohlin.

According to opportunity theory, a youth aspiring to adult criminal status goes through role preparations such as petty theft and need not be psychologically different from an adolescent aspiring to a law career who practices status mobility in the Boy Scouts and develops verbal skills in high school debating.

Yet one feels intuitively that something is missed in this version of the adult criminal model. It is difficult not to speculate about the considerable personality modification needed to fit a narcotics dealer or pusher for doing business with his customers; or about the pimp who may have very special sentiments and motives regarding his stable of girls and the men who patronize them; or the burglars, pickpockets, "fences," and cliques of robbers who may be more profoundly alienated from and exploitative toward their fellow men than other, legitimate artisans; or big-time gamblers and policy men, who may share ideologies regarding human nature which are full of disparagement for others and self-centered striving.

It is hard to believe that some of these men are not hardened personalities, and that their presence and activities do not constitute a brutalizing view of male adult identity for youths exposed to them. Perhaps psychiatry might find no notable incidence of symptoms or diagnoses among them, but a systematic psychology of the successful criminal might teach us much regarding cultural patterning of delinquent personalities.

Hardening may occur through regression in the service of the ego. The peasant who struggles grimly with an impoverished earth may see it as starving him, or withholding or demanding from him. In the interest of achieving a sense of masterful and effective exchange with his environment, he may mobilize not only knowledge and learning abilities, but also old introjects and fantasies from object relations earlier in his life. Examples from clinical literature of this type of ego adaptation may be cited. For example, the very young child who adapts to enforced, repeated use of an enema in a toilet struggle may be assimilating the pleasures of passivity and penetration of an opening (Silverberg, p. 138). Similarly, the adolescent girl confronted with the shock of menstruation may include in her attempt to master the physical and emotional sensations, elements of her earlier struggles with sphincter control (Kaufman, Makkay, and Zilbach, p. 131).

Assuming that our hardened peasant was subjected to an unremittingly cruel soil and sky since infancy, we might, without invoking cultural transmission processes, expect him to "redintegrate," to use the old word, any experience he has had in coping with conflict, including experience from socialization conflicts. After all, withholding submission from that which demands, or attacking that which denies succor, might be the very elements of his infantile and childhood experience which most precisely and profoundly define the relation between his land and himself.

Ego theory (Erikson) suggests that once the individual's self-definition forms about meanings that provide the most reliable interpretations of reality, that identity and those interpretations are likely to endure in his lifetime. These aspects of object relations may be transmitted by socialization of the young. Through them the deprived parent prepares the child, as best he understands, for the burdens of being deprived.

The same process of hardening may be applicable to the family aspects of culture conflict. Handlin indicates that dissension ripped immigrant peasant families when they discovered that the family as a collective economic unit was obsolete in industrial America. This familial strife was augmented by the absence of the peasant village as a sanctioning agent to control both children and parents. He also points out that, to the immigrants' children, the whole complex of tradition based on parental and patriarchal obedience was experienced as an obstruction to the new American ways. Handlin captures the many unrelenting contests that must have taken place in quoting what was apparently an adage of the time: "*So it is now, a brother stabs his brother, a sister drowns her sister, for profit's sake.*"

A hardening process may have occurred here, in the brutalizing effects of guilt, and in the parents' curse. Children repudiated the identities of their parents, and the parents repudiated their children as aliens. A consciousness of self in transition was instituted in the children that was hostile to what went before, to the heritage of identity belonging to the minority group. Erikson makes a similar observation when he notes that "Such excessive contempt for their background occurs among the oldest Anglo-Saxon and the newest Latin or Jewish families" (1959, p. 129). Many sons and daughters, it is suggested, caught between shaping a view of life that would serve themselves, and their parents' need to regenerate themselves in their children, may have reexperienced, with great intensity, old struggles of love, control, and rivalry. Bereft of a bridge to the past, and seeking a purchase on their alien present and future, these children may have reverted to modes of relating when they felt estranged from or threatened by their socializers. They may have reidentified themselves as the one who needs more, or the one who must retain power, or the one who must possess in the service of allaying guilt from the condemnation of abandoned parents.

It would be difficult to believe that such inner and outer discord as is suggested could have been prompted and fixed in children of stable, loving parents. It is tempting to cite evidence that adult immigrants underwent great external stress, but the facts of dislocation would not solve a problem of psychological analysis. *The erosion of the accumulated characterologic achievement of generations* need not have been so dramatic nor so abrupt.

In fact, we have good reason to believe that the conditions for family struggle may have continued unabated over generations among European peasants. Handlin indicates that population increase and refusal to relinquish improvident agricultural practices combined to produce an almost impossible survival situation for two hundred years in peasant Europe. Families were wracked with terrible conflict between the old and the young, and between younger and older brother, for control of the land. The victims of dispossession and depletion of extended family and community, and finally of famine, yielded up their land, only after generations of slow defeat, and, it is suggested, charactero-logic erosion.

Erikson's speculations on the history and the psychology of the Russian people, based on his analysis of Maxim Gorky's life (1950), illustrate many hardened adaptations. The sadomaso-chistic bonds between peasant father and son mirrored the re-lationship between feudal tyrants and Russian serfs. The peasant also felt a maternal bond between his earth and himself and identified with his long-suffering and submissive women. (Fromm also describes matriarchy in terms of ties to incest, blood and soil, and suggests that matriarchy is a form of anachronistic enslavement surviving from medieval Europe in modern totali-tarianisms.) Infantilized submission and brutalized mastery, Erik-son suggests, were "temptations of the Russian soul" that Gorky abjured in his identity formation. Delinquents from deprived subcultures may also try to eject the incubuses of their "native souls" by repudiating legitimate ideologies, as suggested in Chap-ter 3—most often far less successfully than Gorky.

The dramatic strife of family culture conflict witnessed by American sociologists (a generation ago they viewed it as the cli-max to which delinquency was the denouement) was the de-nouement to crisis recreated for perhaps ten generations between brutalized parents and hardening children. The constriction of character structure certainly may not have been uniform, and the degree may have varied enormously. The rapid mobility and the acquisition of relatively successful and secure life-patterns on the part of the bulk of immigrants' children may attest to this variation. On the other hand, the appreciable number of deviance-breeding, multiproblem families of "left-over ethnics" in our inner-city areas may be evidence of the extent of char-acter erosion that many immigrant parents bequeathed to their children. Hollingshead indicates that a transmission of character defect is the cardinal factor in the school drop-outs of Elmtown's lower-class youth.

> Tentatively, we believe that the *significantly poorer family heritage* . . . among the out-of-school Class IV youth gives rise to their poorer adjustment to the demands of the school. . . . Moreover, we are con-vinced that this pattern has been handed down in many cases *from grandparents to the parents*, and on to the adolescents' generation. We

shall go one step further and say the adolescents may be expected to transmit this to their children through the subtle processes of social learning in the family and the community (p. 337; my italics).

The Stirling County study of sociocultural factors and mental illness reports similar observations of generational transmission within its Depressed Areas (Hughes, *et al.;* see also Fisher and Mendell on the transmission of the same neurotic patterns within families over two and three generations).

It is thus suggested that, in the case of the European peasant, widespread impoverishment did harm to his indigenous integrating institutions: seasonal migration in search of work weakened village solidarity and family cohesiveness; parents fought their children instead of fostering them; the children discarded parents instead of cherishing them; the land was too grudging to give a man a sense of mastery no matter how hard he worked; the plight of family and self was too desperate to afford a proud or secure identity or a basis of justification for life. Behind the impoverishment lay the peasant's inability to alleviate his poverty, or to seek whatever other integrating means may have existed in the wider society: he was, for example, ineligible by caste to acquire the power to increase his resources or his education. There were no culturally valid means at hand to integrate a specifically human maturity. His realities pressed in on him in a constant threat to survival, and I suggest that he made a cumulative series of small adaptations, drawn from the struggles of his own development, which fitted him to be The Man with the Hoe, the tyrannical father, the ruthless son, the hungry wanderer.

Kardiner and Linton make much the same assertions when they indicate that frustration of needs in the developed personality will lead to regression to dependency states; chronic frustration of needs will produce certain stable effects on thinking processes (pp. 419–35). When the "world seems to withdraw its hospitality," the functions by which accommodations are effected become inhibited and are no longer at the individual's disposal, as in the case of traumatic war neuroses (p. 436). Thus Kardiner and Ovesey find a dullness in cognitive functions among their Negro subjects, a loss in capacity to make precise distinctions among stimuli, both in interview and Rorschach data. These subjects live in a society to which they are often denied access on the grounds of inherent stupidity.

Seward argues similarly when she cites Hallowell's studies of the Ojibwa Indian tribe; the Berens River branch displayed a regressed form of the Flambeau ego, because of the loss of their indigenous belief system resulting from the incursions of white men (Seward, 1956, pp. 16–19). Ego deterioration may be seen in studies, reviewed by Seward, of the incidence of psychosis, reactive depression, and paranoid states occurring among displaced persons and immigrants as a function of insecurity and lack of linguistic and other skills (1956, p. 216). It is interesting also that Opler reports that first admissions of mostly native-born German, Irish, Italian, and Puerto Rican minority groups to public psychiatric facilities had risen 28 percent since 1940. One may infer from this fact that surrender of ego strength may go on over generations.

I mention again the fact that in the lower class, where several sources of inaccessibility apply, the higher incidence of relatively grave mental illness, found by Hollingshead and Redlich and Langner and Michael, has been confirmed by studies in other cities, as Miller and Swanson indicate (p. 46). The latter two authors hypothesize two families of defense mechanisms, on the basis of Anna Freud's work, one developmentally more primitive and the other emerging at a higher level of personal development. Mechanisms of denial, of obliteration of objective events, and of substitution of more tolerable fantasies allow for gross distortions in reality assessments and create social difficulties; these responses are available shortly after birth and are applicable to most kinds of conflict. Defensive acts, on the other hand, involving reversal or displacement of objects, acts, affects, and agents, require complex skills; each is applicable only to certain kinds of conflict, results in minimal distortion of actual events, and is usually of a type which avoids social difficulty. Miller and Swanson theorize that the first, more primitive mechanisms of denial will occur more frequently in the lower class, and the second more frequently in the middle class. They speculate that in the lower class early and prolonged harshness, lack of reward, and pain are more likely. These experiences would fixate the use of denial mechanisms as they became available to the individual; furthermore, denial might be especially effective in relieving such traumata. Miller and Swanson's findings regarding class differences in the employment of denial mechanisms were negative, but their samples did not include children from broken homes, where one might expect the most severe early experiences to occur. Thus, their hypotheses have not been fully tested.

A variety of data supports the assertion that suppressed subgroups establish infantilized, "regressed" relations with representatives of the dominant culture. Ruesch, on the basis of studies conducted at the Langley Porter Clinic, concludes that

> class membership as such seems to be related to disease. . . . In the lower class, where expression of anger is permitted, and where nonconformance and rebellion are sanctioned by the class ideals, there exist other means of expressing conflict. Therefore, we are not amazed to see that the diseases of the lower classes are connected with exposure to machines and expressions of hostility as found in the incidence of fractures, accidents and traumatic disease. . . . the lower class culture favors conduct disorders and rebellion (pp. 130–31).

Ruesch's point is that in the lower class, where almost all suppressed subcultures may be located, some injuries sustained in relation to the industrial order, as an aspect of the dominant culture, are symptomatic of conduct disorders and rebellion, terms which may cover a multitude of regressed object relationships.

Frazier (1940) describes the manipulative and exploitative servility of some lower-class Negroes toward whites, and contrasts this with the attitudes of some of the same Negroes' parents who consciously mean to be servile, who demean themselves in accommodating to white supremacy. Kardiner and Ovesey describe similar supine positions and reaction-formations against them, adopted by their Negro subjects towards whites, which may be related to narcissistic injury and to dependency feelings. Karon makes thirty-three comparisons between correlated samples of northern and southern Negroes on responses to a projective personality test measuring variables related to aggression, emotionality, work motivation, and feelings of masculinity. He obtains evidence striking in its uniformity regarding higher levels of disturbance in all these dimensions among southern Negroes. Although he does not explicitly examine the matter of white-Negro relations (see Burton's reservations, 1959, regarding Karon's study), his data clearly indicate the deteriorative effect that cultural suppression may have on personality. One may presume, furthermore, that defects in these traits would show themselves in relations with the representatives of the culture which initiated the deterioration. Finally, no better illustration of individual regression and social disintegration under persecution may be found than those in Bettelheim's classic account of experience in those laboratories of psychological destruction, the Nazi concentration camps. Not only was there the regression into infantile behavior which Bettelheim describes, but the accommodation with the aggressors, including identification with their cruelty.

PROPOSITION SEVEN

Parents who have cramped themselves into a system of social and cultural disadvantages regarding access to end-state activity will deal with their children's strivings as they have dealt with their own. Parents may define their children's strivings as rebellion, intrusion, competition, withholding and rejection; the children's responses to these definitions, although varying, will generally resemble those made to an adversary. Thus, it is suggested, only the personally limited (and discontented) parent will behave like the repressive socialization agent of Freudian theory to set himself against his child's "instincts." The character changes resulting from regressive socialization will be present in the organization of personality, family, and larger group. Family and social institutions that emerge in these circumstances will operate semi-independently to obstruct full growth in ego capacity and access to integrative activity. Some of these normative arrangements are destructive child-training practices that overstimulate, deprive, or threaten stages of development; defective sex-role models in the person of the parents; discontinuities and other forms of systemlessness among the family and other social institutions of a class or ethnic subculture; hardening role sequences which capitalize on asocial traits fixed in childhood socialization and process them toward criminality and other forms of adolescent and adult deviance. Further psychological shifts in the socializers accompany their continuing sociocultural responses to environmental strains, and further changes in institutions result in part from the character formation that they introduce in the young, all operating in a spiralling, interdetermining process. Delinquency, as well as psychiatric disorder and other kinds of deviance, results partly from conditions of inner strain induced by these adaptations. As Kerr remarks regarding the people of Ship Street, delinquency is "merely one symptom of a much more fundamental personal and social disorganization. This group is not sick but socially immature" (p. 124). As stated, the spiralling process may be viewed from three vantage points—personal, familial, and sociocultural.

A. *Personal.* The literature on American Negro personality may be taken as representative of self-defeating character formation in suppressed subcultures (Dai, Kardiner and Ovesey, Karon, Rohrer and Edmonson). The extensive description of character limitations found among the "Depressed Areas" in the Stirling County Study of sociocultural conditions and mental illness is probably among the best available material on hardened personality in submerged population segments.

> The essential striving sentiments [of adults in the Depressed Areas] of giving and receiving love are not only malformed but are intercepted by other sentiments of hostility, suspicion, the enjoyment of aggression, and the fear of attack. . . . This lack of affection is, we think, an almost inevitable concomitant of the lack of communication, of association, of leadership, of followership, of family stability, and the other related deficiencies in socio-cultural patterning. It goes, in short, with systemlessness. . . . Inconsistency in loving is, of course, not the only kind of erratic behavior displayed. Adults with whom the child has contact are undependable in almost all dimensions. . . . Such a chaotic social environment offers few patterns as models for the development of consistent and stable sentiments in the child's personality. These behaviors are also the experience of the adult in relation to his fellows. Impulsiveness and lack of dependability characterize interpersonal relations, and this cuts deeply into the possibility of functional stability for all the essential striving sentiments (Hughes, *et al.*, pp. 412–13).

B. *Familial.* The socialization practices in these Depressed Areas (Hughes, *et al.*, pp. 281–95) provide a detailed picture of destructive family experience, from infancy on, in a suppressed subculture. The following data are selected from a wealth of similar information: Only about 35 percent of the families have average or better family integration; infancy experience includes late and abrupt weaning with a severe reaction common among the children; cold mothers, absent fathers, neglect, and long and severe toilet training; childhood experience includes low sex-role differentiation, positively rewarded dependency behavior, physical punishment, and cold fathering.

Rohrer and Edmonson discuss the autocracy of lower-class Negro matriarchs and the infantile demands they make on their children. Miller as well as the last two mentioned co-authors represent the male adult in the most marginal groups as ineffectual and scorned by children as well as wife—a poor role model by all standards. Rohrer and Edmonson, as well as Frazier (1937), report the increasing stability of the Negro family and the growth in effectiveness of the adult male at higher, more advantaged socioeconomic levels. Other studies have already been cited, by Davis, Cavan, and Frazier (1940), of the atmosphere of conflict and assaultiveness that exists in some Negro and other lower class families. In a later paper (1950), Frazier specifically discusses the impact of disorganization in Negro LL family life on the children and youth involved. He stresses particularly the absence, or destruction, of personal values that would orient the young toward collaboration. There are an absence of family traditions; an absence of consistency and even of sense in the parents' lives; maternal rejection and lax, spasmodic discipline; and, a lack of family living which might provide a reality of "fellowship, communion [and] ceremony" (p. 274).

Hollingshead was quoted earlier on limitations transmitted over generations in some lower-class families. Two other pieces of data support the continuation of psychosocial adaptations over generations within families. A study utilizing projective techniques as well as psychiatric interviews found the same core conflict and levels of fixation showing up in two and three generations of a family (Fisher and Mendell). The other evidence is the finding by Rohrer and Edmonson that membership in the types of subculture which they observed among New Orleans Negroes is maintained over generations. They distinguish among subcultures on the basis of differences in values and relationships, both inside and outside the family, to which the members of the respective subculture adhere. These authors found only two cases of marked shift in subcultural membership in two-and-one-half generations of subjects; they see an association between the present position of the individual and consistent patterns of family experience which are traceable to the preceding and the following generations. They further assert that this relationship is not explainable by "a vague cultural determinancy," but must be explained by particular kinds of identity formations arising from distinctive childhood experiences (p. 85).

These authors plotted each of their subjects on a scattergram, with number of years spent with father and with mother respectively as the coordinates. The respective subcultures were so closely clustered that I became interested in a statistical measure of the relation between this gross index of child-parent interaction and subcultural membership. I performed a nonparametric analysis of variance among the five subcultures on the proportion of time each subject spent with father as compared with mother. The results approached the .05 level of statistical significance; as might have been expected, subjects who had spent less of their childhood with father than with mother found their way as adults into the matriarchal and gang subculture, while those who had had relatively more time with father became members of the middle-class subculture, with its stronger family relationships and greater male effectiveness. In an informal communication, Rohrer indicated his confidence that, were the same measure computed for other study subjects not included in the published analysis, the statistical test would yield highly significant results. When one considers the gross nature of the socialization variable utilized in this test, the myriad other influences to which a growing child is exposed, and the alternatives laid open during the adolescent identity crisis, this tentative finding would seem to be an impressive reminder of the important bearing that early family experience has on the ultimate psychocultural fate of the adult.

There are theoretical reasons to assume that the mother-based household, prevalent in the lower class, is itself a limiting sociocultural factor in personality development. In Parsons and Bales' model of family socialization, a basic differentiation within personality that occurs in early childhood is that between the instrumental and the expressive functions, those of negotiations with the environment and of tension reduction within the family unit, which the child in the nuclear family internalizes from the role models and interactions of his parents. It seems reasonable to infer that the son in a mother-based household is handicapped in his preparation for a sex role which obliges him to be primarily responsible for adapting to the outside environment, since this function is less differentiated in his mother's role. Indeed, the instrumental aspect of his mother's functioning consists fairly commonly of maintaining an indigent relation to the larger society, for example, as a recipient of welfare payments. Further, if one pushes beyond the usual concept of "feminine identification" to what *kind* of feminine personality the lower-class boy may be identifying with, one may find reason to believe, in view of the psychocultural considerations raised, that there is a greater likelihood that these mothers will be indulgent, violent, and selfish in dealings with their children. One would expect fixations and intimidations to further personality development to follow from these circumstances.

C. *Sociocultural.* Residents of the Stirling County Depressed Areas held these views toward self and others:

> People here are mentally and morally inferior; it is good to be with people, but you have to watch your step; people are changeable and shifty, and you have to stand by yourself in life; people in authority should not be trusted, but you have to show them respect to their faces; defying authority is a good way to gain prestige . . . self-improvement is practically impossible; work should be avoided if possible . . . the best thing to do in life is escape from your problems as quickly as possible; new things should be looked at with considerable suspicion (Hughes, *et al.*, pp. 295–309).

Hollingshead also describes much the same profound sense of defeat, fatalism, and social alienation among the lower classes in Elmtown. (References have already been made to other studies indicating the same alienation within disadvantaged groups, such as Cohen and Hodges' and Langner and Michael's.)

It is proposed that these subcultural conditions obstruct the development of competence necessary to surmount the crises of psychosexual development and to guarantee psychosocial achievement. A process of psychocultural involution is proposed here; in its advanced stages, the normative state will be one of conflict, and the role structure one of discontinuities; the subculture will have crystallized norms governing the behavior of the peer groups, and role sequences preparatory to adulthood, which clearly compete with the norms of the dominant culture and perhaps with some of the norms of the family as well.

PROPOSITION EIGHT

Every subculturally definable group in our society may generate a degree of anomie, depending on the kind and the extent of its access to culturally defined means of attaining integrative end-states. Parental adaptations to these limitations may generate personal immaturity; normative inconsistencies, as well as normatively-based group conflicts (within a subculture), may interfere further with the consolidation of ego strengths. The anomie prevailing in a subculture may allow the emergence of deviant behavior in youth who are predisposed to it (by ego limitations and externalizing); where the anomie includes competing illegitimate norms, it facilitates the emergence of delinquency among such youths. The anomie not only triggers the release of self-discontent in deviant behavior, but the subcultural limits to securing satisfaction as an adult, which generated the anomie and which are encountered by the child at adolescence, may trigger delinquency as a form of social protest.

This proposition has been entered in order to reconcile the historical-psychological processes preceding it with the emergence of subcultural delinquency as described in Chapter 3. Observations by Bloch and Niederhoffer and by Gans tend to support the idea that delinquency is a form of social protest.

Bloch and Niederhoffer comment that a subordinate group, in this case delinquent youth, can invert the power relation between itself and a dominant group (adults, especially middle-class adults) by controlling the actions of the dominant group, or at least by forcing it to act. Adults need to maintain their status, such as that based on middle-class respectability; challenges to their status, in the form of defiance of their norms, necessitate counter-action. Delinquents are therefore serious enough challengers of adult status to require the respectful attentions of police and other caretakers. These authors also suggest that delinquency is a rejection of what they take to be certain bankrupt aspects of adult conformity, such as the monotony of suburbia (p. 70). I think there are serious defects in their choice of presumed targets for delinquent rebellion, rather than in their argument: It is hard to link up limitations in middle-class adult life-styles with the identity problems of lower-class youth; and other general evaluations of our society (notably Parsons, 1962) do not conclude that our social system is interfering with the personal satisfactions of all adults in it, as Bloch and Niederhoffer and Goodman suggest, but that it is fulfilling its basic cultural imperatives rather well. I do believe, however, that delinquency is directed against threats to the actor's prospective adult integrity, but these are threats which, in this theory, arise *within* the actor's subculture.

Gans' male urban villagers nostalgically relived their moments of adolescent "action" (which may have involved some delinquent acts) in their social get-togethers. Adolescence was remembered as a period of control over one's drives and over the world, "when (a boy) could make things happen. . . . The stories reinforce the belief that one can fight back, outsmart, and even defeat the outside world" (pp. 87–88). The implication is clear, it seems to me, that a part of the satisfaction in this "action" lay in the sense of defiance and conquest of certain restricting realities, the nature of which Gans' subjects did not spell out for him.

part four

paradigms

The following four chapters are illustrative descriptions of psychocultural processes which may lead to delinquency. I believe that they are currently in operation, and that each process is producing young norm-violators who are neither "sociological" nor "psychological" delinquents. They are "normal" in their respective subcultures. They may even evince psychiatric symptoms to lesser degrees than some of their conforming (but self-discontented) peers. The latter may be symbolizers while the delinquents may be externalizers.

These processes are applications of the psychocultural theory in this book. Each process is introduced by a consideration of a particular set of sociocultural constraints operating at one of four social class levels—LL, UL, LM, or UM. Personality adaptations of some people to the set of constraints affecting their class subculture are indicated. Family relationships and childhood experiences which follow from these adaptations are then considered. The effects of these relationships and experiences on prospective delinquents are also discussed. These personalized consequences are then carried through to descriptions of four different kinds of identity crises, each crisis accompanied by different reasons for delinquency—differing pressures, that is, to deviance.

The reader will bear in mind that the title of this section, "Paradigms," means just what it says; these are models or examples. These four processes are not the only four delinquency-producing sequences operating in our society, nor are there any pretensions to offering a comprehensive typology of delinquency. I am trying to show that any *specific* sequence of strategic determinants in delinquency is at once more complex and more coherent than our present, disparate scientific approaches to this problem seem to suggest.

Because each is a *psychocultural* process, each is neither fish nor fowl. The following descriptions may strike some, perhaps, as marriages of oversimplified sociology with overextended clinical generalizations. That may well be. But if these case illustrations show how plausible it is that the personalities of delinquents may fit their places in history and society, then they will have served their purpose.

chapter 10

process I

*T*HE ostracism and the degradation of LL Negroes, in slave and caste society, have imposed profound ego failures on them. The LL Negro matriarch may attach her sons and daughters to herself by fixating their needs and weakening their ego autonomy, because of her distrust of social reality and her fear of being isolated. The fear of youth raised in this setting to exercise independence and initiative, and a deep conviction that one must submit to another's will, may be seen in their interest in certain kinds of homosexuality.

They disbelieve in relatedness between separate individuals, and they strive for psychologically quite primitive and narcissistic interpersonal arrangements. They wish to have sole power over all people and things important to them; this is their pressure toward deviance.

The Process I adolescent experiences a great diffusion of time perspective; he has only, or primarily, illegitimate ideologies around which to form his identity; he assumes a self-certainty that is based more on fantasies of omnipotence than on resources for negotiating his satisfactions with others. He is also capable of experiencing enormous insecurity as a result of projecting this omnipotence. Sometimes, these projections provoke delinquent acting-out; at other times, they may precipitate psychosis. This boy rarely escapes the miserable psychosocial heritage to which he is heir.

Destruction of Integrity in the Negro

The suppressed Negro subculture is an apt example of factors determining the emergence of a very severe adolescent crisis. Great segments of the Negro population have been sunk in cultural degradation and ostracism for three hundred years. The suppression and exploitation of this group was probably nowhere matched in Europe, except perhaps among the Russian serfs, who were emancipated in the same decade as the American Negro. Emancipation of the Negro has meant, as Kardiner and Ovesey and others point out, exposure to general cultural criteria of human worth, but with accompanying denial of means to arrive at culturally defined forms of dignity.

The productivity of the Negro belonged to another, and this fact, in terms of theoretical proposals advanced earlier, would require specialized personality adaptations to his work role in slave and caste society. Kardiner and Ovesey detailed the adaptation of self-rejection and depression from identifying with figures he both loved and hated. There were institutionalized interferences with sexual mutuality of a kind that has probably not existed in as extreme a form since the exercise of seignieurial rights in European feudal society. Male slaves were allowed to breed but not to form durable relationships with their women, and white men usurped the sexual favors of Negro women. Since this was (and may still be, to some extent) one of the few avenues to goods and status for the Negro woman and her children, she was given added reason to reject the Negro male's claim on her. It has been suggested that the white usurper thus reinstated and transposed to his culture his Oedipal drama: As the interloper between the woman and her rightful mate, he projected his guilt in a stereotype of Negro hypersexuality and sensuality. We are not dealing here with a purely historical aspect of role patterning. Karon has observed that the clearest prescriptions and proscriptions of current race etiquette, backed by the most powerful sanctions, particularly in the South but in the North as well, pertain to cross-sex relations between the races, and specifically to white male privilege and Negro male taboos.

Some of the personal consequences of exploitation of an outcaste by a dominant caste are eloquently expressed by Erikson:

> Consider our colored countrymen. Their babies often receive sensual satisfaction of oral and sensory surplus, adequate for a lifetime. It is preserved in the way in which they move, laugh, talk, think. Their forced symbiosis with the feudal South capitalized on this oral-sensory treasure to build up a slave's identity: mild, submissive, dependent, somewhat querulous, but always ready to serve, and with occasional empathy and childlike wisdom. But underneath a dangerous split occurred. The humiliating symbiosis on the one hand and, on the other, the necessity of the master race to protect its identity against sensual and oral temptation established in both groups an association: light-clean-clever-white, and dark-dirty-dumb-nigger. The result, especially in those Negroes who have left the poor haven of their Southern homes, is often a violently sudden and cruel cleanliness training. This, in turn, transmits itself to the phallic-locomotor stage in which the restrictions as to what shade of girl one may dream of and where one may move and act with abandon interfere at every moment of waking and dreaming with the free transfer of the original narcissistic sensuality to the genital sphere. Three identities are formed: (1) mammy's oral-sensual "honeychild": tender, expressive, rhythmical; (2) the clean anal-compulsive, restrained, friendly, but always sad "white man's Negro"; and (3) the evil identity of the dirty, anal-sadistic, phallic-rapist "nigger."
>
> When faced with so-called opportunities which only offer a newly restricted freedom but fail to provide an integration of the identity fragments mentioned, one of these fragments becomes dominant in the form of a racial caricature; tired of this caricature, the colored individual often retires into hypochondriac invalidism as a condition which represents an analogy to the ego-space-time of defined restriction in the South: a neurotic regression to the ego identity of the slave (1959, pp. 37–38).

The problem is not one of establishing a relation between subcultural adversity and personal disorder: The only three Negroes in the Kardiner-Ovesey sample who were characterized as stable or effectively "normal" were all born in the North. The Northern-born Negroes' maladjustments are described by the authors as displaying the same kind of neurotic problems as those of neurotic whites. Karon found too that Northern Negroes differ from Southern Negroes in precisely the same characteristics and in the same way as do Northern whites. Perhaps the personality differences and the underlying cultural realities are captured in Frazier's (1940) assertion that the middle-class Negro may be distinguished from the lower-class Negro in possessing "a more developed sense of personal dignity."

The question is not whether, but to what level of infantilism, modal lower-class Negro personalities have been driven back. Although Kardiner and Ovesey's descriptions are not couched explicitly in terms of developmental stages, we may surmise the crudeness of defenses and the weaknesses of ego and superego structures from their catalogue of traits. As general attributes among their subjects they cite unrealistic aspirations, apathy, hedonism, suspicion, interpersonal distance, oversimplification of perception and cognition, and impulsive discharges of affect. But to their lower-class subjects, they further ascribe deep distrust, projection of hostility to the outer world, a low degree of emotional relatedness, a confusion of sex roles, and absence of a strong conscience. The generality of their findings has been criticized because the N was small, because the study was made in New York City, and because many subjects were patients. But these criticisms cannot apply to Karon's work. In every one of thirty-three comparisons, he found that Southern exceeded Northern Negro samples in externalizing aggression, in denying its existence, in emotional lability, and in attributing the need to work to outside circumstances. Anna Freud (1946) indicates that denial of an impulse in fantasy is a primitive defense mechanism that will interfere with ego maturation if not relinquished in early childhood. Lability and possible impulsive behavior correlates are most often attributable to very early developmental levels. Furthermore, the disturbance of initiative, implicit in work motivation difficulties, would suggest not only the social realities of unattractive work but also some widespread failure in the psychosocial crisis of initiative accompanying the Oedipal encounter.

The Matriarch and Her Children

Nowhere in the literature on disadvantaged groups in our society is the mother more explicitly depicted as a loveless tyrant (Kardiner and Ovesey), or as extremely overindulgent and overprotective (Miller, *b*), or so full of contempt for men (Rohrer and Edmonson). Karon makes a distinction between the mother-dominated house of the rural South, which takes the form of "a more or less stable extended matriarchal family" (p. 32), and urban, lower-class, mother-centered families, which he views as more often a malfunctioning and disorganized form of American family structure. It would seem a safe assumption that the maternal character in the latter situation is as alienated from a womanly identity, as our culture might know its forms, as any retrogressed modal female personality in our general culture.

In these female-based households, mothers and their young sons, and mothers with daughters, who are no longer so young, are engrossed in each other. Each pair is a microcosm of its isolated world, the womb and limbo of families of outcasts. In the ways she attaches her children to herself the matriarch recreates her fear of separateness; her wish to be absorbed into a social organism so like herself she need not become aware of any dangerous individuality; and her distrust of things outside her skin, except for what enters it or passes out of it, such as children. With her son, she constitutes a self-sufficient symbiosis, compensating for her loss of a man through mutual distrust. She makes an appendage of her son to make up for her vulnerability to male exploitation (to which her own masochistic and oral wishes may have made her a willing party).

Her son also becomes her organ of revenge for the abandonment and exploitation to which she has felt subjected: she imbues him with exploitative justifications and counter-ideals, to the effect that the world is an atomized space, each greedy speck in it cold and set on its own selfish course. The narcissism and the "psychopathy" of some very tough Negro boys whom I have seen reflected not only what socializers did with and to them, but also hardened elements of conscience which their socializers taught them. These boys not only worshipped their mothers; they also almost universally scorned their fathers and imagined a day when they could (or actually did) humble their fathers and drive them out.

This was more than Oedipal animosity; these boys often provided hints and anecdotes indicating a put-up job. Their mothers had said, or enacted, "Get him before he gets you, for all he has done to both of us." Cassius Clay shouted on the night he took the heavyweight championship from Liston, "I am the king . . . I upset the world . . . [I beat] that big ugly bear . . . Look at me, I'm so pretty!", and some of this, it was reported, was said to his mother. I recall boys with family experiences of the sort being described self-delightedly and spontaneously putting on shadow-boxing exhibitions before their therapy group and proclaiming similar sentiments, worshipping themselves, it seemed, through their mother's eyes.

In Parsons' terms, what the young child internalizes in these families never proceeds beyond the mother-child subsystem to internalization of a nuclear family system. The type of sexual reciprocity that the child would internalize from his or her perception of mother's expectations of men, and of men's expectations of her, would again be that of an infantile, dependent relationship. The man's infantile posture would in all likelihood be overt, with damaging consequences for the male child. It is important that mother's expectations of men, and of her children, as well as her grievances, would seem to stem from the same infantile level of need and relationship, albeit more covertly. The extremity of mother's regressed position toward men, children, and self is clear in the following statement by a matriarch: "What's love? Ain't no sech thing as love. I love this here (pointing to the baby). *I love what's part of me—what comes out of me.* But love a man? Ain't no sech thing. I tell my girls: don't hear what no man say, but see how much he got" (Rohrer and Edmonson, p. 133; my italics).

The grown daughter is bound to her mother by her indoctrination regarding men as maurauders, and by the characterologic crippling resulting from adaptation to her mother's needs. The younger women in matriarchal families are often chronically depressed, deeply passive, engaged in magical thoughts, and are capable only of the shallowest interpersonal relationships. Of the men, it may be said initially that the male gang subculture is seen by Rohrer and Edmonson as complementing the matriarchal subculture. The sexual aspects of identity in male gang members, adult as well as adolescent, entails aggressive independence (often meaning freedom from familial responsibility), a "touchy and exaggerated virility," and a victimization of women. One is reminded of the Negro male who, according to Frazier (1940), offered as his rule of life, "Jive women and whites." The alienation of these men from manly initiative and independence, as exercised conventionally, may be seen in their profound suspicion and scorn for men who strive to achieve by legitimate means. They view occupational and educational achievement as effeminate. Their exploitation is directed not only at women; "Rather the enemy of the gang is the world of people (especially men) too unmanly for survival in what has often been described as a social jungle" (Rohrer and Edmonson, p. 160).

Homosexuality and Unrelatedness

A notable feature of gang life in this subculture is the importance of homosexuality in initiation ceremonies and in ideologies. Cross-cultural evidence has been reported of a relationship between feminine identification and brutal rites of passage, sometimes including homosexual activity (Burton and Whiting). Gang ideology makes constant distinction between the bully and the sissy, and Rohrer and Edmonson report that the novice may undergo homosexual degradation in becoming one of the

> tough but embattled "mama's men": The feelings of inadequacy of the gang members are specifically related to sexual confusion. Extensive homosexuality is institutionally a part of gang life, and the subsequent insistent masculinity protests too much to be anything other than a necessary reassurance against self-doubt. Such feelings date from a childhood in which being a male in a matriarchal home is equated with being unworthy (p. 167).

I have observed in a training school setting a proclivity among Negro boys, of subcultural background very similar to that described in the New Orleans study, for pederastic assault. The victims, the "punks," are often white boys who appear to the Negro attackers to be infuriatingly and contemptibly passive and effeminate. Verbalizations presented in group psychotherapy by the attackers suggest great alienation from their own passive wishes and great skepticism regarding masculinity.

It seemed that an aim of the assault was to express aggression toward the white embodiments of surrender to adult male authority. The subordinate role in a relationship between males is dramatized, in this act, as one in which a body opening is forcibly penetrated by the superior one. Aggressive maleness is caricatured as sadistic, phallic gratification on the body of one like oneself, but one who surrenders. Narcissism is inherent in commerce with the body of another like oneself, as is a profound alienation from the possibility of developing attachments between self and another, different human being.

It has been proposed that in suppressed subcultures, social and cultural constraints force ego failures on people, and these failures promote infantilizations—adaptive psychosocial and psychosexual fixations. In the LL Negro subculture, object relations of prime importance may become those related to oral, and by substitution other orificial satisfactions. Some of these people have become mired down in the most elemental issues of relatedness, because of ostracism and the passivity demanded of slave and untouchable. Differentiation of independent sexual identities has reverted, and the dominant subcultural figure which emerges is that of the oral matriarch, one representation of which may be the jovial, loving, and shapelessly fat "mammy," who is the more intensely gratified participant, through her body openings, in relationships. Silverberg describes a type of homosexual strategy in a boy's Oedipal strivings to break up the parental sexual couple

> by means of using the father's orifices for the phallic gratification of the boy. The father is to be converted into the equivalent of a female, and it is assumed by the boy that the father will be so gratified by this that he will no longer seek gratification by means of his own phallus. . . . [This adaptation] . . . is based upon the . . . conviction [that] parental sexuality is kept going by the mother's drive for vulvar [or vaginal] pleasure. This would signify that boys making this solution have tended to identify themselves with the mother . . . as the more intensely gratified participant. In its turn, this would imply that such boys anticipate more intense pleasure from stimulation of their orifices than from stimulation of the penis, and reasoning by analogy with themselves, makes this identification with the female. . . . They ascribe to the father this same preference for orificial pleasure over

phallic pleasure and hope therefore to prevent parental sexuality by offering orificial pleasure to the father (p. 226).

Thus these same adolescent Negroes shared fearful stories, as a part of their folklore, regarding female bulldykes who would tear with their labia at a male whom they had forced to enter them, or who would turn the tables on a would-be rapist and forcibly pedicate him with oversized clitoral organs; these may have been projections of oral fixation and of identification with the type of maternal figure Silverberg describes. Thus also, the meaning of their pederasty, as seen in their verbalizations, is that a male wants to be a passive recipient of gratification.

In ego terms, this kind of homosexual contact epitomizes disrespect and the opposite of self- and other-respecting separateness. One approaches the other from behind rather than from his front, where his organs of perception and decision-making are and where the other would be able to make his best, rather than his worst, showing. The inserter degrades the recipient by contacting the latter's lowliest parts; and the recipient ridicules the "aggressor" by turning his back to him, by showing him how little of others assertiveness gets him, even, what parts of people the "male" one really wants them to show him. The assaulter coerces another to take part in a ritual degradation of himself as much as of the other; in this way a cultural castaway may mock and scorn himself, not in his consciousness, but in his actions.

Identity Crisis I

The prospective identities of little boys are prefigured by the matriarch. "They are clearly convinced that all little boys must inexorably and deplorably become men, with all the pathologies of that sex" (Rohrer and Edmonson, p. 161). The matriarch projects the blame for her son's downfall on the "bad boys," and her harsh and erratic punishment, deriving from her own impulsivity, "frequently masks *her own unconscious expectations* of her son, and may do a great deal toward shaping him in the image of men she *knows and approves* or fears and represses" (my italics). The phrases regarding tacit approval are stressed because the exploitativeness of her son towards others would fit well with the underlying enmity toward men that may be characteristic of the matriarch in this setting.

As for such a son, he would be a sometime host, sometime parasite in a symbiotic attachment which, in important ways, antedates incest, and which forecloses the achievement of a secure autonomy or of an assertiveness toward male authority which is not destructive. He would be taught that he has no real father, that his destiny is to replace the man, and in learning to fulfill his mother's heart's desire he is alienated from the possibility of his own separateness. At adolescence he would have only the most fragmentary and primitive notions of masculinity from which to fashion a self-respecting identity. The world of school and work, with its requirements for relatedness between independent individuals and for controlled striving, is alien to him. His daydreams and nightdreams repeat a fantasy, perhaps of the savior, or of a world-bestriding giant with the dreamer's face, or of world destruction, which expresses the one overriding wish to be reestablished at whatever cost in the oceanic bliss of unity with the mothering one. (One such boy dreamed repeatedly that he was a colossus with the world in one crushing hand.) He abhors relatedness because it requires separateness, which implies loss, and so he attacks its representation in people about him. He fears order and mastery because they require delay, partial satisfaction, and relatedness, and so he becomes the enemy of law, vocation, and learning. His pressure toward deviance is a strain toward omnipotence.

His identity problems are multiple because his ego is fixed in a premature simplicity. (The comments below follow Erikson's dimensions of identity formation, 1959.) The son of an overweening matriarch escapes his mistrust of the future by living in a perpetual here-and-now, similar to the blindness toward past experience and future exigencies that a psychopath may show, relating only to what he can sense and act toward and against. His is a kind of primitive empiricism, an ultimate orientation to happenings, which may lend him the spring and alertness of a fighter in a ring—a favorite fantasy of his for other reasons, I suspect, than the fact that it is one avenue of opportunity open to his race and station.

He exists alone in his present, as if he has no connection to events which have gone before and which may yet occur. He has no family or subcultural history of which he feels proud (although some of his peers may be making one, in their demonstrations), none, at least, that binds him to the larger society. He is unable to make those beginning commitments to an ideology and to an adult leadership that would help secure him an integrative identity. His identifications run rather toward local underworld figures and drifters with a personal style, embodiments of alienated individuality and exploitation. He does away with any subsequent sense of social isolation, and with feelings of insignificance, with a stage actor's sense of presence in the present.

This premature self-certainty (premature because it does not allow him a realization of belonging to a larger time and place) presumes the possibility of gratification by magic, like the baby who hallucinates the nipple into being. It also presupposes that relations between himself and another may be ordered in an autocratic way, without taking chances on any risky autonomy in the other, and without risking shame or doubt of self. This in turn interferes with his establishment of a sexual identity which would depend on reciprocity with a complementary, and independent, person. He fantasies satisfaction and commands it, and when it is not forthcoming he seizes for it or attacks those in his way.

Projectively, he may attribute the same omnipotence and tyranny to those who might retaliate; sometimes his delinquency is a pre-emptive strike against his projections. Performance of a delinquent act may fill him with frightening fantasies that his own self will be invaded and subjugated. These inner consequences may provide further delinquent flights into the teeth of reality for those who have sufficient ego strength, or, for those who have gravely weakened egos, paranoid or catatonic breaks in which the boy is terrified that he is going to be punked.

There were boys like this in my training school experience, who seemed to use psychosis in the service of their egos: When misbehavior was discovered by institution authorities, or under the chronic pressures of dormitory living, they might undergo a break, which would remit almost immediately and spontaneously on their transfer to a hospital for psychiatric observation. They would then be returned to the institution. The cycle might be repeated, once or twice again, before the boy might finally be committed, and commit himself, to psychiatric hospitality. These oscillations between a psychosis and a delinquent identity were instructive for me; they indicated the truth in Erikson's suggestion that delinquency may be a lived-out analog of psychiatric disorders.

This first psychocultural process, then, depicts a boy who may be heir to the attitudes of a mother profoundly cut off from collaboration with effective men; and, who is heir also to a male identity that lives as best it can with its own undependability, indigence, and impulsivity. The boy's inner strictures are too binding, his ego resources too meager, for him to do much more than attack his environment. At the end of adolescence, he may slump back into the misshapen identity of his origins, a cultural discard. We may see in this process the antithesis of what Erikson conveys when he states that "A lasting ego identity . . . cannot be completed without a promise of fulfillment, which from the dominant image of adulthood reaches down into the baby's beginnings and which creates at every step an accruing sense of ego strength" (1959, p. 91).

chapter 11

process II

THE fundamental alienation from self and others indicated in Process I could have occurred among some very oppressed European peasants, and it could have been perpetuated in some of their descendants in America. However, other descendants, perhaps those in UL, working-class, ethnic subcultures, have maintained considerable authority in the role functioning of the father. Here, the pressure toward deviance in some adolescents is a rebellion, coached and nurtured by a discontented matriarch, against a patriarchal authority that has historical roots in feudalism.

It seems a reasonable historical speculation that some impoverished peasant men adapted to their caste situation by taking on the absolutism of secular and church authorities and by taking out their frustrations on their families. The women would, in turn, have gradually turned against their men. They would have encouraged the hostility of sons against fathers. Current constraints on workingmen in our social structure might keep these adaptations alive.

Process II youth invest their rebelliousness in gang ideologies which are based on opposition to adult male authority. Their fear of their own inclinations to submit guiltily to another's will also generates rebellion as a reaction-formation. Their self-doubt creates an acute identity consciousness which they deny in the exhibitionistic imperviousness of a working-class tough.

Processes I and II: Distinctions

The psychocultural adaptations to be described in this section may be found among members of ethnic subcultures descendant from those European peasants who may have undergone the characterological erosion suggested in Chapter 9. In this process the focal person for our purposes, the adolescent boy (and his counterpart, the adolescent girl turned mother) struggles against a type of masculinity which is much more available and viable than that described in Process I.

Modal traits in LL Negro family life were used to describe Process I. The same adaptations might be found to occur among LL Italian "maladapted" people (Gans); among some inner-city "ethnic left-overs"; and among very disorganized, impoverished, multiproblem families. Process I may also occur significantly often in some of the English slum families described by Kerr and Spinley. However, when the father exercises functions and powers accepted and recognized in these English families, this second process, which is less destructive to ego resources, may occur.

The cutting point, so to speak, between the levels of ego limitation and adaptation attributed to people undergoing Process I changes and the psychocultural shifts to be outlined now, is the degree of personal maturity of modal female personalities in the subculture. A woman raised with ambivalent attitudes toward men may still enjoy some ability for mutually rewarding transactions with males who retain a degree of independence and authority. The negative side of her ambivalence pushes and supports her boy in his rebellion against male authority. His strain toward deviance, therefore, is a pressure to rebellion. Now, and in the past of his subculture, this mother's son would have a difficult time establishing an identity that would grant him the right to initiative; he must struggle against shackles of incest, guilt, and hatred. (Aside from our interests here, I wonder how often discontented wives and mothers raise revolutions.)

As suggested, however, the degradation and the poverty of centuries might have so eroded the integrity of many European peasants that they too adopted the more deeply estranged and dependent adult identities described in Process I. If I might anticipate just a little here what will be described in more detail below: Mother's hostility, in past generations and other places, to the European peasant father's subservience and failure to provide for his family might have profoundly alienated daughter from father and, in time, from her own man. The mother might have played upon and mobilized any inferiority or envy that her young girl may have experienced regarding males in the course of growing up, to protect her from and prepare her for the disappointments and resentments that mother may have harbored. As decades eroded character, the daughter become mother would have conspired with her own daughter against the men, and would have made any reconciliation with a trusting and collaborative womanhood more and more difficult.

Then, as in Process I, the mother's son would have begun to fulfill a newly paramount aim: He would symbolize her rivalry with her man and the end of her dependence on men; since he was *her* son alone, she would try even harder to keep him from his father. In seeking his father's good faith, the son would have had to risk his mother's anger and withdrawal. Male identity would have taken on a different meaning as the object and in the service of woman's hostile wishes. Flight to the New World would not have delivered mother and son automatically from such inner bondage to each other. In Europe, the Virgin Mother had deep personal significance to the peasant women; in America, a lower-class Irish mother inquired perfunctorily regarding the whereabouts of a certain young man, then enthusiastically welcomed her daughter's illegitimate pregnancy: "I hope it's a boy! We haven't had a boy in the family in a long time!" (W. B. Miller, *b*)

The Italian working-class (UL) subculture, as described by Gans, will be the context for Process II (in which the estrangement between the sexes does not reach the proportions of Process I). Gans distinguishes between routine-seeking and action-seeking subgroups in this ethnic subculture. Routine-seeking adults have one-sex peer group associations related to very stable, "expanded" family and kinship groups. Action-seeking men continue their peer associations away from their families after marriage, living episodically and perhaps having extramarital affairs. They are, Gans says, lower-class by life style and working-class by occupation and income. Gans did not observe or hear about any delinquency among the children of routine-seekers; on the other hand, he did not observe the family lives (such as it may have been) of action-seekers. I am assuming that some of the children of the latter were delinquent. I am assuming further that the attitudes and traits of the routine-seekers, and especially those characteristics which might produce negativism and hostility, apply even more to the action-seekers, since both are members of the same subculture, and since one distinguishing characteristic of routine- and action-seeker is that only the former is concerned with behavior controls.

Patriarchy and Matriarchy

An older sociology of delinquency indicated that European ethnic groups contributed disproportionately to delinquency rates early in their assimilation to American culture. Those of their descendants still located in relatively disadvantaged sectors of our society still contribute to this problem. Immigrant fathers were often rigid, authoritarian individuals who controlled their childrens' lives and demanded strict obedience. The Italian father, for instance, required respect of his sons, performance to his expectations, had little interest in their needs or problems, and made quick physical retribution for transgressions. The sons were and are, as a result, fear-ridden regarding him. This may well be characterized as a patriarchal familial arrangement (Barabee).

However, we have other information that matriarchy is probably nowhere more evident in our society than in these same groups, or at least in those segments of these groups located in the working and lower classes. Gans asserts that a strong attachment to mother, contrasted with ambivalent ties to father, is a universal working-class pattern; Miller states that the mother-son relationship is the dominant one in lower-class culture, that it is "held sacred" by the lower class male (*b*, p. 19); and Hollingshead reaches a similar conclusion (p. 117). It has been repeatedly reported that fathers are weaker and less dependable, and the families more clearly matriarchal, the further down one goes in the social order. This state of family affairs is usually explained by sociological and anthropological observers as an outcome of the functional failure of the man as provider; he is rejected by wife and children, deserts or abdicates responsibility in demoralization, and power devolves on the woman.

It is interesting that even UL, routine-seeking, second- and third-generation Italian males, who pride themselves on their manliness and family authority and who apparently meet the functional requirements of the male role, fear female domination. Men avoid conversation with women on the grounds that women are more facile and will control their thoughts. They are afraid that women will undercut what Gans calls their "nominal dominance" (p. 48). Their dominance in childrearing would appear to be nominal also: Gans observes that the mother is almost totally responsible for the children, and, while the father acts as disciplinarian, it is the mother who calls him for this service and who is able to govern the degree of punishment imposed. Lower-class delinquency has been related to weak as well as to absent fathers.

Psychocultural considerations offer a line of speculation about mothers who seem to control controlling fathers. European peasantry was, to the time of the great westward migrations, locked in a patriarchal social order. The princes of state and church demanded uncomplaining submission to their authority. Fromm states that "the positive aspects of the patriarchal complex are reason, discipline, conscience and individualism; the negative aspects are hierarchy, oppression, inequality, submission" (p. 47). We may assume that as the peasant population increased, and as the aristocracy increased its exactions, the negative aspects of patriarchy weighed more heavily on the peasant. He was denied ways to human integrity. The human cost of his submission may have been resort to passive ways of dealing with experience, characteristic of infancy and early childhood; a surrender to another of initiative and of control over one's destiny, and the desire to surrender himself to father's wishes that marks the first negotiations of a son with his father. These elements seem implicit in Handlin's belief that "The peasant did not begrudge the magnates the pleasures of their manor houses; let *them* at least draw enjoyment from life."

Matriarchal traditions also went to the roots of peasant life. The ties to that from which one comes are the essence of incest, in Fromm's view, and are the center of matriarchy. The bonds to "blood and soil" (p. 45) could be found in the ancient tribe and its agricultural pursuits and underlay primeval matriarchal religions, according to Fromm's analysis. The European peasant retained these bonds, in his communal village and in his agricultural fiefdom up to this century. Of the consolations of mother church and the worship of the Virgin, Fromm writes, "the masses, oppressed by the patriarchal authorities, could turn to the loving mother who would comfort them and intercede for them" (p. 55). One suspects that the peasant intensely yearned to be requited in many ways for his suffering, and that while he, in his community, gained some "sense of the affirmation of life, freedom, and equality which pervades the matriarchal structure," he lost much also: "by being bound to nature, to blood and soil, man is blocked from developing his individuality and his reason" (p. 55).

One might suppose that the relation of peasant father to wife and children was fashioned in the manner of the surrounding patriarchal structure—that the father was king in his own house—which to some important extent seems to have been the case. More important is the manner in which he exercised his authority. The implication exists in the studies cited in this section and in clinical observations of cases of culture conflict (Seward, 1958) that these fathers can be extremely harsh, furious, in their reactions to wrong-doing. Temperamental, aggressive outbursts of retaliation have nothing to do with the investment of power in and the imposition of rules by the father. It is entirely conceivable that patriarchal authority may be absolute and unrelenting, and yet be exercised in a rational way. The societal apotheosis of this may be seen in the figure of a stern but just judge who metes out penalties on the basis of principle rather than passion.

Similarly, the lower-class Italian boy will not fear a father who is firm but also reasoned in his punishment, but he will hate and fear a father who shows implacable rages when his son disappoints him.

Two sources of this type of paternal violence may be identified. One is in a syncretized, punitive superego that includes sadistic elements in its response to transgression. Such a conscience would be functional in a hierarchical society involving callous subjugation by upper castes and submission by lower (see A. Freud, 1946, on the mechanism of identification with the aggressor).

Another source of father's temper may lie in an aspect of his ego structure which is related to his autocratic ideals and prohibitions. He would deal most securely with his children when they bent quickly to his will; regarding issues of autonomy in his interpersonal relations, he would allow a son little room for maneuver. His own assertiveness would have been shaped in the narrow confines of caste relations between dominant and subservient interests. A son who held onto his interests or pressed them a moment too long in an encounter with his father would run the risk of seeming obstinate or demanding, of opposing his father's will. The father would burst into crushingly decisive aggression against such an obstruction. In matters of control and decision, this kind of Old World father's ego operations were probably simple and absolute. An upwardly mobile man in his mid-thirties received a phone call at eleven at night from his senile father, a first generation Italian-American, to come immediately to the father's home across town for a conversation. The son made hasty preparations to leave. His wife demanded to know whether he was still a child, to run at father's command. Without a word in his own defense, the son left. Tradition is tenacious, even when conflicting with contemporary culture.

Manliness: A Style or a Function?

How do we explain these patriarchs who may have felt vulnerable to their wives, and who may have reacted impulsively and explosively to frustrations of their will, like a child in a tantrum?

I want to digress here to a consideration of an issue that has been broached by others regarding the relation of sex-role preparation and delinquency, because it has implications for the maturity of the parents which may be instructive to the question just raised. Cohen has cited Parsons (1947) to the effect that feminine identification in the middle-class boy, because of father's unavailability, leads to sex-role anxiety and to aggressive compensations in adolescence. Cloward and Ohlin say that there is a discrepancy between Cohen's location of this anxiety in the middle-class boy and Miller's attribution of it to lower-class youngsters of female-based households. They conclude that since one cannot attribute sex-role anxiety reliably to either class, it cannot be used to explain lower-class delinquency. It might be said initially that the terms sex-role anxiety and even feminine identification are relatively crude and not susceptible to clear distinctions. Nevertheless, in addition, other important dimensions of sex-role preparation may be introduced and may shed some light.

One should consider whether there exists in these analyses a confusion of sexual *expressive style* and sexually differentiated role *function.* For example, there are references to "feminization" (Ebaugh) of the modern upper-middle-class male, who imposes fewer fiats, negotiates decisions with his wife, and shares disciplinary aspects of authority with her. On the other hand, there is the implication that the lower-class male whose expressive style is more physical, or "motoric" (Miller and Swanson), and who may react with dramatic impulsiveness when crossed by wife or children, is somehow more masculine than his middle-class counterpart. Another important dimension of sex-role patterning is the type of sex-role *reciprocity* that exists between the parents. The ultimate masculinity of the growing child may possibly gain or suffer as much by what his mother *expects and values in a male* as by the kind of fathering he has. (Parsons, 1958, states very clearly that it is the coalition of the parents in family leadership, their role reciprocation, and not just the role of the father, that is the main sociological mechanism for learning the masculine role; see also Bandura and Walters on the hostility of mother for father in the background of aggressive disorders in children. In Chapter 7, it was suggested that the boy's enlistment by mother in her hostility to her husband male a daily reality out of his Oedipal conflict.) It is possible that a study correlating the masculinity of fatherless sons with the womanliness of their widowed or otherwise bereft mothers might clarify some of the issues in the problem of masculine identification.

Similarly, one might make useful distinctions between a mother-centered middle-class household, in which the mother has a reasonably adequate adjustment with a father who must spend ten hours a day at his job in the city, and a lower-class matriarchal household, in which a father or a gigolo "uncle" is present but constantly derogated by a mother jealous of her prerogatives and control. One would think that there are fundamentally different consequences for a male child from the relative *unavailability* of an adequate male model and the *disparagement* and *inadequacy* of the model. The different kinds of felt sexual inadequacy generated would in fact correspond roughly to some of the differences in offenses observed between middle-class and lower-class delinquents. The middle-class youngsters' acts are frequently of a relatively benign, compensatory variety, as in violations growing out of drag racing and unauthorized use of cars. It is as if they were acting out a felt distance or difference between themselves and a known masculine ideal; they "burn rubber" and "tool around" without any real departures or destinations. The more destructive, assaultive behavior of some lower-class gang delinquency, on the other hand, may attest to a commitment, with a vengeance, to a negative identity—what a male should not be but is. One LL boy, a tough recidivist, told me: "She said my old man was no damn good. S——, I did better than that. I been *bad*."

One might assume that a phallic component is emphasized in the lower-class male's identity more than it is in a middle-class male's, in the sense that considerations of physical size and powers may be central and outstanding in lower-class self-conception (Miller and Swanson). It could be confusing, however, to assume that, because his style of expression is distinctively "male," he experiences adequacy in his sex-role performance. Schilder cautioned that

> The ideology of our civilization is based upon the wrong assumption that masculinity and activity are identical and that femininity and passivity are the same. Human beings therefore live with the fear of

> being too feminine and too passive when they are men. The fear of castration is closely linked with the fear of being too passive. . . . The questions arise: . . . Can you be passive and receptive with good conscience? Must one fight? Must one feel masculine? . . . The courage of being passive and of accepting one's passive side is a necessary step for a deeper adaptation (p. 31).

The upthrusting and self-displaying masculinity of some lower-class fathers may ward off fears of submitting to another's will, of being shamefully exposed, of having less to put out than is needed.

Parsons and Bales suggest that a man's performance of his role outside his family weighs more heavily on his personality than does the female's in the same society. The lower-class male is much more liable to the danger of not earning enough to support his family adequately, and, as I have indicated, the function of the mother-based household has been related to this liability in the father.

Insofar as a man tries to realize initiative and autonomy in his work, a subcultural tradition of defeats and compromises may be experienced as weaknesses in his capacity to stand up for himself and look out for his own. He is denied affirmation of these components of masculinity in restrictions on his role functioning. Then he must jealously guard against any other encroachments on his worth and competence; he has to find reasons or scapegoats for his defeat; and he must live with defeat. Male children in such a subculture have poorer prospects of finding identity with a man who feels as competent as he may look.

Familial Effects of Male Insecurity

Gans provides some interesting indications that male sexual insecurity is indeed present in working-class Italian subculture. In an earlier unpublished version of his book he pointed out that fathers, uncles, and mothers not only teach male attributes, explicitly and intensively, but taunt a child with femaleness when he fails. He commented that

The fact that children are being taught explicitly in this way does not necessarily guarantee that they will internalize this image; in fact, one might argue that the explicit emphasis on the subject would be a sign that there is some widely felt insecurity about the male image.

He notes that there are indications of latent fear of homosexuality among some adolescents and men in his subject population.

Evidence has been offered that dependent relations of husband to wife are explicit in the lowest, marginal social strata, and that implicit fear of submission to women exists among some relatively more adequate males of the Italian subculture. One might expect, then, that the particular subculture would also show expressions of possessive urges regarding women, of a type that might be expected of a male child engrossed in an oedipal situation. This is the case in the Italian subculture studied by Gans. He reports that men and women who are not married are never left alone together, because of "the traditional Italian belief that sexual intercourse is unavoidable when a man and a woman are by themselves" (p. 49). A general subcultural concern with self-control is particularly evident in the fear that "undue contact with a woman may produce sexual desire that cannot be satisfied" (pp. 48–49).

Subcultural emphases on demandingness, possessiveness, and rebellion against authority in males is given added dimension if we think about a possible female character is this setting. I suspect that some of the women in this subculture, wives of the action-seekers, themselves have a demanding and critical posture toward their husbands, and identify with their young sons' opposition to paternal authority. More or less consciously, they would encourage their boys' opposition to father, would keep alive their boys' impatience with postponement of gratification and angry reactions to frustration. "People believe that discipline is needed constantly to keep the child in line with and respectful of adult rules, and that without it he would run amok" (Gans, p. 59). It has been noted that mother can and does control the degree of father's punishment; Gans indicates that the boy's attachment to mother as his defender against father is general in this population. Barabee has also taken note of spoiling and overprotectiveness as traits of Italian mothers, and W. B. Miller has made a similar observation regarding lower-class Irish-

American mothers (to touch on another ethnic subculture in which Process II may occur often.)

Although Gans gives us no direct evidence of wives' hostility, his description of maternal disciplinary behavior reflects other suggestions regarding the strength of the bonds between mother and child. They expose their children to furious controls; they chew their children out and nag at them for wrongdoing. It is difficult to believe that such oral aggressiveness and relentlessness is always restricted to their dealings with their children:

> Punishment is both physical and verbal . . . the mothers slap and beat their children, tell them not to do this or that, and threaten to tell the fathers when they come home. Indeed, to a middle class observer, the mother's treatment of the child often seems extremely strict and sometimes brutal. There is a continuous barrage of prohibitions and threats, intertwined with words and deeds of reward and affection. But the torrents of threat and cajolery neither impinge on the feelings of parental affection, nor are meant as signs of rejection. As one mother explained to her child, "We hit you because we love you" (Gans, p. 59).

Marital Conflict and Filial Rebellion: Historical

The European peasant underwent prolonged disadvantages on account of his caste status and economic exploitation by his superiors. He may have been authoritarian within the family, but it was also likely that his family witnessed his denial of his own power to control and command, in his supine obedience to landowner, official, and priest. Authority as a property of the male role may have been further compromised by the peasant father's own rebelliousness, the retaliative wishes he must have experienced, perhaps verbally expressed or acted out in avoidance of planning or decision, or in outbursts of aggression.

What of the woman's part in bringing about and maintaining such a male identity and role model? It seems plausible that the man's uncertainty about his own worthiness would have been expressed in reliance on her. The references which have been made to a matriarchal tradition suggest this; his dependence on her would have put greater power to coerce him in her hands, a power she may have prized if she had lost respect for him. It is possible that these marriages could have been harmonious and quite stable despite occasional blowups and nagging, and with a distinct style of manliness in evidence—a style involving touchiness and impulsivity, valued and encouraged by the wife and mother. This certainly seems to have been the pattern of many marriages that Gans observed, among descendants of peasants. Delinquency does not come of it, so far as Gans could determine.

I have in mind, however, a further process of adaptation in the establishment of this second deviance-producing process. Suppose that the male's adaptive hardening implanted cruelty and submission so firmly in his character that his wife alternately had great power over him and hatred for him. She might also have undergone a similar displacement of objects and aims, attaching firmly to her female identity sadomasochistic ways of relating to him, in envious scorn for his bullying and martyred sufferance of it. The peasant father was exploited at his family's expense. A peasant wife and mother might have been chronically dissatisfied with her state, spiteful and resentful toward her husband in her very fear of him.

When not taking it out on her, the hardened male would have gone to his wife to placate her and for some solace, impelled by a submissive and masochistic streak in himself, by the matriarchal traditions, and by his guilt. She could have relieved herself of her malice in at least two ways. She could have assumed the role of the carping, hostile wife, whose ridicule would have been powerfully rewarded by the man's chagrin and misery in his rejection. And she might have readied her sons for rebellion against him. Also, certain role expectations regarding masculinity would already come naturally to the mother, by prior psychocultural adaptations in which women before her had grown to cherish impulsive and possessive maleness. A bitter reality, too, made sons turn like a primal horde on their father and then perhaps against each other: Handlin and other historians indicate that grim family battles were fought over possession of the scrap of mother earth each peasant got, or had to take, from his father before him.

The discontented mother whom I am imagining would have augmented this sex-role preparation by imparting her dissatisfied, resentful attitude toward her husband to her sons, and by championing and sympathizing with them in their struggles against his authority. These sons would have presented their fathers with mother's dissatisfaction and contempt, whether veiled or manifest, first decked out in Oedipal terms and then in the terms of the adolescent identity crisis and their struggle for adult prerogatives.

Contemporary Pressures

So far, this has been historical conjecture. I proposed in Chapter 2, however, that ULs today live under normative constraints. It is possible that these constraints are maintaining the same adaptations in these people that have been ascribed to their ancestors. The success of the American free enterprise system in creating wealth and in distributing it among urban industrial workers and service employees does not alter the fact that the laborer's effort still makes others' profit, and that as a consequence they tell him how his work life is to be organized, what product he is to make, or service to perform, and how he is to do it. Added to this ongoing cultural pressure to adapt submissively to his work role is the fact that the urban laborer has had to accept the paternalism, and at times the authoritarianism, of his great unions in order to wrest from corporate management the economic advantages he now enjoys.

The industrial worker may be confronted today not so much with exploitation of his labor for profit as with an exploitation of the market for his income with its increased purchasing power. The UL person is persuaded to devote himself primarily to the acquisition of goods and services by a mass entertainment medium which seduces with passive pleasures. The dominant culture takes much less initiative in encouraging community organization and action in the lower class than it does in selling that class its goods. The steady resistance of the business community to welfare legislation at all government levels must be attributed, at least in part, to the view that lower-class families are first and foremost a source of profit, and that these profits must be protected against taxation. Taxation would, of course, provide public services, living areas, and recreational facilities to these same lower-class families.

It is thus proposed that the lower-class male is prompted to make and maintain a regressive, compliant adaptation in relation to representatives of government and business interests which are often unresponsive to his needs. He is induced to relate to others, in work and leisure, as if he were by turns a coordinated set of gross muscles, a mouth, an eye, a reflexive urge. A sense of purpose and self-command, of a reality of proaction rather than reaction, may be lost; authority as an element of his sex role is attacked, and a dependent adaptation to the stimuli and demands of the dominant culture may occur, or recur. Thus it is possible that current factors in our society are maintaining the Process II adaptation in some UL industrial workers, which their European ancestors may have undertaken generations earlier.

Identity Crisis II

These men may feel intransigence and rebelliousness in reacting to constraints that their consciences impose on their egos. Gans' observations suggest how self-defeating such externalizations can be, as in their stiff-necked refusal to put their heads together in order to save their neighborhood from physical destruction. If they become as estranged from their wives as is suggested in Process II, their sons may live out the fathers' sentiments in delinquent ways through which they may feel that they can indeed "fight back against, outsmart, and even defeat the world." They live out these deviant sentiments partly for their fathers, as successors to alienated family and subcultural traditions, and partly against them, as bearers of identity problems that parental estrangement has forced on them.

These boys often have very great idealism; sometimes they behave and dress as if they are enacting a fantasy of being an errant knight, who is determined to prove the strength of his lance and to display the splendor of his armor to win the favors of some secret lady. These kinds of boys love to serve a moral purpose in their delinquency, as in punishing other gangs for wrongdoing and in playing Robin Hood to the undeserving rich. They love to go down fighting the Black Knight: Unlike Process I boys, these youths will occasionally talk proudly about their fathers' physical strength or fighting or drinking capacities;

in the next breath, they curse their fathers for throwing them out of the house or beating them up.

A white boy from New Orleans, of French-American working-class background, was an inmate of the training school of which I have spoken before. He had already proved himself incapable of resisting challenges, and unable as well to resist throwing the gauntlet in the face of injustice, injustice as he defined it. He had been committed after rebuking the judge for disparaging him in court. I tried to make some sense with him, but gave up when I decided that he was no more interested in coming to terms with me than he had been with other men, including his father.

When I saw him several months later, I was shocked by his appearance. There were two sutured scars on his face; one of his front teeth was broken, and the other knocked out. He had been thrown in the institution's "can" repeatedly, and had lost his chance for parole because of an endless series of fights with the most powerful clique in his dormitory. He had championed the cause of every "weak" boy whom the clique was exploiting and who had appealed to him for help; and he fought clique members, no matter how outnumbered he was, if they made insinuations against him. I suggested that he might let some of these insults pass by, save himself physically and get out of that place. He rebuked me, but softly, for my naivete: "Aw, Doc, dey's such a t'ing as pride." A short time after winning a parole, he was shot resisting arrest.

Youths who emerge from Process II have had a different sort of early mothering experience than those of Process I. They were the babies of women who, because they were economically supported by their husbands, were able to bring a good deal more dependable support to their children's first years. Process II youth are therefore spared, or suffer less, that untimely self-differentiation of the very young child whose most basic experiences in being safe with another may have been violated (see Erikson on identity formation, 1959). They are able to attach goodness to their mothers and others, and it is this capacity for romanticizing friendships and idealizing friends that helps create a gang solidarity which may last a lifetime and a loyalty to gang leadership and ideology. It is, however, a peer leadership and ideology as alienated from adult authority as they feel, and as their fathers may have felt before them.

This devotion to boy friends, one suspects, also makes it hard for them to establish intimacy with girls (unfortunately for some of the children in the next generation) and perhaps adds to their nervous interest in homosexuality. Another element in the sex-role anxieties of these boys is the heavy hand their fathers and mothers laid on them. Their parents' gestures and countermeasures, during these boys' earlier crises of self-assertiveness, must have generated fantasies and experiences of having one's will and body broken, of being exposed and humiliated. The male vanity and exhibitionism of working-class subcultures would provide excellent examples, and mothers' admiration ample encouragement, of reaction-formations against self-doubt and feeling puny; but their earlier subjugation may have created in many a temptation to sweet surrender, wishes which might be so abhorrent to many of these boys as to prompt a flight into rebellion.

Nevertheless, secret feelings of self-doubt might cling in the form of a consciousness of being too visible and open to disparagement. They deny this painful self-consciousness in the exhibitionistic imperviousness of a young working-class tough. Such a boy needs to shout out his self-reliance, to maintain constant vigilance in order to forestall what might be shameful submission. As much as his desire to dispossess male authority, this boy's quixotic pride probably prompts his commitment to the negative identity of a young rebel, a jouster, an idol-smasher, and a raider.

chapter 12

process III

BUREAUCRACIES exercise pressures on white-collar LMs to suppress and narrow their emotional expressiveness, to intellectualize their experience, to emphasize routines and cautiousness, in short, to adopt personality characteristics similar to those of an obsessive-compulsive person. As a result, some LMs fear ego autonomy, and overtrain their child in obedience, creating considerable self-doubt in him.

In their marital relationship, they are covertly hostile, because of dependency feelings resulting from self-doubt, and manipulative, because they fear independent action in each other. The Process III child suffers from their manipulativeness and from their displacement of hostility to him. Limitations on his will and initiative make achievement situations threatening to him, so that he performs inadequately in the primary grades. A desire to avoid planful effort is his pressure to deviance.

If he is not trained to disguise this avoidant impulse, he will in adolescence repudiate school and conforming effort openly in misbehavior and delinquency. His identity crisis consists of a general ego constriction, in which he deals with his inner experience by denial and by interpersonal distance maneuvers, sometimes acted out in flight from situations. The crisis also consists of work paralysis; of identity consciousness involving a fear of shameful failure to achieve, and of inferiority feelings which he dispels by repudiating conventional normative evaluations regarding achievement. He resorts to defeating the rules and limits set up by others as a way of perversely asserting his will, since his parents gave no consistently satisfactory outlet for self-assertion during his developing years.

Family Consequences of LM Adaptations—An Overview

The delinquent child of some lower-middle, white-collar parents opposes himself to what he sees as grim and grudging, self-denying identifications, to a relentless instrumentalism which perhaps has some ideological roots in the religious doctrine of predestination. (The pattern described here may also hold true for many families who may be middle-middle and upper-middle economically but who share the same orienting values and identities.) His parents have learned a tradition of serving the enterprise and the initiatives of others, and in doing so have carried duty to such an extreme that they efface their own individuality.

Such parents suppress ambition and separateness, experiencing these qualities as a closely guarded ambivalence toward authority and as an unwillingness to take interpersonal risks with their marriage partners as well as with others. Their wills become absorbed in stubborn, smoldering feuds and in withholding from each other no less than from themselves. Frequently, it is a part of their unwritten, unspoken marriage contract that one will save the other, somehow, from the dangers of spontaneity—that two can live more obsessively than one.

When one of them discovers that he has taken on an insufferable dependency in this kind of marital symbiosis, then the other partner clutches all the more tenaciously to his private version of their tacit agreement. His terror of facing life on his own two feet becomes a sense of outrage that the other has reneged. He nurses an indignation that ruminates endlessly over catalogues of slights, rebuffs, unkindnesses. Sometimes the husband, the wife, or both, have dogged and punished the other for years with a withdrawn and unforgiving sullenness.

What makes matters worse from a treatment standpoint, even this resentment, this marital externalization of self-denial, is itself denied and masked, so that the parents often present themselves to the therapist as bland, compatible people who have no problems except for the black sheep who has inexplicably appeared in their midst. I have often heard parents say, "The only disagreements (far be it from them to have had out-and-out fights!) we have ever had have been over our son (or daughter)." They have been disagreeing, vehemently, with each other and with the child since he has had sphincter control with which to resist them, hands to grab things that they did not want him to have, legs to carry him out of their reach.

In such instances the parents seem actually to maintain their child's acting-out. A twelve-year-old boy, for example, was already demonstrating his need to seize what was not his by stealing bicycles, when his father bought him an old car to rebuild. The boy was four years younger than the statutory age at which the state permitted young persons to drive. Five years later, after a long series of automobile offenses and smashups, he was faced with an indefinite revocation of his permit, possible commitment to a state training school, and a bitter, no-exit deadlock with his father. The boy committed suicide—by closing himself inside his father's car and piping in the exhaust fumes.

The parents support the acting-out in ways and for reasons very similar to those by which other families disguise and externalize their conflicted relations in keeping one of their members schizophrenic or profoundly neurotic (Abrahams and Varon; Boverman and Adams; Jackson and Weakland; Will; Wynne, *et al.*). The child acts out their hostility, while they in their vicariousness are safe from their consciences; they can use him as a scapegoat for their frustrations; they can escape the problem of their individuation by preoccupying themselves with his, and by not letting him or enabling him to achieve self-reliance; and they can blame each other for the mess in which his young life is entangled, as a substitute for an honest confrontation of the other with personal grievances. Such encounters would risk the surrender of glorious hopes and guaranteed moral superiority for the more limited realities of mutual respect and help.

It seems plausible that one reason many of these delinquent youngsters are not simply driven crazy, considering the incompatible directives that their families thrust on them ("Control yourself but let us do it," the parents seem to say) is that their parents encourage conflict with the environment rather than, or at least as much as, within the child himself. The parents have harped on self-control for as long as the child can remember, but what they chiefly convey is that the child is incapable of effective self-guidance and is foredoomed to overwhelming environmental deprivation or punishment (Leventhal and Sills).

Several mothers have confided to me in quite similar expressions poor opinions of their sons' ego strengths, and their involvement in the sons' impulse life: "Even as a little boy, he grew up too fast. . . . He's always been too much ahead of himself." As one such boy described such parental overconcern, "It's like you push and push against a door and somebody is holding it shut. . . . Then they don't just let go, they pull it open. Now, I don't know what I want to do with myself. But I do know that if anybody pushes on me, I push back." This boy promoted his shoving matches from parents to school authorities and finally to the police.

Cultural Constraints

The lower-middle class marks the beginning of participation in a subculture determined by the upper-middle and lower-upper classes. Entry into the dominant culture is signalled by the emergence, in socialization and in adult action, of a dispositional system which may be an integrative need in itself or a common component of other integrative need systems, notably, those of creativity, mastery, regeneration, and belief or faith—the pervasive achievement orientation of the middle class, the striving toward standards of excellence (McClelland, *et al.;* Atkinson).

McClelland and Friedman provide cross-cultural evidence that the achievement motive is not limited to the middle classes of industrialized Western societies, not, in other words, an artifact of contemporary success strivings. The existence of the achievement motive at the middle-class level suggests that cultural conditions may free modal parental personality sufficiently from conflict regarding developmental needs to invest conflict-free ego energy in independence training (Winterbottom). The existence of the achievement need in the lower-middle class indicates greater cultural enfranchisement than lower classes have.

This is not to say that there are no disadvantages in lower-middle status, and that no characterologic erosion may ensue. "This cultural emphasis on achievement," Davis says, "arises largely from social insecurity; in lower-middle groups it arises largely from the fear of loss of occupation or respectability, which would plunge the family into lower class life" (p. 530). This threat may be particularly vivid and personal for recently mobile, especially Negro, families who continue to be exposed to a type of inaccessibility of integrative channels like withdrawal of eligibility by lower- and upper-middles. At the end of the Eisenhower administration, newspapers reported racial discrimination in hiring for Federal white-collar jobs and admittance to the older trade unions, many of whose members are of lower-middle status.

This fear of slipping back into lower-class life, as Davis puts it, reminds one of the theological doctrine of predestination. The doctrine is secularized by a society that measures a person's worth by the goods and status he acquires in this world; God's foreordainment is not explicitly stated. Nevertheless, a lower-middle-class person must show, by his daily observation of middle-class proprieties and pieties that he is one of God's elect who deserves to share success. Only those with superior innate gifts will win power, respect, and material comfort, so Little Orphan Annie's Daddy Warbucks, Ayn Rand, and the success ethic tell us; the underprivileged simply demonstrate their unworthiness and deserve to lose. One wonders, in passing, which segments of the middle class are the most numerous supporters of the Daddy Warbucks philosophies of right-wing political movements.

Structural Constraints and LM Adaptations

As suggested in Chapter 2, several social-structural processes may constrain some LMs toward self-limiting adaptations. Business enterprise is steadily bureaucratized and decision-making regarding production may be devolving on fewer and fewer people as all work roles continue to differentiate and become more specialized (Parsons, 1962). Furthermore, specialization may make jobs more routine, not in the sense that they become technically simpler, but rather that the rationalization of work establishes fixed procedures.

LMs are either skilled technicians or white-collar workers in public or private organizations which are becoming increasingly bureaucratized. It might be valuable to review Merton's discussion of the impact of bureaucratic structure on personality. Merton maintains that bureaucratic organization molds its own formality into the personalities of people working within it; they learn to "restrain the quick passage of impulse into action" (p. 151). The generality of procedural rules trains people in categorizing other people and situations (which reminds one of Fromm's "abstractifying" in alienation); bureaucracy maximizes security and minimizes various kinds of risk-taking; it stresses technical efficiency, and "approaches the complete elimination of personalized relationships and nonrational considerations (hostility, anxiety, affectional involvements, etc.)" (p. 152). Furthermore, bureaucracy, Merton maintains, encourages secrecy regarding decisions and information.

Merton considers these structural characteristics functional, in the sense that they serve bureaucratic operation. They can have dysfunctional consequences interpersonally, as in family relationships. Merton also examines certain aspects of bureaucracy which can render the structure itself inefficient. He mentions a "trained incapacity," in which the bureaucrat's skills get in the way of his coping with certain situations. Trained incapacity in bureaucrats produces rigidity in the face of change, Merton says, and an overconformity that induces "timidity, conservatism, and technicism."

The concept of trained incapacity is quite similar to the idea introduced in Chapter 2 that people restrict their ego capacities when they idealize constraints in the social structure. Moreover, the process of internalization is the same in both personal adaptations. Merton speaks of the transfer of the above sentiments from organizational ends to the details of instrumental behavior; in the development of ego constrictions, individuals invest limiting social realities with the possibility of satisfaction or perceive them as means to satisfactions. In both instances, people cathect social-structural limitations on personal action as objects or agents of personal gratification. These cathexes are then expressed as more generalized, and personalized, sentiments and values in the people who have formed such attachments.

As has been suggested, these cathexes may be achieved by regression in the service of the ego. I have said that people may search their personal histories until they identify elements of past object attachments and identifications that provide the best ways of living with depriving realities. They may also sift through their satisfaction potentials, ranging over and scanning their libidinal traits, to squeeze what satisfactions they can get from "given" sociocultural situations, and in order also to bind themselves more loyally to social norms from which they do not choose to deviate. (Again, for emphasis, instead of saying that people look for ways to become infantile, to "rebel" against "reality," it is proposed that people may exaggerate needs in the very act of trying to live with difficult situations.)

The ego characteristics and the impulses related to the era of sphincter training might be among the sources of adaptive responses to the rules and rationality that bureaucracy rates so highly. The psychoanalytic literature is replete with ideas and examples regarding issues of control of inner experience and over others' actions which may arise out of bowel- and bladder-struggles with socializers. Erikson has described some of the more aggressive ego aspects of this stage of development in terms of coercing others by withholding affect and response (1950). The obsessive-compulsive neuroses may be viewed as extreme illustrations of processes by which many other people cope with institutionalized routine and orderliness.

Bureaucratic situations, Merton maintains, stress categorizing, security, technicism, the elimination of affect, rigidity, and overconformity. Toilet regimentation and the accompanying ego crisis of autonomy—the era of "independence training" of the general behavior theorists (Child; Sears, Maccoby, and Levin; Whiting and Child; Winterbottom)—may produce character traits based on "anal" forms of aggression and on experiences of shame and doubt, which match these institutionalized requirements. A person with anal fixations and with accompanying ego limitations may orient much of his living by such rule-making and -following.

He tends to mistrust his own emotions as well as others' and maintains constant intellectual surveillance over them. He is attracted to fiats and prefers his authority relationships absolute and impersonal. The fear of shame (and of shameful exposure, psychoanalytic theory and practice tell us, of the servile and aggressive turns his sexual and other libidinal wishes have taken) drives him to preoccupations with interpersonally and socially safe routines. His character structure tends toward clinical descriptions of obsessiveness; his characteristic living patterns and social values follow Merton's description of the ritualist's life-style, and he is pre-formed for bureaucracies.

This is not to say that bureaucrats are all obsessive-compulsive neurotics, and certainly not that all or even most LMs are. I do assert, with Merton, that obsessive traits are "presumably more frequent" (p. 142) in this social class than in others. So too has Jurgen Ruesch:

> The lower-middle class with its preponderance of psychosomatic conditions can be characterized as the culture of conformance and excessive repressive tendencies. Because of lack of expressive facilities, the only possible solution for unsolved psychological conflicts seems to remain in physical symptom formation (pp. 130–31).

Possible Ideological Basis of LM Adaptations

Merton leaves open the question why obsessive personality traits are concentrated in the lower-middle class. Only speculations on this question, neither very detailed nor systematic ones at that, can be ventured here:

Bureaucracy is only one institutional expression of an instrumentalism that is a root premise and value of our culture. Neither the social machinery of bureaucracy nor the physical machinery of our technology could have come into being without a profound adherence to a belief that man, to realize himself, must subordinate his faculties to the production of things and services that others recognize as valuable. The inner dialectic between subordination and mastery is probably personalized for all of us in our private oedipal dramas, and in their re-enactments in our adult lives as we aspire to our superior's status and keep subordinates from our own. The theological assumption that men are instruments of God's will on earth is a fundamental value that Parsons (1962) has called "instrumental activism."

One might conclude that there are innumerable constraints on people, particularly on those in the broad middle class, to identify themselves as rational instrumentalities of God's (secular rendering: society's) will. The working-class boy who takes his education more seriously than do his friends has been instigated by some of these constraints, operating in his own life and through his parents; we say that he is upwardly mobile or middle-class-oriented, labeling values which are actually culture-wide as middle-class because they are clearest there.

Particular patternings and emphases are put on the ideology of instrumentalism in the lower-middle class. Merton has suggested, in his discussion of ritualism, that this adaptation results from child disciplining for conformity among LMs. However, as Merton indicates himself, this puts the cart in front of the horse, because the issue of LM parents' preoccupation with conformity is left unclarified.

There may be a differentiation among class subcultures of instrumentalist ideology and therefore of adaptive personal characteristics in each class. Certain kinds of obsessive rigidities occur more frequently in the characters of lower-middle class people. LMs implement and complete the activities of UM entrepreneurs, managers, and experts, who make decisions, initiate policies, or modify technology. UMs are the activists, LMs their loyal instruments. LM participation in the general culture requires them to be willing recipients of modification that UMs introduce.

In terms that were used earlier, LMs cathect this specialized function and tend to crystallize their ego and libidinal resources about it. Such characterological adaptations can clamp limitations on negotiating the satisfaction of other socialized strivings and may generate considerable hostility; the hostility will in turn follow the channels laid down in the character structures of these constricted individuals. The excesses of zealous and talented bureaucrats who have perverted instrumentalism to their highest ethic are detailed in some of Franz Kafka's stories and in the career of Adolph Eichmann.

This selective and fixative process would occur among those groups which may have had stable, lower-middle-class membership for generations, as for example, among some descendants of the earlier immigrations. A selective factor may also function in upward mobility and recruitment to the lower-middle class: only those members of newly mobile groups, like Negroes and descendants of recent immigrants, who are particularly fitted by their socialization to modal lower-middle traits will attract, and be attracted by, acceptance. Furthermore, the more obstinately the established lower-middles withhold eligibility, the greater the aspirants' compulsion to hold onto their new-found status, to put off complaints, and do away with aggressive feelings in themselves and their children.

Transmission of LM Self-Discontent: Developmental

Erikson has commented that the mobile Negro, in order to expunge from himself the white stereotype of "dark-dirty-dumb-nigger," has adopted a "violently sudden and cruel cleanliness training" (1959, p. 38). In another context Erikson comments,

> Minority groups of a lesser degree of Americanization (Negroes, Indians, Mexicans, and certain European groups) often are privileged in the enjoyment of a more sensual early childhood. Their crises come when their parents and teachers, losing trust in themselves and using sudden correctives to approach the vague but pervasive Anglo-Saxon ideal, create violent discontinuities (1959, p. 90).

His assertions are supported by the results of Davis and Havighurst's study of social class and color differences in child-rearing practices. While Negro middle-class children had consistently richer oral experience than their white peers, bowel training was begun earlier (87 percent at or before their sixth month) and completed earlier; bladder training was instituted and accomplished earlier than among the middle-class white families. The relative rigidity of lower-middle adults is suggested by the findings of a questionnaire study of class morality (Rettig and Pasamanick). Lower-middle white-collar workers who recently moved up to LM status have stronger strictures regarding general and economic moral issues than either blue-collar workers or middle-class professionals.

In the case of the potentially delinquent lower-middle-class child, certain elements in the socialization of achievement motivation, notably those of self-reliance and autonomy (Rosen and D'Andrade), may become progressively deemphasized. On the other hand, certain other, more restrictive elements in independence training, notably denial, delay, and self-control, may be over-emphasized, because these latter traits integrate the distinctive ways in which lower-middle-class people participate in the general culture. Strivings to compete and excel are shaped by emphatic cleanliness training and restrictive conditions on the exercise of ego autonomy.

Beller makes certain speculations in this vein. He predicts, and obtains empirical confirmation, that signs of oral and anal fixation in nursery school children would correlate positively with expressions of dependency and negatively with autonomous achievement striving. He predicts the negative correlation on the grounds that complications in sphincter training will have an adverse effect on exploratory activity, which he defines as a component of achievement striving.

He goes on to assert that

> Extreme conflict and frustration reaction to training toward sphincter control may produce certain heightened forms of autonomous achievement striving which, however, would fail to meet some of our criteria. Examples of such cases would be a heightened striving to achieve with impaired ability to complete work, with extreme frustration reactions to interferences and obstacles, with over-emphasis on details, with lack of satisfaction with work itself. Such manifestations would result in low scores on our measure of autonomous achievement striving, although more precise control will eventually be necessary to differentiate between these phenomena and the ones we set out to study (Beller, p. 292).

Transmission through Family Experience

"Extreme conflict and frustration reaction to sphincter training" will occur when the parents' regimes seem too hard. The poor frustration tolerance and the irritability which Beller sees as consequences are often the reactions of a child who feels control wrested from him and who doubts his own effectiveness because he has been disrespected. Parents who operate in such coercive ways have so enshrined obedience and control among their own personal sentiments that they have forgotten the meaning of personal freedom, and in fact disrespect their own autonomy.

They disrespect each others' autonomy as well. They rely on techniques of manipulative control as a principal way of having their wishes met. These tactics consist, for example, of disparaging what the other gives so as to get more, or of threatening to carry a grudge unless one has things his way, or of arranging circumstances so that the other is confronted with what seems an accomplished fact. These tactics are designed to avoid the possibility that the other might exercise a free choice.

There are at least two great advantages in free choice, as an ego value and as a sociopolitical value in our culture. It maximizes the chances for mutual satisfaction (through mutual regulation) between individuals. In the case of individuals or groups in relation to society, it optimizes the possibility of individuation of interests and actions—itself a basic evolutionary trend, perhaps, in Western culture—without forcing a choice also between normative conformity and deviance.

These advantages are lost on overcontrolled and overcontrolling parents, their lip service to the value of free choice notwithstanding. Instead of deriving benefits from getting something in exchange for giving—the benefits, that is, of a policy of live-and-let-live—they only fear negotiation as an exposure to the dangers of being helpless and exploitable. Indeed, a central problem of the kind of person I am trying to describe is the same dilemma that an "anally fixated" person experiences: He abhors dependency as much as he craves it, because he is afraid that he will be made to serve another's wishes against himself; consequently, he is chronically dissatisfied and hostile, and he both disguises and displays his dependent resentment in the control he exerts over his feelings and those of others.

Reiner and Kaufman describe anal-character-disordered parents of delinquents, highlighting the details of family and personal dynamics by examining a clinical extreme. Certainly, such clinically disturbed parents will make a much bigger mess of their lives (at least superficially) than those indicated here. Their egos, as Reiner and Kaufman describe them, are much weaker and more controlled by strategies of self-defeat. The relatively successful LM parents whom we are considering have more ego strength to begin with, and furthermore, they maintain a quid pro quo in their externalizations that affords each parent greater conscious feelings of security. But the needs, the fears, and the preoccupations of both kinds of parents are similar in kind, if not in quality and degree.

These LM overcontrollers of acting-out children have a tendency to thought-control of their children, arising from their general preoccupation with putting right thoughts over wrong feelings. Sometimes they spy on their children, or each other, and invade privacy. I had one such mother send me a note, from her daughter to a boy friend, that mother had intercepted. The note was taken up with plotting ways of manipulating the girl's parents. The mother had no realization of how much of her own plotting and prying she had shown me. At the bottom of the note the mother had circled the word "Christ!" and had appended the question, "Why does my daughter have to use such language?"—this piety in the middle of an intense struggle with her daughter, centering around the mother's vast projections that the girl was misbehaving sexually.

This tendency to self-righteous moralizing is a part of these parents' great concern about shoulds and oughts—that behavior must after all be governed by edict—and with their tendency toward arbitrary and oversimplified distinctions between good and bad and right and wrong. Ambiguity and complexity threaten their own impulse control.

Such parents often make a great fuss over their children's lack of personal responsibility, because of the parents' middle-class acculturation. They usually mean responsibility for one's actions and not for personal feelings, since the latter are to be disguised and secreted away. Often, the parents are themselves quite irresponsible regarding their private feelings and the consequences that these feelings engender in others. They rely on denial, avoidance, and projection of feelings as a way of handling their own responsibility for provoking hostility and aggression on the child's or marital partner's part. Then, often as not, they are astonished and aggrieved to discover that their child lies to them or employs such indirect forms of hostility as stealing from them.

These parents also teach their children to run away from trying situations. Some of these mothers characteristically evade disciplining the child. After making it clear that he must be punished, they leave the dirty work for father. Sometimes they compound this flight from the situation by manipulating their husbands. They may not directly ask him to punish, but they coerce the husband by acting so upset about the child that he punishes in order to "keep peace in the family," as many fathers misguidedly put it.

Often, the father administers his punishment cruelly or impulsively because he is displacing, from wife to child, a rage he may feel regarding his wife's more general, dependent hostility. Her dependency is plain in her failure to manage the situation. She may be acting out her hostility toward him by making him her executioner, by creating an antagonism between father and child. The "peace" that these fathers may be buying, at the price of their children's love and loyalty, is their euphemism for flight from confrontation with marital problems. His own dependency may make him afraid to deal with a sharp-tongued or grudging wife, or he may be gratifying his own hostility toward her by watching endless bickering and baiting between wife and child. Father, too, shows the child how to run away from things. Again, these parents are perplexed and righteously indignant when their child is expelled from school for truanting, or steals a car to run away from trouble.

Such parents' fear of unrequited dependency needs, which was mentioned as a nuclear problem in their relationships, breeds still another, the fear of intimacy. This fear of intimacy contributes semi-independently to their estrangement, since it would operate against any resolution of differences which might bring them closer. They fear closeness because they fear opening themselves to another; in their black-and-white terms receptiveness means passivity, and passivity threatens some of them, at the most profoundly private levels, with the possibility of homosexual submission. Sexual ambivalence is a trait of the anal-character-disordered parents whom Reiner and Kaufman describe; the wish submissively to gratify an aggressive other, and the fear of this wish, are also traits of the adults described here.

This fear of intimacy, by the way, is an instance of a sacrifice in ego capacity which interferes with an integrative end-state, as discussed in Chapters 2 and 3. The consequences of parents' strictures on their own ego autonomy limits their capacity for intimacy. In turn, psychosocial conditions for leading their children toward maturity are lacking.

Both father and mother have their respective ways of showing the ambivalence mentioned above, as a character trait and in their sexual feelings. The father may express his sexual insecurity, that is, his anxiety regarding underlying passive wishes, in his inadequate performance of his sex role. He is hostile about his wife's and, in turn, his children's flouting of his authority; yet, ambivalently, he submits to belittling. Often, he drones away when his children misbehave, with boring and ineffectual lectures in high-flown terms and with a distant manner, hoping that his wife will catch the note of aggrieved righteousness in his voice and take it to heart herself.

For her part, the mother frequently has remained absorbed in an extremely infantile relation with her mother throughout her marriage. If the maternal grandmother is not physically established in her daughter's home, she often lives close by. She continually intrudes on her daughter's marriage and on her management of the children. Whether the married daughter cravenly plays up to her mother or keeps up a running feud with her, her husband and children are sometimes left to pick up whatever emotional scraps are left over from a relationship that is primary for both women; or they have to take care of, or put up with, mother when she is feeling neglected by her first and real love.

His parents' reiteration of rules and punishment convinces the child that if he asserts his will he will be dealt overwhelming humiliation. One result is that he worries when he sets himself a goal or is presented with an achievement situation. Another is that, very early, he starts to recoil angrily or rashly from any prospective failure, as Beller suggests and as Leventhal and Sills observe in the delinquent boys they treated. His problems with self-control and his resistance to external control take another turn during the Oedipal phase of his development. His mother, who is as unsatisfiable with him as she is with her husband, leads him on nevertheless because he is anxious to please, and because he may be more pliant and available than her husband.

A resentful disappointment becomes evident in the boy's manner with mother that revives sharply during his adolescent quarrels with her. Mother is the one who is *really* on his back; he maintains that he cannot get a pleasant word out of her. He means more than her Oedipal betrayal of him for his father. In her hostility, mother built up his hopes and his susceptibilities to her and then withholds her affection or carps at him. His interest in his mother's attentions and her divisive tactics with father and son leave him antagonistic and guarded toward father, guilty and fearful of punishment for his ambitions and hopes.

Inferiority, Achievement, and the School

Psychological analysis is inadequate if it does not reckon with the consequences of earlier experiences in school adjustment, especially for a middle-class child. Success or failure in school is obviously much more important for middle-class people than it is for those in lower social strata. I believe that the outcome of the first achievement experiences (in the primary grades) of the LM child who has lived with the people just described, and with their effects on him, finally determines what he does about his self-discontent during adolescence.

When he begins in first grade, he is deservedly suspicious of external controls, and these would include, to his mind, those limits the school sets around proper efforts and behavior. He doubts his ability to bring off independent action successfully, that is, without humiliating consequences. He has been provided no suitable sublimation for his will, which has been curbed by conformity training, or for the sense of enterprise, which is a casualty of his entanglement with mother and his estrangement from father. Autonomy and initiative, in Erikson's terms, are encumbered by self-doubt and guilt.

Whether these forms of self-discontent are displaced to other people and external situations and begin to be expressed in norm-violative behavior, or develop into a private, symbolic symptom pattern, depends on the outcome of the child's encounter with the school and learning, during latency. If the child obtains some security or accomplishment in school he will get a personal stake in continued participation. If his failure mobilizes so much parental attention that he does not dare stop trying openly, the boy will join the adults against his own private wishes. He will struggle with indifferent success to read the words that the adults put before him. His memory will fail him on tests for which he has studied. He will attend in class but make his homework too difficult to complete. He will be engrossingly afraid of teachers. If, however, the boy fails in school early or continually, and does not meet effective parental intervention, he will begin a process of conscious repudiation of school achievement and conformity.

The Process III boy enters the school with limits wrought on him by his class-engendered socialization: a clamp on spontaneity, a fear of initiative, and guilty subordination to those who take it; a socialization that overemphasizes the security and recognition to be gained by renunciation of impulses, and that neglects to provide a mastery or pleasure which might sublimate powers that are also being renounced. His subculture deprives him of the means to launch himself with an enterprising curiosity on the quest of learning; he ends without the personal means for learning. He loses, during latency, the development of the cognitive and the perceptual facilities required to learn. The failure to organize these ego skills results in a desire to escape planful efforts which constitutes the strain toward deviance in Process III. His early socialization makes him the object of a subcultural deprivation of motivational and emotional means for reaching end-states. This deprivation precipitates a critical loss of structural (ego) means, creating a powerful avoidant motive which determines him on a path of deviant adaptation.

A forced achievement need may result in a failure of development in late childhood. According to Beller's estimate, this type of achievement training would facilitate high standards with low stamina and poor frustration tolerance, further beset by obsessiveness and dislike of work. Without success, the Process III child will not extend himself to learn. Without educative effort, he will not lead out and command the cognitive faculties available to him. And so the resistiveness, obsessiveness, and compulsivity modeled into the grain of the child's early strivings, later institute the latency failure in Process III.

Only when the personality finally concerts, with some provisional effectiveness, its bodily realities with the bodily realities of others, does it seem free to further differentiate capacities latent in its current organization. These capacities include "perception, intention, object comprehension, thinking, language, recall-phenomena, productivity . . . and . . . the maturation and learning processes implicit in all these and many others" (Hartmann, p. 8). The maturation and learning necessary to effectively manage and use these perceptual-cognitive functions are absolutely essential to a fruitful educational experience. One must learn how to learn, and one must be free to grow and learn.

Erikson's psychosocial crisis of latency is between a sense of industry or one of inferiority and inadequacy. It assumes a further elaboration of cognitive functions in latency, and it relates the fate of these functions to the nature of the child's learning experience. "(T)here is the danger (probably the most common one) that throughout the long years of going to school he will never acquire the enjoyment of work and the pride of doing at least one kind of thing well" (Erikson, 1959, p. 88). Erikson remarks on an aspect of the crisis of industry that is crucial for a peculiarly American (or Western industrial society) identity, the child's derivation of a sense of equality in industrial association. It is, he says, "equality of all those who apply themselves wholeheartedly to the same skills and adventures in learning" (p. 91).

The Process III child, however, is psychologically handicapped in this quest for a feeling of industrious equality. His achievement need is freighted with ambivalent sentiments toward the conditions set down in school for achievement, and it is hedged in by his personal insecurities. This child is predisposed to intimidation by the school's learning requirements and by the competitive aspects of the learning situation. He probably starts resisting the educational process early. This writer's experience with the Wechsler Intelligence Scale for Children is that one is likely to find the typical test score pattern in an acting-out adolescent, that is, a pattern consisting of lower verbal than performance scores—representing long-standing retardation in developing verbal abilities and difficulties with classroom tasks—whether the child is LM or lower-class.

Identity Crisis III

Deviant behavior in Process III may begin during latency in the form of provocative, aggressive, or destructive behavior against the school and repeated, compulsive flight from it. But the final push, the transformation into gang delinquency with norms organized about theft and destruction of others' property, illegal drinking, and disorderly behavior, etc., may come only at the onset of adolescence. Then, the inferiority that the youth has been seeking to escape and deny is finalized, so to speak, by the higher performance requirements of the intermediate grades and by the conforming rejection of more favored and accomplished peers.

The Process III youngster deals with some of the important changes and challenges of adolescence by taking interpersonal distance from them, and so appears to be a stranger to teachers, family, and sometimes to himself. The estrangement is usually not complete, however, nor is it always a marked characteristic of this type of youth; it usually depends on the degree to which his parents have dealt obsessively with each other and with him.

In this matter of expressive style, he is less likely to resemble the kind of acting-out adolescent described by Leventhal and Sills. Their picture is that of an expansive, breezy, and disturbed youth who tries immediately to take over in situations. The Process III youth is more like an extreme of the "normal" adolescent as he is described by Adelson: He is constricted in his approach to situations and guarded in his verbal reactions. Often, he denies the ambiguity and the intensity of his feelings, or tries to funnel all of them into anger. Consequently, he sometimes seems deaf, dumb, and blind to his inner life, even when he tries to grasp it. He tries to express and fight out all of the important wishes and choices which beset him in terms of the teen-age trivia of cars, pocket money, clothes, curfews, and, less trivially, in terms of school failure and law violations.

Often, he can only watch adults distrustfully, resenting their power over him, and yet, both fearfully and withholdingly, dodging confrontations of them when opportunity offers. When questioned about himself, even when his trust—such as he can muster, that is—is won, his answers tend to the monosyllabic and uninformatively banal, as if he were abiding by the articles of war in the presence of captors. He can abandon himself to action when that action conveys his nosethumbing at rules and conforming effort—in car thefts and drag races on open highways, in neighborhood and school hell-raising that brings school expulsion and charges of incorrigibility, disturbing the peace, and vandalism against him. This abandonment occurs in the company of friends all of whom agree tacitly never to intrude personal uncertainties or feelings of isolation into their mutual search for action and distraction. He is, in this sense, a stranger to his friends and they to him.

The marked scholastic difficulties that often show up in intermediate and junior high school are only a finalization of his failure to identify himself as a worker and a doer. Long before adolescence he had foresworn the possibility of earning status and equality through efforts. (This resume follows Erikson's dimensions of the adolescent identity crisis, as did the closing passages of Processes I and II.) His identification with father had been impeded by antagonisms; those partial identifications which he may have managed also include negative elements in his father's conformity, those characteristics based on self-doubt and guilt.

Thus, his acting-out conveys certain fixated and regressed trends in his parents' personalities. It betrays his commitment to self-limiting life-styles forged by those who preceded him. It also is a limited protest against his parents' psychocultural adaptations, like lower-class, Processes I and II youth whose delinquency is a more obvious living-out of and resistance to sentiments prevailing in their subcultures.

The compulsions of the Process III youngster's parents, regarding limit-setting and housebreaking, gave him an acute awareness of self as risking failure in new ventures instead of a reasonable self-assurance. He gave back to his father, on his own behalf and his mother's, some of the same estrangement his father showed him. As a partial result, he acquired a negative sense of being different from his father, rather than a security, which he might have acquired through identification, to play-act different kinds of male roles. Indeed, he may also have acquired a sense of negative differentness from his other siblings, when his mother needed a ready scapegoat. Before the machinery of community and police label him a delinquent, his parents and teachers attach to him the negative identity of a rule-evader and -breaker, of being impulse-ridden and unreachable through ordinary appeals and threats.

He no longer hopes for conforming achievement; he rationalizes away the value of education. His previous repudiation of responsibility brings about a profound work paralysis that sets him on a seemingly downward-mobile course. Only his wanderings and adventures with his companions, with their occasional delinquencies, appear to provide the Process III youth with a dependable escape from relentless pressures to aspire to goals which he believes (usually secretly) are beyond his powers. He is willing to go to great lengths, including the violation of conventional norms, in order to controvert the sense of inferiority he must experience if he were to accept their legitimacy.

Accomplishments are barred to him by limitations and injuries to interpersonal functions of his ego, and by syncretisms of objectivating ego functions as a result of failure in the primary grades. As a consequence, he would rather feel the power of defeating the efforts of others to direct and control him than to experience himself as a passive, weak agent of other's wishes—even if the assertion of his will in this way is itself ultimately self-defeating. He would rather be a stranger than a class dunce, or a pushover for someone else's pieties. "There are only two places to be," one such boy said. "Everybody inside the system is controlled by somebody else. I'm outside it."

chapter 13

process IV

SOME UM people disregard their own worth in their slavish devotion to the ideology of success. They believe that they are nothing other than what the world says they are. Consequently, they are driven to acquire adulation and power in their interpersonal relationships as much as in the success symbols they seek. They are vain, exploitative, and insensitively self-serving marriage partners and parents. Often, they want to be worshipped by their marriage partners; and, often as not, this desire is defeated by private guilts and inadequacy feelings, stemming from developmental experiences which predispose them to a feverish pursuit of success.

Because so many of their interpersonal strivings are based on vanity and feelings of unworthiness, their marriages are frequently shallow, unstable affairs. They are unfaithful to each other and to their child's needs for dependability and for elementary considerateness. The cynicism and self-centeredness that he acquires, in his reactions and by their example, make it extremely difficult for him to give fidelity to any of the values and ideals on which conforming, achievement-oriented behavior is based.

He does not believe that any significant adults take their ideals seriously enough to value any commitment he might make. His pressure to deviance, then, is his distrust of legitimate ideals and values. His refusal to obligate himself to any prospective integrative goals leaves him mired in the immaturity and the insecurity with which his childhood experiences have saddled him. In order to escape the regressive pull of his fixations, on the one hand, and the lack of inspiriting ideological choices on the other, he flees into a negative, hedonistic identity that obliterates past and future in the moment, and that conveys his rejection of conventional values.

As I wrote the previous three examples of psychocultural processes leading to delinquency, it became clear that each process is only one way of organizing a variety of related material, and that each "type" is, like so many typologies, a stereotype. Three main themes were selected out of many possible others: matriarchy and mistrust among the banished; patriarchy and rebellion among the patronized, and the over-piety of some of the "backbone" and the over-private desperation of some of their children. The possible variations on each of these themes became more importunate with each page written.

Permutations and combinations have been crooking their fingers at me, or waggling them reproachfully for being ignored. I have had the feeling that I had to keep my wits about me for fear that some of these stray thoughts would take over my theory and revise it to suit themselves. At any rate, a theory is made to be questioned. So I'll finish proposing, and the reader will dispose as he pleases, of themes, variations and all.

Family Consequences of UM Adaptations—An Overview

The UM delinquent of this fourth process is a cynic who has had so many articles of faith traduced that his youthful capacity for devotion has failed. (This process may also be found among some middle-middle and lower-upper delinquents whose family situations may correspond to what will be described.) His parents are thralls of success; they believe in little else besides conspicuous acquisitions and visible signs of power and status. They have exaggerated the significance of opportunity as a value and have oversimplified it to mean opportunism. They translate individuality into careerism, and initiative and industriousness into ruthless self-service and exploitation.

Both parents seek self-display and adulation above most other experiences, and may have been quite fickle and faithless in feeding their vanities. The child may have been dragged through one or two previous marriages before his adolescence, and lobbed back and forth among several households and private schools while his parents pursued their respective fantasies through various partnerships. Moreover, the set of parents with whom he is residing during adolescence may openly show their scorn and the shallowness of their feeling for one another by carrying on extramarital affairs that are thinly disguised or are open family scandals.

Frequently, the parents may show an amazing insensitivity or an appalling indifference in their own acting-out, to their child's most elementary needs for security and dependability. The Process IV youth may present the same callow and self-indulgent view of life's purposes and of relations with others. But he will do so in a gross, adolescent way, "with the bark on," and without the superficial niceties of manner and the pleasantries with which his parents have learned to decorate their secondary relationships.

Underlying this boy's suspension of belief lies a history of betrayals and bad faith by his parents toward some of his most essential feelings about himself. His delinquency is a flight into a negative identity from his scorn for a beginning ideological commitment, essential to a resolution of the identity crisis. Though his scorn for new commitments merits respect on its face, it also masks the backward-looking, fearful tenacity of an insecure child.

Sociocultural Constraints and UM Adaptations

The following passage from Fromm is quoted because it captures the loss of mature ego activity—what was referred to earlier as the attainment of integrative end-states—which may result from an obsessional pursuit of financial success:

The alienating function of money in the process of acquisition and consumption has been beautifully described by Marx in the following words: "Money . . . transforms the real human and natural powers into merely abstract ideas, and hence imperfection, and on the other hand, it transforms the real imperfections and imaginings, the powers which only exist in the imagination of the individual into real powers. . . . It transforms loyalty into vice, vices into virtue, the slave into the master, the master into the slave, ignorance into reason, and reason into ignorance. . . . He who can buy valour is valiant although he be cowardly. . . . Assume *man* as *man*, and his relation to the world as a human one, and you can exchange love only for love, confidence for confidence, etc. If you wish to enjoy art, you must be an artistically trained person; if you wish to have influence on other people, you must be a person who has a really stimulating and furthering influence on other people. Every one of your relationships to men and to nature must be a definite expression of your *real, individual* life corresponding to the object of your will."*

* "Nationalökonomie und Philosophie," 1844, published in Karl Marx' *Die Frühschriften*, Alfred Krämer Verlag, Stuttgart, 1953, pp. 300, 301 (My translation, E. F.). (Fromm, p. 132.)

Individuals may perform important community and economic functions and acquire symbols prized in the culture without acting integratively. Participation in corporate enterprise, communications, or political life (to select the three prime targets of contemporary social commentary) can be highly integrative or conducive to personal integration; still, some of the people doing this work operate successfully by other means to other ends: to be "successful," in the sense of acquiring the cultural trappings of significance, by manipulation, conscious or unconscious, whether of others or self.

Merton has said that

(W)hen . . . success becomes construed as "winning the game" rather than "winning under the rules of the game," a premium is implicitly set upon the use of illegitimate but technically efficient means. . . . The process whereby exaltation of the ends generates a literal *demoralization*, i.e., a de-institutionalization, of the means occurs in many groups. (pp. 128, 129) (C)ontemporary American culture continues to be characterized by a heavy emphasis on wealth as a basic symbol of success, without a corresponding emphasis upon the legitimate avenues on which to march toward this goal (p. 133).

On the top economic levels, the pressure toward innovation not infrequently erases the distinction between businesslike striving this side of the mores and sharp practices beyond the mores. As Veblen observed, "It is not easy in any give and take—indeed it is at times impossible until the courts have spoken—to say whether it is an instance of praiseworthy salesmanship or a penitentiary offense" (pp. 134–35).

Merton also reviews data that norm-violative behavior, specifically felonies, was so prevalent among a large sample of conforming, middle-class adults that it could properly be called a statistically normal characteristic of this group (pp. 135, 136).

An upper middle-class person who has obligated himself to success—a "wheeler-dealer" entrepreneur, some salesmen, a supremely ambitious corporation executive, the professional devoted basically to accumulating prestige and money—turns himself and others into instruments of his passion, or neglects and discards those aspects of his experience, including some relationships, which do not serve it. In his idolatry he has to serve and submit to the vagaries of taste and economic opportunity; he is under pressure to treat most of his attachments to people and situations as subject to change without notice. As a result, he cannot allow himself deep attachments, but more than that, he is constrained to disregard his own needs to be trusted and prized for his personal qualities by others. Such seekers of power and admiration tend paradoxically to disrespect themselves. They give themselves too little opportunity to enjoy family, friends, and community. They have devalued the more intimate, and in some ways simpler, adult satisfactions, and in doing so disparage their own worth. They hope to compensate for a private emptiness by empire-building and by conquests of other men and adventures with women. Failure to them means to be inept and useless and to be outmaneuvered by those few people for whom they have regard, other operators and manipulators. They live from coup to coup, and in between they nurse their vanity.

The businessman may employ "wealth and power" to achieve his asocial ends: He forces or buys that which the norms forbid him to force or buy. An approximate psychological rendering of this kind of innovation (of norm-violative means) would seem to be found in the notion of manipulation, "the use of man by man," to use Fromm's phrase. If we discover that someone has enlisted our actions, ostensibly for our personal, or for mutual, advantage, but really so that he might gain, and we gain nothing or lose, we say that the other is selfish or that he has used us. The matter may be a swindle or not, depending on whether legal norms have been violated; sociologically, "selfishness" refers to his neglect and violation of normative obligations on his behavior which are intended to assure mutual security in the social system. If the other intended his own advantage, and we accepted on the pretext that we would gain, then even if we actually do benefit, he was still manipulating us, and so perhaps were we manipulating him (if we were "on to him" but "played along"). This is the criticism Fromm makes of the ethic of "fair play," and the basis of his assertion that twentieth-century capitalism, as much as was the more exploitative nineteenth, is based on the use of man by man (p. 93). Furthermore, duplicity is not essential since the innovator-manipulator may employ his money and power in violation of others' interests very openly.

Psychologically, in order for the other to manipulate our efforts to his advantage, he must relate to us as if we were objects, as instrumentalities who are for the moment less real in human dimensions than he is. He must disregard or deny his perception of us as like beings with similar histories, predicaments, and prospects. Or he must perceive only our acquisitive and self-seeking similarities to himself to justify his acts; but then he is making a prophesy regarding our motives which we must fulfill if we are to survive with him (Merton, pp. 179–95). He must "abstractify" our wishes, he must deny us; he must alienate himself from *the possibility of any mature wishes in himself that he might integrate with us.* That is, the manipulator cannot possibly commune with his object to enlarge his realm of belonging, clarify and verify his belief, and unify himself; nor can he make or adorn anything which has relevance to this community, since he prevents its existence in himself. He is, in the manipulative act, an organization of energy, will, wits, knowledge, and feeling, functioning alone in a collection of similar monads, who never have had or will have any bearing on one another except those of utility or obstruction.

Put this way it sounds improbable or overdone; yet I am trying to suggest an image of personal experience and behavior which is not incompatible with the anomie by which Durkheim and Merton explain massive social deviance. It is also an image that approaches Fromm's conception of alienation—without the attribution of self-denial applicable in Process III, and emphasizing here the acquisitive function of this adaptation. Again, this definition of self creates its own reality; it must bring consequences, in the reaction and proaction of others, which will prove the value of that self-definition. Behavior among such atomized people will prominently display distrust, deceit, or ruthlessness.

UM Adaptations and Family Experience

And what do the children see?

Erikson has said that

> (O)nly through constant rededication will [social] institutions gain the active and inspired investment of new energy from their young members. . . . (O)*nly by maintaining, in its institutionalized values, meaningful correspondences to the main crises of ego development*, does a society manage to have at the disposal of its particular group identity a maximum of the conflict-free energy accrued from the childhood crises of a majority of its young members (1959, p. 155; my italics).

We might ask what levels of ego development children and youth in the dominant classes may see represented in the activities of their parents; how an adolescent's conflict-free energies, in search of absorbing, worthy forms, can be attracted to manipulation, alienation, vanity, and the accumulation of things.

The boy's father at the time of his adolescence may not be his natural father. Mother may have traded the latter in on a new model who may himself have come and gone from the boy's life. Sometimes the several men whom the boy called father have shared many of the characteristics to be described, because of mother's interest in this kind of man. He may have paid the child incidental attention, enough to persuade himself of his merits as a father, but in fact has often considered the child a part of the baggage that came with his wife, or worse, an obstacle in the way of his making full claim on her attention and favors. This kind of man is interested in enhancing himself in his own eyes and others', and his wife is, much more than other men's, a sexual object and a decoration that he likes to display.

With this sort of indifference and hostility to the child, the father may deprive him of many essential ego experiences, breaking the child's faith in those of his own characteristics and of others that are most critical at the several stages of the child's ego development. The mother's self-centeredness, and disruptions of her married life during the child's babyhood, may already have provided him with poor experiences in trusting. After that, this father, or his predecessors, may have ignored, scorned, or punished the child's assertiveness, humiliating or frightening him into feelings of insignificance.

Father's resentment of the boy's claims on mother would prompt him to drive the boy off or override him when he might try to initiate an activity with the father as well as mother. It is likely, therefore, that the boy will have failed to establish sufficient work identifications with his father to put any zest into learning. As a result, he may pass through a latency period that is, at best, undistinguished by achievement and which gives him no strong sense of industriousness. At worse, the boy's ego deficiencies may be so great that he begins to show a pattern of underachievement and misbehavior in the primary grades, similar to that of the Process III child.

Sometimes his parents respond to this school failure by placing him in a private or a military boarding school, late in latency or even earlier. They thus solve several problems at once: Father rids himself of the interloper, mother is free to pursue her romantic adventures (sometimes the placement is made just before a marriage breakup or between marriages), and both are emotionally freed of disturbing reminders of the boy's resentment toward their selfishness.

The boy's mother is often a very attractive-looking woman. Sometimes she has a flashy and overly made-up attractiveness to go along with her being overly on-the-make. She cares more for self-display and for the admiration of men and the envy of other women than for most other things. She wants their admiration, but she rarely reciprocates. Sometimes she claims that she likes only men or gets along with them better, but this usually means that they will join her in games of seduction and conquest. In fact she does not like people, usually, and does not trust them very far. Often, she feels a contempt for her husband that is partly founded on a self-contempt: "He can't be much if he likes me."

The general shallowness of her feelings for others and of her commitments to them are related to her experiences with her parents and with the kinds of people they were. Her mother was dissatisfied with her own husband and made the daughter a confidante of her contempt and disappointment. Her mother (our Process IV youth's grandmother) also encouraged her to live out the mother's grievances and daydreams: It is a sad fact of life that it is a man's world; men are out for what they can get; therefore, a girl either uses her wits and charms to get what she can, or else she is a fool.

Some of the maternal grandmother's hostile attitudes were externalizations of her poor opinion of herself and of being a woman. Therefore, she also directly disparaged her daughter's femininity. As a result the Process IV youth's mother may have grown up feeling insecure as well as acquisitive and manipulative. These feelings were confirmed by her father's relationship with her. Either he disliked her, treating her as a scapegoat for his problems with his wife, or else he acted seductively and disrespectfully. He may have played with her as if she were a pretty toy, interesting himself only in her appearance and caring very little for what she thought or felt. He thus corroborated his wife's version of men's attitudes toward women, and substantiated daughter's feelings that what she was as a person was of little value.

The mother of the Process IV youth plays seductive games with her son. She tries to "save" him from the indifference or cruelty of his father or step-father, and she wants to mold for herself a little man who, unlike the big ones, will do her bidding. Sometimes, in between marriages or during separations, she may shunt the boy over to her mother. The latter often spoils the boy, and for similar reasons, despite the fact that by now grandmother may have grown sons who have not been able to accept their own work and family responsibilities, because similar overindulgence and seduction made it impossible for them to achieve adequate masculine identifications. One such boy was living with his mother and his second step-father in what was a disastrous marriage. His favorite fantasy was to return to his maternal grandmother's home with his mother and have both women keep him in expensive cars, clothes, and pocket money. This boy made open sexual grabs at his mother.

The Process IV boy's father has had his own experiences and

reasons to account for his desperate ambition and insensitive selfishness. Often, his mother was both extraordinarily ambitious for him and dominant in her marital relationship. She may have been insensitively insulting to her husband. The latter (the paternal grandfather) was, frequently, impotently hostile toward the son, unable to get past mother's protection; or he meekly accepted mother's major investment of affection in her son, thus tacitly admitting his son's primacy over him.

The Process IV father thus grows up with a burning desire to live out his mother's wishes and with an arrogance born of his father's defeat. But he also grows up with a great unconscious guilt born of the same defeat. This guilt makes him feel a secret unworthiness, which on the one hand drives his sore and bedeviled vanity, and on the other, prompts him to deprive himself in doing without trust, friendship, community, and sense of belongingness. His Oedipal guilt overdetermines his slavish, self-sacrificial worship of success.

Thus, Process IV families would include those highly mobile people whose needs and wishes fit them for an overbearing success ideology. One might predict that their class origins were lower than their attained status. They might be found more frequently in those occupations where status rewards are high. Also, the occupations of the fathers offer great financial returns, as in the communications industries and in booming entrepreneurial ventures, such as real estate development. One would expect them to reside in the expensive, prestigious new suburbs of metropolitan centers.

Thus, adults may perform important socioeconomic functions for other than integrative purposes. Indeed, our society as it is presently organized is in some ways well-served by the drive of these entrepreneurs and operators. Furthermore, their self-discontent is sociologically a functional equivalent of the self-realizing of UMs performing the same roles, because the differing psychological motivations get the same work accomplished. (See Chapter 2 for a discussion of the functional equivalence, sociologically, of differing personal incentives.) These negatively conforming parents (see Chapter 3) transmit their self-discontent to the child, not just by direct role-modeling but also by imposing on his ego development. He translates ego constrictions into personal discontent and eventually into social discontent.

The Process IV youngster accrues a margin of psychosocial failure and of psychosexual limitations as he approaches adolescence. He externalizes personal discontent in his refusal to grant fealty and fidelity to any of the social values and ends around which most of his peers organize achievement-oriented identities. (See Erikson, 1962, on the importance of a sense of fidelity to youth.) His mother's emphasis on achievement and conformity strikes him as hypocritical in the light of her past disloyalties to him and to men. His father always seemed to take what he wanted, and was proud of his treachery and defeats of others; the boy does not see why he should be called on to have regard for others' feelings and to mesh his interests with theirs. This youth refuses to credit any endeavor with deserving his devotion, and his faithlessness is founded on his broken trusts.

Identity Crisis IV

An adolescent must be able to find in available identity models ways that will enable him (1) to bind up, for once and all, the old counter-claims against his adulthood of early ties and wishes, stirred up now by a revolution of growth, and (2) to find some coherent yet multiform, familiar yet unique shape to express, integratively, the free energy and the ego skills available from earlier psychosocial successes. Furthermore, these models must (3) comprise leaders, valued in the culture, who call for organization of self because they value it in themselves and others, and (4) the models must also impart the *meaning and value for the culture* of these renunciations and integrative commitments. (See Erikson on leadership polarization and the function of ideology in surmounting the identity crisis, 1959, pp. 120, 142, 146; and 1962.)

In other words, the adolescent will identify and obligate a significant portion of his acquired and created potentials *if and only if* the adult culture recognizes them, beckons to them, makes and keeps a place for them, and welcomes them. The privileged, anomic, manipulative, shallow, and quietly desperate milieu that may exist in some segments of the upper-middle and lower-upper classes would not have models to embody the renunciation, integrity, ideology, or authority for securing relations between adolescent identity and culture. And the adolescent will not leap into nothingness—unless he becomes convinced that the alternatives are worse.

Some of Goodman's comments are peculiarly germane to the problem of the Process IV boy:

We live increasingly, then, in a system in which little direct attention is paid to the object, the function, the program, the task, the need; but immense attention to the role, procedure, prestige and profit. . . . (T)he task is rarely done with love, style, excitement, for such beauties emerge only from absorption in real objects (p. xiii) [Growth requires adequate objects in the environment to meet growing needs and capacities; delinquency is not a matter of poor influences or bad attitudes, but is] an objective question of real opportunity for worthwhile experience. . . . (O)ur abundant society is simply deficient in many of the most elementary objective opportunities and worthwhile goals that could make growing up possible. It is lacking in enough man's work. It is lacking in honest public speech, and people are not taken seriously. It is lacking in the opportunity to be useful. It thwarts aptitude and creates stupidity. It corrupts ingenuous patriotism. It corrupts the fine arts. It shackles science. It dampens animal ardor. It discourages the religious convictions of Justification and Vocation and it dims the sense that there is a Creation. It has no Honor. It has no Community (p. 12).

I am not sure that I subscribe to Goodman's evaluation of our society, but this passage is an eloquent statement of the Process IV boy's nihilism.

Two other of Goodman's observations are also relevant: Delinquency is a sign of, as much as anything else, unutterable boredom with the culture (p. 72); and, an individual who is deprived of faith in the possibility of his cultural order will be without a vocation (in the strict sense of a calling) and without honor, as based on a faith in self, which is a different thing from the woundable conceit of the organization man or of the subcultural delinquent.

Delinquency as Social Protest—A Resumé

Each delinquent type that I have discussed is in some way aware of the cultural adversities besetting him and is directing his efforts against them; he is not just responding in terms of the regressed impulses and restricted relations bestowed on him by these adversities. In each process, for example, a negative relation that the dominant classes hold to the class level in which the process occurs may be specified; one can also specify behaviors by which the delinquent seems to symbolize his rejection of the relation that the normative order is in a sense forcing between him and itself.

In Process I, a lack of relatedness among members of marginal groups results in an infantile character formation in youth which strains toward unlimited power and gratification. The destruction of character was initiated by ostracism, and the current attitude of the dominant classes to these groups is still that of ostracism. I am reminded of tough Negro delinquents from such slum areas, caricaturing with deadly overstatement, for each other's amusement, in a psychotherapy group, the impassively polite or pompous tone of a middle-class Anglo-Saxon authority. The impersonator would finally make his point: the white male's appeals to reason disguise an attempt to gain a personal advantage. Abruptly they became young Negroes laughing uproariously, "giving each other skin"—touching palms—in knowing comradeship. Their great scorn for white boys who submitted sexually had an unrelievedly stereotyped quality; it was as if they were giving back to the whites their version of a racial caste system, with the very same aggressive and animal sexuality that the white had projected on them.

In Process II, a rebellious mother's son shares and suffers from a subcultural resistance to male authority. The relation of dominant groups, in the European peasant origins of this process and in our contemporary society, to the class level involved is one of exploitation for economic advantage. The relatively favorable position of American industrial labor does not detract from the basic consideration that, as Fromm says, "the employer has bought the services of the worker, and however human his treatment may be, still commands him, not on a basis of mutuality, but on the basis of having bought his working time for so many hours a day" (p. 94). A Process II delinquent will readily inform a listener of the illicit ways in which the dominant classes acquire and use wealth. But his cynicism is not just a rationale for the loosening of his own normative controls; it is an objective assessment of a particular state of affairs. He may reject middle-class respectability and manners and want only money, not just because he is identified with his own class as opportunity theory allows, but because he views the middle-class emphasis on amenities as an instance of hypocrisy masking disrespect for all but financial success.

One might say that the relation of members of the upper-middle and lower-upper classes to the members of the lower-middle, site of Process III, is colored by attitudes of patronization. In turn, Process III fathers progressively develop a kind of latter-day Calvinism, believing that they are only what they should be, what their defects have predestined. They do their daily penance in work that is dead to them. They live in a penury of satisfaction and hoard up their sacrifices, hoping thereby to prevent further socioeconomic backsliding; they acknowledge their faultiness each time they shrink from their wives' accusing demands. Process III sons sometimes show an outraged contempt for their fathers' morality. They suspect all lower-middle-class virtues, especially the virtue of any abstract product of one's labor; they trust only what their hands can do with their cars. They deny their stock and parentage, frequently affecting the indigenous speech patterns and manners of local lower-class boys. They share with the latter a scorn for conforming age-mates, who are "punks," surrendering, they think, to a system which does the conformist no good. Similarly, in Process IV, the young person, witness to manipulation within his class context, finds this system of action and its ends profoundly pointless and boring. He loses faith in it, but his life offers him no substitute except hedonism to divert him from his unsettling inner tentativeness, and a perverseness which serves to convey his rejection of and to the adults.

Delinquency is an adaptation to current realities to be sure, but it is a half-truth to maintain that this quality is its sole, most significant aspect. Adolescence grants freedom to know and act against an unfavorable truth; but childhood has bound some to personal legacies of untouchability, servility, inferiority, alienation. They are not only subjects acting against a reality inimical to their interests, but they are also the objects of that same reality. It is probably this duality which sets off so much of the theoretical controversy in delinquency studies, and that has, I suppose, prepossessed this writing. In fact, it may be said that this theory differs from others in that it takes into account both resentment and rebellion as necessary conditions in delinquency. Social theory stresses delinquency as protest; psychological explanations generally dwell on manifold clinical forms of resentment in delinquency. This theory maintains that much delinquency is generated only by the dialectical tension between resentment and rebellion. If either is predominant, the inner dialectic disappears, and the deviance that emerges is something else, not delinquency. Without conscious rebellious impulses the resentful individual displays clinical symptoms. If the force of resentment were much weaker, many delinquent youths might adopt the more positive ideologies and actions of social and political protest movements. The truth, as the native said to the missionary in Michener's *Hawaii*, lies somewhere between.

Identity Crisis IV (Concluded)

The Process IV adolescent hangs suspended between his particular bonds to childish objects and his dismay and disinterest in the way adults around him live their lives.

> (A)ny marked *avoidance of choices* . . . leads to a sense of outer isolation and to an *inner vacuum* which is wide open for old libidinal objects and with this for bewilderingly conscious incestuous feelings; for more primitive forms of identification; and (in some) for a renewed struggle with archaic introjects. This regressive pull often receives the greatest attention from workers in our field, partially because we are on more familiar ground wherever we can discern signs of regression to infantile psychosexuality. Yet the disturbances under discussion here cannot be comprehended without some insight into the specific nature of transitory adolescent regression as an attempt to postpone and to avoid, as it were, a psychosocial foreclosure. A state of paralysis may ensue, the mechanisms of which appear to be devised to maintain a state of minimal actual choice and commitment with a maximum inner conviction of still being the chooser (Erikson, 1959, p. 124).

Erikson is referring to the general problem of identity diffusion. It is suggested that Process IV delinquency is a foreclosure of inner dispersion of this nature by negative choices (in the sense that the choices negate that which their subculture asks of these youths), which grant a pseudo-security from inner threats and outer entrapment. The automotive escapades and disorder, the drinking and sexual misadventures, the occasional felonies of

Process IV youth dramatize the momentary experience that obliterates past and future—an expression of their need for an uncompromising contemporaneity that might lend a semblance of meaning to this denial of past and future. Their occasional, unaccountably vicious acts are vengeful expressions of their nihilism.

Process IV youths fear giving up what they had, or had not enough of, in exchange for the parental and adult patterns that they see. They fear equally and more urgently, the "regressive pull" that Erikson speaks of, because it possesses them, they are its objects. Their delinquency represents simultaneously a denial of the pull to early objects and a means of securing a measure of those early satisfactions. They reject and demand, at one and the same time. Their age-mates who adhere to more conforming variants of the middle-class youth culture are not nearly so involved in provoking the adults. They are too absorbed in keeping their hands free—from external and internal restraints, in order to explore and experiment—to wish on themselves the particular consequences that delinquency begs. They want adults to let them be. The Process IV youth cannot let the adults be; he demands that they be other than what they are. The Process IV youth clutches tenaciously to being in and of the moment, while his non-delinquent peer is less afraid of having been and is interested as well in becoming.

chapter 14

conclusion: on programs and prospects

FOR those who bear some responsibility to intervene and change, this can be a gloomy theory. It is rather like the prayer of the martyred Rabbi Amnon of Metz which the orthodox Jews recite on the New Year: The prayer portions out a different doom to each man. Here, there is a doom for each class. This has been a theory of lives miscast, as well as cast out, by culture and society. The mold is not easily melted or broken. I endorse Goodman's belief that delinquency is not just a matter of "poor home influences," any more than it is a reaction to lack of money or status or any other relatively external privation. It is both.

Any clinical effort, no matter how "detached" or "aggressive," can do no more than influence the lives of the individuals it touches. But because the individuals, parents and children alike, are objects of collective action by individuals elsewhere, the clinicians will inevitably fail to contain the contagion. Without wishing to sound uncharitable, I should think that a social-change program which really does nothing more than enlarge opportunities for making money is in danger of repeating the charming naivete of a Lady Bountiful off to the poor with a basket of fruit. Putting more of society's goods in the hands of the economically disadvantaged does not alter the way they have been taught to live. There are other disadvantages. But while one may regard the failure of social-change programs from the standpoint of what they have not tried to change, there is room for hope in the resources which these programs muster. Intervention efforts teach us to include within our population-at-risk, people and behavior we formerly viewed as outsiders. Perhaps we are experimenting in whom and what to ask and how to ask it.

This theory would ask business management to invest profits in providing more economic opportunity and stability for seasonal and unskilled labor. It would also direct attention toward providing more livable, human-scale, physically integrated community developments for lower-class families; toward providing more challenge, responsibility, and creativity in semiskilled and lower-status white-collar jobs; and toward the educating of men in the importance of making a venture into such work. Legislators and governing officials need further acquaintance with the functional relation of these economic and cultural aspects not only to the culture of poverty but also to delinquency. Methods are required to convey to trade union rank-and-file members, and to their leaders, the mutual advantages of judging a man other than by his skin and the necessity of yielding up the economic privileges of disbarment. The processes wherein significant numbers of relatively successful and, in the narrowest sense, well-adjusted parents fail in some important measure—miss out on important parental work and its own rewards—need to be understood and to be effectively explained.

Compared to these possibilities, a technology is evolving of engaging in absolutely essential efforts to change the population-at-risk, lower-class people: Area projects in New York, New Haven, and other cities are providing certain blueprints, mandates in terms of legitimate areas of professional effort, and some experience to evolve new, more intensive effort on the part of change agents to collaborate with these people and to further change. Political, business, and dominant class interests would have to be persuaded not only to finance such area work but also to get ready to accommodate some of the collective demands which would be forthcoming from these groups as they find their voice.

No amount of jargon borrowed from scientific management and industrial engineering—with copious references to gearing, meshing, processing, activating, and phasing people, programs, staff, and facilities—can make a social-change program which has been committed to compromised assumptions and goals any the less limited in its ultimate effect. Nor can this scientizing and technologizing mitigate the fact that the scientist may have unscientifically avoided probing into arduous, resistive regions, on the pretext that these were not, after all, affairs that he could or should do anything about in his professional role. The behavioral scientist, pure and applied, brings to the problem of delinquency a mandate to control and his professional privilege to engage in preventive and experimental measures to establish that control. The delinquency problem, like other grave social issues, challenges the scientist to consider the behavioral sciences themselves as an experiment.

On the other hand, delinquency control programs that do call for simultaneous efforts to alleviate root conditions such as prejudice and poverty are as romantic, and, in a way, as presumptuous as they are necessary. Programers and interventionists probably have to wait for protest movements to build up social and political power strong enough to force accommodations from established interests. In other words, some of the more pervasive, fundamental deprivations and inequities will yield to nothing less than culture change. These changes will result from direct negotiation between the parties most affected—the deprived and the privileged—and the negotiation depends on ideological invention and the spread of mass movements, such as the current civil rights movement.

Special preschool work with extremely deprived LL children will probably require greater budget increases for school systems; where is the political pressure to come from, for the levying and appropriation of additional tax moneys, if not from those whose welfare is at stake? Until such educational measures are more fully developed and implemented, the scholastic achievement of lower-class people may remain about the same. In the age of automation, their need for unskilled and semiskilled jobs will probably increase. Assume that retraining programs aimed at LL youth and dropouts successfully prepare significant numbers of them for one of the newer service occupations that these programs initiate. There are limits on the economy's capacity to absorb large numbers of retrained youths and adults, limits which can probably only be estimated at this time, since our society is only beginning to experiment with large-scale manpower retraining programs. How can employment possibilities be increased without a radical expansion of the economy? And what combination of forces will provide enough impetus for an economic expansion that will sweep the disadvantaged along? The Kennedy Administration pushed and propagandized for two years for a simultaneous tax cut and deficit spending, unsuccessfully; President Johnson obtained the tax cut only by promising a balanced budget. Moreover, it has been claimed that most of the benefits of the tax cut went to those already inside the closed circle of economic privilege, and very little to those outside it.

Even if deprived people find an ideology of protest and organize around it, our political machinery grinds exceedingly slow and sometimes not too fine. The economically deprived are often (though by no means always) in urban areas. Their representation in state legislatures and in the Congress has been grossly unfair (because of gerrymandering and other measures) since the rise of our cities during the last century. Decades of frequently fruitless efforts to obtain equitable reapportionment from rural-dominated legislatures preceded the Supreme Court's historic decision of June, 1964, that both houses of state legislatures must fairly represent population. Nor does this mean that now the urban poor may have a voice if they can find one, because there may well be further litigation and redress through the courts. Again in June, 1964, the Supreme Court finally ordered Prince Edward County, Virginia, to reopen its public schools on an integrated basis—thirteen years after Negroes in that county took their case for integration into the courts.

While one need not feel gloomy about the prospects for social and economic justice (one may stand in awe of the fact that democratic processes work at all), there are no grounds for easy optimism either. Under the circumstances, scientific planners and professional interventionists can only do their best and hope for better. The "best" that they may be able to do about basic social problems is to catalyze, to start more than they can finish. For every intervention program has the potential for fanning social discontent; in view of the human suffering and waste caused by the misdirection of this discontent, at least from the theoretical perspective of this book, the hopes that a program raises may be more important than those it satisfies, because social discontent may then be given legitimate purposes and goals. The mobilization of discontent may in fact be the most important consequence of most programs planned or in operation now, nor is it a consequence for which planners need apologize. They do need to anticipate it, however. Very powerful political and economic interests, even some of those which may have originally supported a program in a given locality, may oppose the goals of a protest movement as its adherents free themselves from client status and paternalistic control. Planners need to make personal and professional decisions well ahead of the fact, regarding what their job really is and what new directions their programs might take should the target population begin defining some targets of its own.

But programed intervention in delinquency requires much more refined effort than attempts to increase economic opportunity and employability among LLs. Some very deprived children suffer great learning limitations that cripple their futures as surely as bodily disasters. There are the private instabilities and enslavements that I have tried to indicate, which are the silent partners of public misconduct, in youth and in adults. Delinquency occurs in an anomic context, including, among other things, the rootless life of the adult male corner group, and the sometimes desperate isolation of the women who try to keep their children together under one roof. We are still at the beginning of developing and testing special methods of dealing with these particular aspects of delinquency; indeed, some experts will argue that these are not "aspects of delinquency" at all but social problems, and that LL delinquency may be reduced by efforts addressed only to the delinquents and not to their surroundings. The fact that this kind of dialogue still persists means, to this opinionated writer, that we are without a priority list of conditions which affect delinquency rates, let alone an established set of methods for making changes.

The school, for example, is only beginning to appreciate the magnitude and complexity of its educational task with deprived children. It must take on some of the functions of parent and home, if it is to hold many of these children and succeed with them. Highly promising, but still experimental, work is being done at the preschool and primary levels, to help LL children catch up in maturation with middle-class children of their age. But modifications in curricula and methods will also be needed through the intermediate and secondary school levels.

Modifications not only in programs but also in personnel are needed. New kinds of educators will be needed; in fact, the development of new enabling subprofessions, and new functional differentiations within the established helping professions, is probably a major technological need in delinquency control. Teachers who can teach arithmetic and basic language skills while being work-crew foremen and group counselors; women who can instruct in the elements of home management while mother-helping and providing supportive casework; new kinds of correctional workers (along with new kinds of facilities) for delinquents, are among the roles that some programs are currently developing.

Still to be considered remain techniques and types of people to get adult, corner-group "action-seekers" to make solid commitments to retraining and higher work aspirations and, no less important, to families and neighborhoods. When I have raised this matter of intervention with colleagues, veteran community workers tend to scoff that these LL men tend to be stuck, passive, distrustful, exploitative. What is more, the counter-argument runs, there is plenty of work to be done with greater promise than this; better to help the young in their formative years than to pit oneself against the accustomed life-styles of adults.

However, the adult males are a part of these youths' formative experience, mostly in negative ways, and more importantly than is generally thought. Programs are initiated and workers detailed to help mothers in female-based households, because they have immediate care of and contact with potential or actual delinquents. It is less well realized, I think, that the boys first despise manhood as it is interpreted and enacted in their mothers' homes; then, to escape their mothers, they run to the values of these same male floaters and exploiters. An adult male may be missing from the house, but the male image of the subculture is reflected all about them.

Furthermore, if there is serious hope of changing a neighborhood as a *community*, or of welding it into one, it is a staggering prospect to plan on winning over a metropolitan slum on a house-to-house, Stalingrad basis, but with social workers instead of soldiers. Plans to restore communality and to organize local action must, somehow, reach the men on the corners and in the bars; women and children cannot build collaborative neighborhoods without them. It is likely too that these "ineffectual" males could effectively sabotage a community action program, and would, if they felt by-passed and ignored.

In view of what is not known and what is only now being learned regarding delinquency intervention, it would be mistaken, I believe, to expect or promise too much benefit from the basic poverty and employment programs under way and planned, and from the more specialized delinquency programs, most of which are in a test-run, "demonstration" phase of their evolution. The penalty for such a mistake might be a backlash in loss of public confidence and support that might unnecessarily set the cause of intervention back several years.

Nor should interventionists be overly modest or defensive about their modest knowledge and technology. After treating the American electorate, during the previous two years, to a classic display of how agonizingly they can drag out the public business, congressmen turned their attention in the summer of 1964 to an extension of federally authorized delinquency-control programs and immediately began grumbling about the slowness of these programs. According to news reports, they complained that excessive time and money had been spent in planning and that little or nothing had actually been done. These congressmen are very much like the parent who ignores or rationalizes about a problem he has had with his child for fifteen years, hoping that it will go away; when the child finally becomes delinquent, the parent then goes to a therapist and insists on immediate transformation of the troublemaker. These legislators should be informed that we are dealing with matters that are in some respects more complex than the development of an economically backward country, and that they require more than the best brains and long-term planning that the nation is now able to devote to the problem. It is one person's opinion, at least, that the legislators should be told what can be done and over what period of time, rather than how much money should be spent on crash programs, with goals set for the end of one or three fiscal years. Such arrangements make more sense politically than social-scientifically, but that is just the way things are done in Washington and in statehouses and city halls. Professionals should resist crash programs, and, if possible, even refuse them, until government officials are educated to the fact that planned change of this nature cannot always be made to serve political exigency.

bibliography

Abrahams, J., and Varon, E. *Maternal Dependency and Schizophrenia.* New York: International Universities Press, 1953.

Adelson, J. The mystique of adolescence. *Psychiatry, 27,* 1964, 1–5.

Aichhorn, A. *Wayward Youth.* New York: Viking, 1935.

Alexander, F. Psychoanalysis and social disorganization. *Am. J. Sociol., 36,* 1937, 781–813.

Alexander, F., and Healy, W. *Roots of Crime: Psychoanalytic Studies.* New York: Knopf, 1935.

Andry, R. G. *Delinquency and Parental Pathology: A Study in Forensic and Clinical Psychology.* London: Methuen, 1960.

Atkinson, J. W. (Ed.) *Motives in Fantasy, Action, and Society.* Princeton: Van Nostrand, 1958.

Axelrad, S. Comments on anthropology and the study of complex cultures. *Psychoanalysis and the Social Sciences, 4,* 1955, 29–50. New York: International Universities Press.

Baittle, B. Psychiatric aspects of the development of a street corner group: an exploratory study. Institue for Juvenile Research, Dept. of Public Welfare, Illinois, no date. (*Mimeographed.*)

Bandura, A., and Walters, R. H. Dependency conflicts in aggressive delinquents. *J. Soc. Issues, 14,* 1958, 52–65.

Bandura, A., and Walters, R. H. *Adolescent Aggression: A Study of the Influence of Child Training Practices and Family Interrelationships*. New York: Ronald, 1959.

Banfield, E. C. *The Moral Basis of a Backward Society*. New York: Free Press, 1958.

Barabee, P. How cultural values affect family life. *Social Welfare Forum,* 17–29. New York: Columbia University Press, 1954.

Beaglehole, E. Character structure. *Psychiatry*, 7, 1944, 145–62.

Becker, H. S. *Outsiders: Studies in the Sociology of Deviance*. New York: Free Press, 1963.

Beller, E. K. Dependency and autonomous achievement striving related to orality and anality in early childhood. *Child Develpm., 28,* 1957, 287–315.

Bender, L. *Aggression, Hostility, and Anxiety in Children*. Springfield, Ill.: Charles C Thomas, 1953.

Bettelheim, B. Individual and mass behavior in extreme situations. In E. E. Maccoby, T. M. Newcomb, and E. L. Hartley, *Readings in Social Psychology*. New York: Henry Holt, 1958. Pp. 300–10.

Bettelheim, B. The ignored lesson of Anne Frank. *Harper's Magazine, 221,* November, 1960, 45–50.

Bettelheim, B. The problem of generations. *Daedalus,* "Youth: Challenge and Change," Winter, 1962, 68–96.

Biderman, A. D., and Zimmer, H. (Eds.) *The Manipulation of Human Behavior*. New York: Wiley, 1961.

Bloch, D. The delinquent integration. *Psychiatry, 15,* 1952, 297–303.

Bloch, H. A. *Disorganization, Personal and Social*. New York: Knopf, 1952.

Bloch, H. A., and Flynn, F. T. *Delinquency: The Juvenile Offender in America Today*. New York: Random House, 1956.

Bloch, H. A., and Niederhoffer, A. *The Gang: A Study in Adolescent Behavior*. New York: Philosophical Library, 1958.

Bordua, D. J. Juvenile delinquency and "anomie": an attempt at replication. *Soc. Problems, 6,* 1959, 230–38.

Boverman, M., and Adams, J. R. Collaboration between psychiatrist and clergyman: a case report of family therapy for an acute schizophrenic reaction. Clinical Services Division, Pastoral Institute, Washington, D.C., no date (*Mimeographed*).

Bowlby, J. *Forty-four Juvenile Thieves: Their Character and Home Life*. London: Bailliere, Tindall and Cox, 1946.

Brenman, M. The relationship of minority-group membership and group identification in a group of urban middle-class Negro girls. *J. Soc. Psychol., SPSSI Bull., 11,* 1940, 171–97.

Bromberg, W. The treatability of the psychopath. *Am. J. Psychiatry, 110,* 1954, 604 ff.

Bronfenbrenner, U. Socialization and social class through time and space. In E. E. Maccoby, T. M. Newcomb, and E. L. Hartley, *Readings in Social Psychology*. New York: Henry Holt, 1958. Pp. 400–25.

Burt, C. *The Young Delinquent*. New York: Appleton, 1925.

Burton, R. Review of B. P. Karon, "The Negro Personality," in *Harvard Ed. Rev., 29*, 1959, 260–61.

Burton, R. V., and Whiting, J. W. M. The absent father: effects on the developing child. Unpublished manuscript, NIMH, NIH, DHEW, 1960.

Camus, A. *The Rebel*. New York: Knopf, 1954.

Cavan, R. S. Negro family disorganization and juvenile delinquency. *J. Negro Education, 28*, 1959, 230–39.

Child, I. L. Socialization. In G. Lindzey (Ed.), *Handbook of Social Psychology*. Vol. II. *Special Fields and Applications*. Cambridge: Addison-Wesley, 1954. Pp. 655–92.

Clark, K., and Clark, M. The development of consciousness of self and the emergence of racial identification in Negro preschool children. *J. Soc. Psychol., SPSSI Bull., 10*, 1939, 591–99.

Clark, K., and Clark, M. Emotional factors in racial identification and preference in Negro children. *J. Negro Ed., 19*, 1950, 341–50.

Clark, K. B. Color, class, personality, and juvenile delinquency. *J. Negro Education, 28*, 1959, 240–51.

Cloward, R. A. Social control in the prison. In *Theoretical Studies in Social Organization of the Prison*, SSRC Pamphlet 15, March, 1960.

Cloward, R. A., and Ohlin, L. E. *Delinquency and Opportunity: A Theory of Delinquent Gangs*. New York: Free Press, 1960.

Cohen, A. K. *Delinquent Boys: The Culture of the Gang*. New York: Free Press, 1955.

Cohen, A. K., and Hodges, H. M., Jr. Characteristics of the lower-blue-collar class. *Soc. Problems, 10*, 1963, 303–34.

Cohen, A. K., and Short, J. F., Jr. Research in delinquent subcultures. *J. Soc. Issues, 14*, 1958, 20–37.

Cohen, A. K., and Short, J. F., Jr. Juvenile delinquency. In R. K. Merton and R. A. Nisbet (Eds.), *Social Problems: An Introduction to the Sociology of Deviant Behavior and Social Disorganization*. New York: Harcourt, Brace and World, 1961.

Colm, H. The role of affirmation in analysis. *Psychiatry, 23*, 1960, 279–85.

Coolidge, J. C., Tessman, E., Waldfogel, S., and Willer, M. L. Patterns of aggression in school phobia. *The Psychoanalytic Study of the Child, 17*, 1962, 319–33. New York: International Universities Press.

Dai, B. Some problems of personality development among Negro children. In C. Kluckhohn and H. A. Murray (Eds.), *Notes on Personality in Nature, Society, and Culture*. New York: Knopf, 1953.

Davis, A. Socialization and adolescent personality. In T. M. Newcomb and E. L. Hartley, *Reading in Social Psychology*. New York: Henry Holt, 1947. Pp. 139–50.

Davis, A., and Dollard, J. *Children of Bondage: Personality Development of Negro Youth in the Urban South.* Washington, D.C.: Am. Council on Ed., 1940.

Davis, A., and Havighurst, R. J. Social class and color differences in child rearing. *Am. Sociol. Rev., 11,* 1948, 698–710.

Dinitz, S., Kay, B. A., and Reckless, W. C. Group gradients in delinquency potential and achievement scores of sixth graders. *Am. J. Orthopsychiat., 28,* 1958, 588–605.

Dinitz, S., Scarpitti, F. R., and Reckless, W. C. Delinquency vulnerability: a cross group and longitudinal analysis. *Am. Sociol. Rev.,* 27, 1962, 515–17.

Douvan, E. Social status and success strivings. In J. W. Atkinson (Ed.), *Motives in Fantasy, Action and Society.* Princeton: Van Nostrand, 1958. Pp. 509–17.

Ebaugh, F. G. Psychosomatic medicine. *International Forum, 2,* 1954.

Ehrlich, H. J. The study of prejudice in American social science. *J. Intergroup Relations, 3,* 1962, 117–25.

Erikson, E. H. *Childhood and Society.* New York: Norton, 1950.

Erikson, E. H. Identity and the life cycle: selected papers. *Psychol. Issues, 1,* 1, 1959.

Erikson, E. H. Youth: fidelity and diversity. *Daedalus,* "Youth: Challenge and Change," Winter, 1962, 5–27.

Erikson, K. Notes on the sociology of deviance. *Soc. Problems,* Spring, 1962, 307–14.

Finestone, H. Cats, kicks, and color. *Soc. Problems, 5,* 1, 1957.

Fisher, S., and Mendell, D. The communication of neurotic patterns over two and three generations. *Psychiatry, 19,* 1956, 41–46.

Frank, L. K. Cultural control and physiological autonomy. In C. Kluckhohn and H. A. Murray, *Notes on Personality in Nature, Society and Culture.* New York: Knopf, 1953.

Frazier, E. F. The impact of urban civilization upon Negro family life. *Am. Sociol. Rev., 2,* 1937, 609–18.

Frazier, E. F. *Negro Youth at the Crossways.* Washington: American Council on Education, 1940.

Freud, S. *Group Psychology and the Analysis of the Ego.* London: International Psychoanalytical Press, 1922.

Freud, S. *Civilization and Its Discontents.* New York: Jonathan Cape and Harrison Smith, 1930.

Freud, A. *The Ego and the Mechanisms of Defence.* New York: International Universities Press, 1946.

Freud, A. Adolescence. *The Psychoanalytic Study of the Child, 13,* 1958, 255–78. New York: International Universities Press.

Friedlander, K. *The Psycho-analytical Approach to Juvenile Delinquency.* New York: International Universities Press, 1947.

Fromm, E. *The Sane Society.* New York: Rinehart, 1955.

Gans, H. J. *The Urban Villagers: Group and Class in the Life of Italian-Americans.* New York: Free Press, 1962.

Gill, M. The present state of psychoanalytic theory. *J. Abn. Soc. Psychol.*, *58*, 1959, 1–8.

Glueck, S., and Glueck, E., *Unraveling Juvenile Delinquency*. New York: Commonwealth Fund, 1950.

Goff, R. Social and emotional difficulties of Negro children due to race. *J. Negro Ed.*, *19*, 1950, 152–58.

Gold, M. *A Social-Psychology of Delinquent Boys*. Ann Arbor: Inter-center Program on Children, Youth, and Family Life, Institute for Social Research, 1961.

Gold, M. *Status Forces in Delinquent Boys*. Ann Arbor: Inter-center Program on Children, Youth, and Family Life, Institute for Social Research, 1963.

Goldfarb, W. Psychological privation in infancy and subsequent adjustment. In W. E. Martin and B. B. Stendler (Eds.), *Readings in Child Development*. New York: Harcourt, Brace, 1954.

Goodman, P. *Growing Up Absurd*. New York: Random House, 1960.

Gorer, G. The concept of national character. In C. Kluckhohn and H. A. Murray, *Notes on Personality in Nature, Society, and Culture*. New York: Knopf, 1953.

Gould, H. A. Castes, outcasts, and the sociology of stratification. *Internat. J. Comp. Soc.*, *1*, 1961, 220–38.

Green, A. W. The middle-class male child and neurosis. *Am. sociol. Rev.*, *11*, 1946, 31–41.

Greenacre, P. Conscience in the psychopath. *Am. J. Orthopsychiat.*, *15*, 1945, 495–509.

Handlin, O. *The Uprooted: The Epic Story of the Great Migrations that Made the American People*. Boston: Little, Brown, 1951.

Hartmann, H. On rational and irrational action. *Psychoanalysis and the Social Sciences*, *1*, 1947, 359–92, New York: International Universities Press.

Hartmann, H. Comments on the psychoanalytic theory of instinctual drives. *Psychoanalyt. Quart.*, *17*, 1948.

Hartmann, H. Comments on the psychoanalytic theory of the ego. *The Psychoanalytic Study of the Child*, 7, 1952. New York: International Universities Press.

Hartmann, H. Notes on the reality principle. *The Psychoanalytic Study of the Child*, *11*, 1956, 31–53. New York: International Universities Press.

Hartmann, H. *The Ego and the Problem of Adaptation*. New York: International Universities Press, 1958.

Hartmann, H., and Kris, E. The genetic approach in psychoanalysis. *The Psychoanalytic Study of the Child*, *1*, 1945, 11–30. New York: International Universities Press.

Hartmann, H., Kris, E., and Loewenstein, R. M. Comments on the formation of psychic structure. *The Psychoanalytic Study of the Child*, *2*, 1946. New York: International Universities Press.

Hartmann, H., Kris, E. and Loewenstein, R. M. Notes on the theory of aggression. *The Psychoanalytic Study of the Child, 3–4,* 1949. New York: International Universities Press.

Healy, W., and Bronner, A. *New Light on Delinquency and Its Treatment.* New Haven: Yale University Press, 1936.

Henry, J. *Culture Against Man.* New York: Random House, 1963.

Hewitt, L. E., and Jenkins, R. L. *Fundamental Patterns of Maladjustment.* Springfield, Ill.: State of Illinois, 1946.

Hill, M. C. The metropolis and juvenile delinquency among Negroes. *J. Negro Education, 28,* 1959, 277–85.

Hoffman, M. L., Mitsos, S. B., and Protz, R. E. Achievement striving, social class, and test anxiety. *J. Abnorm. Soc. Psychol., 56,* 1958, 401–3.

Hollingshead, A. B. *Elmtown's Youth.* New York: Wiley, 1949.

Hollingshead, A. B., and Redlich, F. C. *Social Class and Mental Illness.* New York: Wiley, 1958.

Honigmann, J. J. Culture patterns and human stress. *Psychiatry, 13,* 1950, 25–34.

Honigmann, J. J. *Culture and Personality.* New York: Harper, 1954.

Hughes, C. C., Tremblay, M., Rapoport, R. N., and Leighton, A. H. *People of Core and Woodlot.* Vol. 2. *The Stirling County Study of Psychiatric Disorder and Sociocultural Environment.* New York: Basic Books, 1960.

Hurwitz, J. I. Three delinquent types: a multivariate analysis. Boston University and South Shore Guidance Center, Massachusetts, 1963. (*Mimeographed.*)

Inkeles, A. Personality and social structure. In R. K. Merton, L. Broom, and L. S. Cottrell, Jr. (Eds.), *Sociology Today: Problems and Prospects.* New York: Basic Books, 1959.

Jackson, D. D., and Weakland, J. H. Conjoint family therapy. *Psychiatry, 24,* 1961, 32.

Jenkins, R. L., and Hewitt, C. Types of personality structure encountered in child guidance clinics. *Am. J. Orthopsychiat., 14,* 1944, 84–94.

Johnson, A. M., and Szurek, S. A. The genesis of antisocial acting out in children and adolescents. *Psychoanalyt. Quart., 21,* 1952, 323–43.

Joyeaux, C. (narrated to I. H. Freeman). *Out of the Burning: The Story of a Boy Gang Leader.* New York: Crown, 1960.

Kardiner, A., *et al. Psychological Frontiers of Society.* New York: Columbia University Press, 1945.

Kardiner, A., and Linton, R. *The Individual and His Society: The Psychodynamics of Primitive Social Organization.* New York: Columbia University Press, 1939.

Kardiner, A., and Ovesey, L. *The Mark of Oppression.* New York: Norton, 1951.

Karon, B. P. *The Negro Personality: A Rigorous Investigation of the Effects of Culture.* New York: Springer, 1958.

Kaufman, I. Three basic sources for pre-delinquent character. *Nervous Child, 11,* 1955, 12–15.

Kaufman, I., and Heims, L. The body image of the juvenile delinquent. *Am. J. Orthopsychiat., 28,* 1958, 146–59.

Kaufman, I., Makkay, E. S., and Zilbach, J. The impact of adolescence on girls with delinquent character formation. *Am. J. Orthospychiat., 29,* 1959, 130–43.

Keniston, K. Social change and youth in America. *Daedalus,* "Youth: Challenge and Change," Winter, 1962, 145–71.

Kerr, M. *The People of Ship Street.* New York: Humanities, 1958.

Kitsuse, J. I., and Dietrick, D. C. Delinquent boys: a critique. *Am. Sociol. Rev., 24,* 1959, 211–12.

Kluckhohn, F. R. Dominant and variant value orientations. In C. Kluckhohn and H. A. Murray (Eds.), *Notes on Personality in Nature, Society and Culture.* New York: Knopf, 1953.

Kluckhohn, F. R. Family diagnosis: variations in the basic values of family systems. *Soc. Casework, 39,* 1958, 63–72.

Kobrin, S. The conflict of values in delinquency areas. *Am. Sociol. Rev., 16,* 1951, 653–61.

Kobrin, S. (*a*) Sociological aspects of the development of a street corner group: an exploratory study. Unpublished manuscript, Institute for Juvenile Research, Dept. of Public Welfare, Ill., no date. (*Mimeographed.*)

Kris, E. *Psychoanalytic Exploration in Art.* New York: International Universities Press, 1952.

Lander, B. *Towards an Understanding of Juvenile Delinquency.* New York: Columbia University Press, 1954.

Langner, T. S., and Michael, S. T. *Life Stress and Mental Health.* New York: Free Press, 1963.

Lee, H. *To Kill a Mockingbird.* New York: Lippincott, 1960.

Leighton, A. H. *My Name Is Legion.* Vol. 1. *The Stirling County Study of Psychiatric Disorder and Sociocultural Environment.* New York: Basic Books, 1959.

Leventhal, T., and Sills, M. R. The issue of control in therapy with character problem adolescents. *Psychiatry, 26,* 1963, 149–67.

Lewis, O. Further observations on the culture of poverty. Dept. of Anthropology, University of Illinois, 1963. (*Mimeographed.*)

Linton, R. *Culture and Mental Disorders.* Springfield, Ill.: Charles C Thomas, 1956.

McClelland, D. C., Atkinson, J. W., Clark, R. A., and Lowell, E. L. *The Achievement Motive.* New York: Appleton-Century-Crofts, 1953.

McClelland, D. C., and Friedman, G. A. A cross-cultural study of the relationship between child-training practices and achievement motivation appearing in folk tales. In G. E. Swanson, T. M. Newcomb, and E. L. Hartley (Eds.), *Readings in Social Psychology.* New York: Henry Holt, 1952. Pp. 243–49.

Maccoby, E. E., Johnson, J. P., and Church, R. M. Community integration and the social control of juvenile delinquency. *J. Soc. Issues, 14,* 1958, 38–51.

Macgregor, G., Hassrick, R., and Henry, W. *Warriors without Weapons: A Study of the Society and Personality Development of the Pine Ridge Sioux.* Chicago: University of Chicago Press, 1946.

McQueen, A. J. Presentation of results of a Flint Youth Project study to PSB (NIMH, NIH, DHEW) study group, Washington, D.C., April, 1961.

Matza, D. Subterranean traditions of youth. *Annals*, "Teen-Age Culture," *338*, November, 1961, 102–18.

Matza, D., and Sykes, G. Juvenile delinquency and subterranean values. *Am. Sociol. Rev., 26*, 1961, 712–19.

Mead, G. H. *Mind, Self, and Society.* Chicago: University of Chicago Press, 1934.

Merton, R. K. *Social Theory and Social Structure.* New York: Free Press, 1949.

Miller, A. *The Crucible.* New York: Viking, 1953.

Miller, D. R., and Swanson, G. E. *Inner Conflict and Defense.* New York: Henry Holt, 1960.

Miller, S. M. Poverty, race and politics. Syracuse University Youth Development Center. Syracuse, New York, May, 1963. (*Mimeographed.*)

Miller, W. B. Lower class culture as a generating milieu of gang delinquency. *J. Soc. Issues, 14*, 1958, 5–19.

Miller, W. B. (*a*) A treatment approach to conforming delinquency. Roxbury Special Youth Project, Roxbury, Mass., no date. (*Mimeographed.*)

Miller, W. B. (*b*) Cultural features of an urban lower class community. NIMH, NIH, DHEW, Bethesda, Md., no date. (*Mimeographed.*)

Miller, W. B. (*c*) Male sexual and mating behavior in male adolescent gangs. In *City Gangs.* New York: Wiley, to be published.

Miller, W. B., Geertz, H., and Cutter, H. S. G. Aggression in a boys' street-corner group. *Psychiatry, 24*, 1961, 283–98.

Minor, C. A., and Neel, R. G. The relationship between achievement motivation and occupational preference. *J. Counsel. Psychol., 5*, 1958, 39–43.

Mobilization for Youth, Inc. *A Proposal for the Prevention and Control of Delinquency by Expanding Opportunities.* New York: 1961.

Myers, H., and Yochelson, L. Color denial in the Negro. *Psychiatry*, 39–46.

New York City Youth Board. *How They Were Reached.* 1954, No. 2.

New York City Youth Board. *Reaching the Unreached Family*, 1958, No. 5.

Noshpitz, J. D. Opening phase in the psychotherapy of adolescents with character disorders. *Bull. Menninger Clinic, 21*, 1957, 153–64.

Nye, F. I. *Family Relationships and Delinquent Behavior.* New York: Wiley, 1958.

Opler, M. K. *Culture, Psychiatry, and Human Values.* Springfield, Ill.: Charles C Thomas, 1956.

Parsons, T. Certain primary sources and patterns of aggression in the social structure of the western world. *Psychiatry, 10,* 1947, 167–81.

Parsons, T. Psychoanalysis and the social structure. *Psychoanalyt. Quart., 19,* 1950, 371–84.

Parsons, T. The superego and the theory of social systems. *Psychiatry, 15,* 1952, 15–25.

Parsons, T. Social structure and the development of personality: Freud's contribution to the integration of psychology and sociology. *Psychiatry, 21,* 1958, 321–40.

Parsons, T. Youth in the context of American society, *Daedalus,* "Youth: Challenge and Change," Winter, 1962, 97–123.

Parsons, T., Bales, R. F., *et al.* Family Socialization and Interaction *Process.* New York: Free Press, 1960.

Parsons, T., and Shils, E. A. (Eds.) *Toward a General Theory of Action.* Cambridge: Harvard University Press, 1952.

Piaget, J. *Play, Dreams and Imitation in Childhood.* New York: Norton, 1951.

Plant, J. S. *Personality and the Cultural Pattern.* New York: Commonwealth Fund, 1937.

Polk, K. Juvenile delinquency and social areas. *Soc. Problems, 5,* 1957–1958, 214–17.

Pollak, O. *Integrating Sociological and Psychoanalytic Concepts: An Exploration of Child Psychotherapy.* New York: Russell Sage, 1956.

Polsky, N. The village beat scene. *Dissent, 8,* 1961, 339–59.

Rabinovitch, R. The concept of primary psychogenic acathexis. *Am. J. Orthopsychiat., 21,* 1951, 231–37.

Radke, M., and Trager, H. Children's perceptions of the social role of Negroes and Whites. *J. Psychol., 29,* 1950, 3–33.

Rapaport, D. A historical survey of psychoanalytic ego psychology. *Psychol. Issues, 1,* 1, 1959, 5–17.

Reckless, W. C. The etiology of delinquent and criminal behavior. *Soc. Sci. Res. Council Bull., 50,* 1943.

Reckless, W. C. *The Crime Problem.* 3rd ed., New York: Appleton-Century-Crofts, 1961.

Reckless, W., Dinitz, S., and Kay, B. Self concept as an insulator against delinquency. *Am. sociol. Rev., 21,* 1956, 745.

Reckless, W. Dinitz, S., and Kay, B. The self-component in potential delinquency and nondelinquency. *Am. sociol. Rev., 22,* 1957, 566–70.

Redl, F. Group emotion and leadership. *Psychiatry, 5,* 1942, 573ff.

Redl, F. The psychology of gang formation and the treatment of juvenile delinquents. *The Psychoanalytic Study of the Child, 1,* 1945. New York: International Universities Press.

Redl, F., and Wineman, D. *Children Who Hate.* New York: Free Press, 1951.

Reiner, B. S., and Kaufman, I. *Character Disorders in Parents of Delinquents.* New York: Family Service Ass. of America, 1959.

Reiss, A. J. Social correlates of psychological types of delinquency. *Am. Sociol. Rev., 17,* 1952, 710–18.

Rettig, S., and Pasamanick, B. Moral value structure and social class. *Sociometry, 24,* 1961, 21–35.

Ribble, M. A. *The Rights of Infants: Early Psychological Needs and Their Satisfaction.* New York: Columbia University Press, 1943.

Ribicoff, A. Statement before Special Education Subcommittee of House Committee on Labor and Education, July 10, 1961. (*Mimeographed press release.*)

Riesman, D., Glazer, N., and Denney, R. *The Lonely Crowd.* New Haven: Yale University Press, 1950.

Rohrer, J. H. Personal communication. 1961.

Rohrer, J. H., and Edmonson, M. S. *The Eighth Generation: Cultures and Personalities of New Orleans Negroes.* New York: Harper, 1960.

Rosen, B. C. The achievement syndrome: a psychocultural dimension of social stratification. In J. W. Atkinson (Ed.), *Motives in Fantasy, Action, and Society.* Princeton: Van Nostrand, 1958. Pp. 495–508.

Rosen, B. C., and D'Andrade, R. The psychosocial origins of achievement motivation. *Sociometry, 22,* 1959, 185–218.

Rubenfeld, S., and Stafford, J. W. An adolescent inmate social system—a psychosocial account. *Psychiatry, 26,* 1963, 241–56.

Ruesch, J. Social technique, social status, and social change in illness. In C. Kluckhohn and H. A. Murray (Eds.), *Notes on Personality in Nature, Society, and Culture.* New York: Knopf, 1953.

Sapir, E. Why cultural anthropology needs the psychiatrist. *Psychiatry, 1,* 1938, 7–12.

Saussure, R. de. Psychoanalysis and history. *Psychoanalysis and the Social Sciences, 2,* 1950, 7–64. New York: International Universities Press.

Scarpitti, F. R., Murray, E., Dinitz, S., and Reckless, W. C. The "good" boy in a high delinquency area: four years later. *Am. sociol. Rev., 25,* 1960, 555–58.

Schilder, P. *Psychotherapy.* New York: Norton, 1951.

Sears, R. R., Maccoby, E. E., and Levin, H. *Patterns of Child Rearing.* Evanston, Ill.: Row, Peterson, 1957.

Seward, G. *Psychotherapy and Culture Conflict.* New York: Ronald, 1956.

Seward, G. (Ed.) *Clinical Studies in Culture Conflict.* New York: Ronald, 1958.

Shaw, C. *Brothers in Crime.* Chicago: 1938.

Shaw, C. R., and McKay, H. D. Juvenile delinquency and urban areas. Chicago: University of Chicago Press, 1942.

Short, J. F. The sociocultural context of delinquency. *Crime and Del., 6,* 1960, 365–75.

Silverberg, W. V. *Childhood Experience and Personal Destiny*. New York: Springer, 1952.

Simcox, B. R., and Kaufman, I. Casework with parents of delinquents. *Soc. Casework*, 1956.

Simpson, G., and Yinger, J. *Racial and Cultural Minorities: An Analysis of Prejudice and Discrimination*. New York: Harper, 1953.

Slater, E., and Woodside, M. *A Study of Marriage Relationships in the Urban Working Classes*. London: Cassell, 1951.

Spiegel, L. A. Comments on the psychoanalytic psychology of adolescence. *The Psychoanalytic Study of the Child, 13*, 1945, 296–308. New York: International Universities Press.

Spinley, B. M. *The Deprived and the Privileged: Personality Development in English Society*. London: Routledge & Kegan Paul, 1953.

Spiro, M. E. Culture and personality: the natural history of a false dichotomy. *Psychiatry, 14*, 1951, 19–46.

Srole, L. Social integration and certain corollaries, an exploratory study. *Am. sociol. Rev., 21*, 1956, 709.

Stott, D. H. *Unsettled Children and Their Families*. London: University of London Press, 1956.

Stott, D. H. Delinquency, maladjustment and unfavourable ecology. *Brit. J. Psychol., 51*, 1960, 157–70.

Strodtbeck, F. L. Progress report: the reading readiness nursery-short term social intervention technique. The Social Psychology Laboratory, University of Chicago, August, 1963. (*Mimeographed.*)

Sullivan, H. S. *The Interpersonal Theory of Psychiatry*. New York: Norton, 1953.

Sullivan, H. S. *Clinical Studies in Psychiatry*. New York: Norton, 1956.

Sutherland, E. H. *Principles of Criminology*. 4th ed., Philadelphia: Lippincott, 1947.

Sykes, G., and Matza, D. Techniques of neutralization: a theory of delinquency. *Am. sociol. Rev., 22*, 1957, 664–70.

Szasz, T. S. *The Myth of Mental Illness*. New York: Free Press, 1962.

Toby, J. Review of R. A. Cloward and L. E. Ohlin, Delinquency and opportunity: a theory of delinquent gangs. Youth Development Program, The Ford Foundation, 1961. Private circulation.

Wattenberg, W. W. *Boy Repeaters*. Detroit: Wayne State University Press, 1947.

Weber, M. The Protestant Ethic and the Spirit of Capitalism. London: Allen and Unwin, 1930.

Whiting, J. W. M. Sorcery, sin, and the superego: a cross-cultural study of some mechanisms of social control. In M. E. Jones (Ed.), *Nebraska Symposium on Motivation*, Lincoln: University of Nebraska Press, 1959. Pp. 174–95.

Whiting, J. W. M., and Child, I. L. *Child Training and Personality: A Cross-Cultural Study*. New Haven: Yale University Press, 1953.

Whiting, J. W. M., Kluckhohn, F. R., and Anthony, A. The function of male initiation ceremonies at puberty. In E. E. Maccoby, T. M.

Newcomb, and E. L. Hartley, *Readings in Social Psychology*. New York: Henry Holt, 1958. Pp. 359–70.

Whyte, W. F. *Street Corner Society*. Chicago: University of Chicago Press, 1943.

Winterbottom, M. R. The relation of need for achievement to learning experiences in independence and mastery. In J. W. Atkinson (Ed.), *Motives in Fantasy, Action, and Society*. Princeton: Van Nostrand, 1958.

Witmer, H. L., and Kotinsky, R. *New Perspectives for Research on Juvenile Delinquency*. Washington, D.C.: Children's Bureau, DHEW, 1955.

Wood, A. L. Minority-group criminality and cultural integration. *J. Crim. Law, Criminol., and Pol. Science, 37*, 1947, 498–510.

Wynne, L. C., Ryckoff, I. M., Day, J., and Hirsch, S. I. Pseudo-mutuality in family relations of schizophrenics, *Psychiatry, 21*, 1958, 205–20.

Yinger, J. M. Contraculture and subculture. *Am. sociol. Rev., 25*, 1960, 625–44.

index